The Financing of Small Business

A detailed empirical study of how small business owners finance their enterprises, this volume compares the experiences of women with those of men. The author redresses an over-reliance on subjective and anecdotal evidence of discrimination in this area with a controlled study of forty matched pairs of male/female owners, and their strategies for raising finances.

The book finds considerable similarities between female and male entrepreneurs in the type and amount of finance used in the business. It also uncovers some significant differences in the banking relationships and networking behaviour of the two groups. The implications of this for academics, policy makers and the financial community are also considered.

Lauren Read studied for her Ph.D. at the University of Southampton. She is currently a senior policy advisor at the Confederation of British Industry, responsible for small firms policy in the SME Unit.

Routledge Studies in Small Business
Edited by David Storey

The Financing of Small Business

A comparative study of male and female business owners

Lauren Read

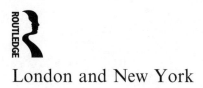

London and New York

First published 1998 by Routledge
11 New Fetter Lane, London EC4P 4EE

Simultaneously published in the USA and Canada
by Routledge
29 West 35th Street, New York, NY 10001

Typeset in Times by Pure Tech India Ltd, Pondicherry
Printed and bound in Great Britain by Biddles Ltd, Guildford and King's
Lynn

British Library Cataloguing in Publication Data
A catalogue record for this book is available from the British Library

Library of Congress Cataloguing in Publication Data
Read, Lauren, 1971–
    The financing of small busines: a comparative study of male and female
    busines owners/Lauren Read.
    p.   cm.
    Includes bibliographical references and index.
    1. Small business—Finance.   I. Title.
  HG4027.7.R397   1998
  658.15'92—dc21   97–40388
                       CIP

ISBN 0–415–16956–9

This book is dedicated to Mum, Dad, Lindsay and Kevin.
Thank you for all your love and encouragement.

Contents

Figures

Tables

Preface

This book is based on research carried out for a Ph.D. thesis between October 1992 and October 1995. It reports on the experiences of eighty business owners in the UK in raising finance to start and grow their businesses. In particular it examines the complex relationship between small businesses and their banks. Interviews with the businesses were conducted in 1994, during a period of recession and great uncertainty, and only one year on from the peak in small firm failures. Anyone looking back at this period will be reminded of the frequent 'bank bashing' that occurred in the media. Readers should therefore bear in mind the impact of the economic climate on the findings contained in this book.

I started the research with the aim of understanding and comparing the experiences of male and female owner-managers in financing their businesses. During the course of the research, however, I found myself exploring much more than just their accounts or their bank statements. Indeed, it was a great privilege for me to be allowed an insight into the whole process of starting and running a business – the stresses and strains, balanced by the joy of making money and being your own boss. It became very apparent that the processes involved, such as raising finance or entering a new market, are not neatly compartmentalised – they are interlinked and inextricably bound into the entrepreneur's life as a whole. Understanding small business is therefore not simply about economics, it is as much to do with understanding people, their motivations, and the environment in which they live. My training as a geographer has therefore been invaluable in allowing me to look at the process of financing a business from the various perspectives, bringing together the relevant disciplines and theoretical strands to form a complete picture. I hope that, as a result, the research is able to offer valuable insights and information, not only to the financial community, but to policy makers and business owners themselves.

Acknowledgements

I would like to take this opportunity to thank a number of people, without whom the completion of this book would have been impossible:

- My supervisor Professor Colin Mason, for his invaluable advice, assistance, patience, and encouragement throughout the research process.
- The Economic and Social Research Council, for its financial support during the course of my studentship.
- All the small business owners who agreed to be interviewed and who gave a great deal of their valuable time. To them I am extremely grateful.
- Everyone who gave me good advice and guidance during the course of the research. In particular, I am grateful to the 'team' from the Scottish Enterprise Foundation, who helped me formulate my research questions.
- My family, for their invaluable financial support and constant encouragement.
- Clare for keeping me relatively sane!
- My final thanks go to Kevin. Without you I would never have made it through.

Lauren Read
July 1997

1 The growth and characteristics of female entrepreneurship

1.1 INCREASING NUMBERS OF WOMEN-OWNED BUSINESSES

Since the late 1970s, most developed countries have experienced a significant increase in the number of new businesses[1] started by women. In Great Britain, between 1979 and 1995, the number of self-employed women rose from 292,000 to 801,000 (Barclays Bank, 1992; *Employment Gazette*, 1995) (Table 1.1). It is estimated that approximately one-third of all new, small businesses in the UK are started by women (Barclays Bank, 1992; *Guardian*, 1992a). A similar pattern of growth in the number of women-owned businesses can be seen in other developed countries, including the USA (Clark and James, 1992), Canada (Atlantic Canada Opportunities Agency, 1992), Australia (Department of Industry, Technology and Commerce, 1991) and the Netherlands (Koper, 1993). In the USA, between 1977 and 1988, the number of non-farm sole proprietorships owned by women increased from 1.9 million to over 4.6 million (USSBA, 1990; 1991). It is estimated that by the year 2000, 50 per cent of all businesses in the USA will be owned and run by women (House of Representatives Report, 1988: p. 2). In former West Germany, 40 per cent of all new business start-ups are by women (*Guardian*, 1992a: p. 14).

Curran *et al.* (1987), however, warn researchers not to overstate the growth in numbers of female self-employed (p. 13). In particular, it is important not to overlook the fact that growth has taken place from a much lower baseline than for men. While the number of women-owned businesses has increased dramatically, there are still considerably fewer than men-owned businesses (Rees, 1992). The relative gender 'mix' therefore remains fairly stable in favour of the male business owner with a ratio of around three men to one

Table 1.1 Self-employment (Great Britain, winter 1994/5)

	Women	Men	All
Total in employment	11,290,000	13,931,000	25,221,000
Self-employment	801,000	2,458,000	3,259,000
% of total in employment	7	18	13

Source: Labour Force Survey, winter 1994/5 (*Employment Gazette*, 1995)

woman (Allen and Truman, 1991: p. 115; Goss, 1991: p. 36). However, according to a National Opinion Polls (NOP) survey for Barclays Bank, the proportion of women starting their own businesses has been falling during the early 1990s from around 33 per cent of start-ups in 1988 to about 25 per cent in 1994 (*Sunday Times*, 1994: p. 13). The NOP survey attribute this, in part, to the more flexible working practices of larger organisations which have been creating more opportunities for women's employment in the labour market.

1.2   EXPLAINING THE GROWTH OF FEMALE ENTREPRENEURSHIP

1.2.1   Introduction

Every new firm formation decision begins with the decision by an individual or group of individuals to make a major change to the life path they are following. Their decision will be influenced by a number of factors. First, there are 'push' factors or negative displacements which might force an individual to consider business ownership. Second, there are 'pull' factors or positive displacements which might attract an individual towards business ownership. Third, there are factors associated with the external 'environment' which facilitate or inhibit small business start-up (e.g. the availability of resources, Government policy towards small businesses and the credibility of entrepreneurship). While most factors are applicable to both male and female business owners, there are a number which are specific to women or which have a gender dimension. In an attempt to explain the rise in the number of female business owners, the remainder of this section examines the importance of various 'push', 'pull' and 'environmental' factors from the perspective of a female business owner, recognising that in most cases an entrepreneurial event is caused by a complex interaction of factors.

1.2.2   A reaction to problems in the labour market

The background to women's participation in the labour market

It has been recognised that the rise in the number of self-employed women and women owner-managers parallels, but with a time-lag, the increasing participation of women, particularly married women, in the labour market (Carter and Cannon, 1992: p. 2). Since World War II, labour force participation by women in OECD countries has increased by at least one-third (OECD, 1990: p. 21). In Great Britain since 1977, the female share of total employment has risen in all occupational groups, with the exception of operatives and labourers (Equal Opportunities Commission, 1989). By Winter 1994/5, there was a total of 11.3 million women in employment, 45 per cent of the total population in employment (*Employment Gazette*, 1995: p. LFS33).

A number of factors have contributed to the increasing number of women entering the labour market. According to McDowell (1991), these are best explored within the wider context of social and economic change which has occurred in contemporary industrial societies this century – the shift from 'Fordism' (or 'Organised Capitalism') to 'Post-Fordism' (or 'Disorganised Capitalism' or 'Flexible Specialisation/Accumulation') (Aglietta, 1979; 1982; Piore and Sabel, 1984; Lash and Urry, 1987; 1994; Harvey, 1989; Lawton Smith *et al.*, 1991; Cooke, 1992; Malecki, 1995).

From the early 1900s, the dominant economic form in industrialised economies was Fordism, an era of 'intensive accumulation' characterised by 'mass production, reduced working hours, relatively high wages (at least for the labour aristocracy), mass consumption based on the "family" wage of the male breadwinner and the commodification of social life' (McDowell, 1991: p. 402).

In Britain, as in other advanced industrial economies, many women entered the labour market to help meet the cost of lifestyles based around consumption. Their entry was facilitated by the provision of care for the elderly and young children from the welfare state (McDowell, 1991). These services themselves created more employment opportunities for women and an increase in the provision of education and training allowed many women to improve their positions within the labour market.

Since around the 1970s, in response to increasing macro-scale *disorganisation* at national and international levels, firms have moved towards a more flexible approach in the organisation of production, the utilisation of labour and the organisation of relationships with other firms (Atkinson, 1984; 1985; Shutt and Whittington, 1987; Gertler, 1992; Miles and Snow, 1992; Imrie, 1994; Malecki, 1995). It has been argued that Post-Fordist business organisation involves substantial dependence on networks of suppliers, a high degree of production flexibility, more decentralised and less bureaucratic management structures, higher skill densities in workforces, more flexible working practices and an increased tendency towards inter-firm collaboration (Cooke, 1992). These changes have been facilitated by new technologies which have helped to accommodate the new style of production (Rothwell, 1992).

The increased need for part-time, flexible labour has therefore increased the number of opportunities for women to enter the labour market (McDowell, 1991). Corporate restructuring has also meant that many large companies now subcontract out services that were previously 'in-house' such as catering and cleaning and also white collar services such as public relations, marketing and computer support services (Keeble *et al.*, 1991). Furthermore, rising consumer affluence and the increase in numbers of dual income households has created a need for 'quasi-domestic' services (McDowell, 1991: p. 416). There has therefore been an increase in the number of jobs available in those types of occupations and industries that have traditionally employed women (Massey, 1984). While such factors are important in explaining the growth of women's participation in the labour market, it is important to remember that such a growth has been an 'integral rather than a coincidental part of the restructuring process' (McDowell, 1991: p. 406).

Another factor which has led to an increase in the number of women entering the labour market is the break-up of the nuclear family (Moore, 1993: p. 11). There are now more single-parent mothers having to go out to work. Within the two-parent family, economic stagnation, the lowering of wages and the threat of unemployment, particularly during the 1990s, has meant that the concept of a family supported by a sole male breadwinner is declining in prevalence. In many cases, the woman's income is needed to keep the family above the poverty line (West, 1982). In other cases, the woman's salary may be used in order to sustain a particular lifestyle. This might include private education, foreign holidays or luxury cars.

Demographic factors have also meant that women are living longer and having fewer children, often later in their lives. This has enabled many women to take up full-time paid employment. Furthermore, the psychological expectations of women have changed so that their identities are now more frequently related to their experiences in the workplace, rather than to their role as a wife and/or mother. Women have been entering the workforce to exercise their rights to an equal role with men in the world economy. Facilitating factors have included an increase in women's access to education, particularly higher education, and the introduction of laws addressing inequalities in access to employment opportunities (Malveaux, 1990).

The question is, how has the growth in the number of women entering the labour market had an impact on the growth of small business ownership among women?

The problems faced by women in the labour market

Despite their increased participation in the labour market, waged labour entry has not had a widespread emancipatory impact on women generally (McDowell, 1991: p. 401). As highlighted by Carter and Cannon (1992), research on labour market segmentation indicates that there are sexual divisions in the organisational distribution of the workforce which mean that women tend to remain at the bottom of the occupational hierarchy in four main ways.

First, women tend to be concentrated in part-time jobs. Indeed, in Spring 1993, 45 per cent of female employees were working part-time, compared to only 6 per cent of male employees (*Employment Gazette*, 1993: p. LFS2). However, 81 per cent of the part-time female employees said that this was by their own choice. While only 10 per cent said that they were forced to take part-time work because they could not find full-time work, it is quite likely that many of the 81 per cent who had 'chosen' part-time work also had domestic responsibilities which would have made it very difficult for them to have taken full-time employment (see section 1.2.6).

Second, the jobs taken by women in the labour market tend to be less skilled than those taken by men. Women are more highly represented in clerical work and other service-related jobs and less so in managerial or technical jobs. A study of employees by occupation shows that 76 per cent of all clerical and secretarial employees in Great Britain are women (*Employment Gazette*, 1993: p. LFS2).

Third, women often find it much more difficult than men to develop their careers in larger organisations because of stereotyped ideas about their ability to succeed in a business environment (Chaganti, 1986) and because many men perceive women to lack managerial attributes (Cromie and Hayes, 1988). While women comprise 34 per cent of all managers, they are still concentrated in traditionally 'female' occupations such as the 'caring professions' (*Employment*

Gazette, 1993: p. LFS2). Furthermore, for those women who achieve upward career mobility, advancement past the ranks of middle management is very often blocked by a 'glass ceiling' (Hymounts, 1986). This has been described as

> an invisible but very real barrier, through which women can see the senior positions for which they have the potential, experience and qualifications, but which for a variety of reasons, including prejudice, they often do not achieve.
>
> *(Guardian*, 1992a: p. 14)

According to Belcourt (1991), less than 3 per cent of the senior positions in Canadian corporations are occupied by women. A Government report[2] in the UK also points out the fact that although today's women are better educated and harder working, their jobs are still lowlier than men's and less well paid. The report shows that even in industries that mainly employ women, for example teaching, while women account for more than 80 per cent of all nursery and primary teachers, only 57 per cent are employed as school heads or deputy heads.

Fourth, it is well documented that women earn less than men (Cromie and Hayes, 1988: p. 88). Not only are women concentrated in the lower paid jobs, but the Northern Ireland New Earning Survey (1985) found that, even in the same jobs as men, women are paid less. For example, in clerical jobs, male clerks were paid 30 per cent more than female clerks. A Labour Research Department report recently estimated that working women will have to wait more than fifty years before they earn the same as men. At present, women's gross hourly earnings are 79 per cent of men's (Wilkins, 1995). In summary therefore, many women in the labour market lack job security, have poor career prospects and few occupational rights and benefits (Carter and Cannon, 1992).

Research indicates that dissatisfaction in paid employment causes many men to start their own businesses (Scase and Goffee, 1980). It is therefore likely that the experiences of women in the labour market will have a similar effect (Goffee and Scase, 1985: p. 7). Business ownership is often seen as an important way for women to avoid 'a labour market which confines them to insecure and low-paid occupations' (Goffee and Scase, 1983: p. 635). Self-employment and business ownership offer the potential for career progression (Batchelor, 1987; Hertz, 1987; Rees, 1992) without the 'supervisory controls of formal employment' (Goffee and Scase, 1983: p. 635). It is perceived as being free from the formal employment selection criteria which often lead to systematic discrimination against women (Hertz, 1987; Belcourt, 1991), chauvinistic recruitment officers (Belcourt, 1991), stereotyped perceptions of women and their abilities (Cromie and Hayes, 1988), and 'male imposed identities which are allocated to women via established societal institutions' (Goffee and Scase, 1983: p. 625). Recent studies confirm that many new businesses are started by women seeking to escape discrimination as employees (*The Independent*, 1991; Reuber *et al.*, 1991; Patel, 1994). Other women, especially single parent mothers, are forced to consider starting their own businesses because of financial burdens which cannot be met through formal employment (Patel, 1994) and because as employees women tend to earn less, they face lower opportunity costs when giving up paid employment to start a business than men (O'Hare and Larson, 1991).

1.2.3   An outcome of the Women's Movement

The growth in women's involvement in the labour market has coincided with the rise of the Women's Movement and feminist awareness. According to Goffee and Scase (1983), the Women's Movement represents a 'collective response to gender-related experiences of subordination and deprivation' (p. 625). The emphasis has been on collective action to eliminate gender-based inequalities by breaking down male-dominated institutions and patriarchal structures. Women, like many ethnic minority groups and immigrants, are often denied access to 'positions of power and authority' (Devine and Clutterbuck, 1985: p. 65). This 'social marginality', as defined by Stanworth and Curran (1976), is where there is an 'incongruity between the individual's personal attributes or self-image and the role he or she holds in society' (Goss, 1991: p. 61). Women in a predominantly masculine capitalist world are also a minority group (Hertz, 1987). Business ownership is therefore seen as a way of providing women with the personal autonomy and self-determination needed to undermine or at least query these structures.

However, the role of business ownership in the Women's Movement has been contested. One of the main areas of contention is the fact that entrepreneurs tend to operate as individuals. Supporters of the role of business ownership in the Women's Movement, particularly US feminists, believe that an 'individual' approach can be a good 'alternative, or supplement, to collective action' (Goffee and Scase, 1983: p. 626) and has more radical potential because it rejects 'the exploitative nature of the capitalist work process and labour market' (p. 627). Furthermore, female business owners who succeed in 'male' sectors of the economy have the potential to undermine 'conventional and stereotyped notions of a woman's place' (the traditionally defined, gender-based divisions of labour – Goffee and Scase, 1983: p. 627). It is seen by many as a chance for women to 'beat men at their own game'. According to one of the businesswomen interviewed by Goffee and Scase (1985), the reason she had started her own business was because she enjoyed 'achieving the things men want to achieve – and doing it better than them' (p. 43).

The counter-argument, particularly from British feminists, has been that female business owners may actually be fostering the capitalist values and institutions which 'sustain the domination of men over women', while ignoring the 'collective nature of sisterhood' (Goffee and Scase, 1983: p. 627). Furthermore, it has been pointed out that there is frequently a lack of choice underlying the decision to enter self-employment for women (Allen and Truman, 1991) and that many women are not necessarily better off out of the labour market (Belcourt, 1991). For example, female homeworkers often continue to be subjected to patriarchal divisions of labour and experience very little economic independence or improved working conditions (Allen *et al.*, 1992). It has also been found that businesswomen earn less than their male counterparts (Allen and Truman, 1991; Clark and James, 1992). White (1984) suggested that female business owners earn one-third less than male business owners. This may simply reflect the fact that businesswomen take a smaller salary from their businesses compared to men or that their businesses are smaller, younger, or less profitable. However, another theory is that the same factors which contribute to women in the labour market earning one-third less than men also apply to small business ownership. These include sex-linked differences in ability, socialisation processes, systematic discrimination and differences in education and work patterns (Belcourt, 1991).

Nevertheless, it has been shown that the independence which many women gain through business ownership can be channelled back into collective action. For example, 'radical' women business owners, that is, women who have a low commitment to both conventional entrepreneurial ideals and traditional gender roles, tend to 'regard their business activities as part of a collective struggle which offers services to other women in ways compatible with feminist ideology' (Goffee and Scase, 1985: p. 139). Many such businesses are co-owned and collectively organised as co-operative enterprises, providing spheres of autonomy which free their owners from male domination. Co-operative businesses are particularly popular with women (Rees,

1992) but are difficult to set up in the UK as financial organisations are suspicious of non-traditionally managed business ventures.

1.2.4 Increasing numbers of female role models

As the number of female business owners has grown, so has the number of role models on whom would-be female business owners can model themselves (Batchelor, 1987; Allen and Truman, 1991). The growing presence and visibility of female business owners has had a two-fold effect. First, successful businesswomen demonstrate to other women that they have a choice in the labour market. In particular, they do not have to suffer the 'glass ceiling' or the poor conditions often associated with employment in the formal labour market (Godfrey, 1992). Second, they provide a potentially important pool of mentors. As mentors, existing female business owners can offer advice and encouragement to newcomers and introduce them to established networks of useful contacts which are vital for business survival and growth. Women generally prefer to use other women for information and advice (Smeltzer and Fann, 1989) and often create their own business networks (Hisrich and Brush, 1985) offering different kinds of support compared to men – social support as well as practical (Smeltzer and Fann, 1989). UK examples of female entrepreneurs' networking organisations are The British Association of Women Entrepreneurs, The UK Federation of Business and Professional Women and the parliamentary lobby group (Women Into Business).

Recent years have witnessed the meteoric rise of businesswomen such as Anita Roddick of the Body Shop, Debbie Moore (Pineapple) and Sophie Mirmam (Sock Shop). In the latter two cases, they have also received public attention over their failure in business. Nevertheless, the visibility and profile of such role models depends largely on the country in question. American women entrepreneurs, as with their male counterparts, tend to enjoy a much higher profile coverage and more energetic public lives compared with their British equivalents (Hertz, 1987). This has much to do with the respective business cultures. In America, being an entrepreneur and running one's own business is a common aspiration. There are dozens of magazines devoted to entrepreneurship in general and a growing number targeting women entrepreneurs (e.g. *Entrepreneurial Woman*; *Women In Business*). In Britain, however, entrepreneurship has a much lower status and female entrepreneurs are often seen as somewhat of an oddity. They therefore tend to be more solitary and isolated in the business world, interacting little with other female business owners

(Hertz, 1987). Indeed, Clutterbuck and Devine (1987) note that female entrepreneurs need to be able to 'develop in a vacuum' (p. 107).

It is also worth bearing in mind, however, that growing numbers of women running their own businesses might actually cause more women to remain in the workplace. As pointed out by Godfrey (1992), if women know that they have the choice to set up their own business and can survive outside the corporate workplace, they are no longer 'victims' of their situation and they can use this knowledge to demand change within the workplace.

1.2.5   The desire for independence

For many women, as for many men, the motivation to start a business is driven by the desire for independence (Hertz, 1987; Carter and Cannon, 1992; Carter, 1993). The independence of running one's own business is usually taken to mean freedom from having to take orders and/or having control over one's own destiny. While these are common aspirations for both men and women, for many women, independence has additional connotations (Carter, 1993). For instance, many women see business ownership as offering them the chance to be independent of men (Goffee and Scase, 1983; Cromie, 1987b; Hertz, 1987). In a study by Hertz (1987), a property millionairess was interviewed and explained that she had started her own business because she was 'fed up with being trodden on or trodden over by men' (p. 60). A single female might consider the independence of business ownership in preference to the only other alternatives perceived to be on offer (being a dependent housewife or a low-paid employee) (Goffee and Scase, 1985: p. 43). For a married woman, business ownership may represent independence in the form of eliminating domestic subordination.

The desire for independence is therefore a very complex issue and can mean different things to different women. This is supported by Carter and Cannon (1992) who demonstrated that women at different stages of their life and from different backgrounds have different definitions of independence. They identified five groups of women united by common experiences and motivations for starting a business. First, they identified *young achievement oriented* women who see business ownership as a long-term career option. Such women will tend to view independence in terms of freedom from the perceived confines of the formal labour market and self-employment as offering better career opportunities. Second, young women who have '*drifted*' into self-employment, either through lack of motivation or their rejection of

conventional employer–employee relationships, generally see the independence of self-employment as a way in which to reject figures of
authority. Third, older, *high achievement oriented* women often desire
the independence offered by business ownership because they have met
with a 'glass ceiling' in their career, are disillusioned with a labour
market which has failed them as women, or want to escape the perceived confines of formal employment. Others want the flexibility to
have a family and a career which is not available to them as employees.
Fourth, *'returners'* to the workforce, usually following motherhood,
generally seek the short-term independence which allows them to be
something other than a mother. However, such women tend to face
real or perceived barriers in their return to mainstream employment.
Business ownership allows these women to return to work. This category may also include women who have been full-time mothers and
suffer from 'empty nest' syndrome when their children leave home.
Business ownership helps such women fill the 'gap' left by the children.
Fifth, in many families, entrepreneurship is a *traditional way of life.*
The independence that business ownership offers women from such
backgrounds is one which enables them to enter into what they perceive as a 'normal way of life' (Carter and Cannon, 1988: p. 12).

However, while it is usually perceived as quite acceptable for a man
to seek independence – 'the tough lone male has always gained the
admiration of men and women alike' – the same admiration is not
extended to the 'tough lone female' (Hertz, 1987: p. 60). She must
contend with disapproval from those around her and often self-doubt
as a result. In addition, the importance of motivational factors such as
'the desire for independence' must not be overstated. Business ownership for both sexes is often a result of the inability to find more
formal, full-time employment (Roberts-Reid and Curran, 1992).

1.2.6 Women juggling their lives

As well as independence, many women choose business ownership in
order to have more control over their lives, in particular, to be able to
co-ordinate their work life with their domestic responsibilities (Scottish Enterprise, 1993b). Through desire or necessity, many women
choose to combine work with raising a family. However, Lonsdale
(1985) has shown statistically that the existence of dependent children
has a detrimental impact on women's employment activity rates.
Indeed, her study showed that in 1981, 84 per cent of women between
the ages of 20 and 24 who did not have children were economically
active, compared to only 16 per cent of those with children. A number

of factors contribute to the lower economic activity of women with dependent children. First, there is a strong ideology present in society that requires women to give priority to their homes and family over paid employment (Cromie and Hayes, 1988). In most cases, the provision of child-care is still regarded as the woman's responsibility. Many women who choose to seek paid employment are therefore seen, or see themselves, as somewhat deviant. Second, many employers are not willing to take on women with domestic responsibilities (Hertz, 1987; Carter and Cannon, 1992). Third, paid child-care is too expensive for many women and few employers provide 'in-house' crèche facilities.

Business ownership offers women the flexibility and often the only option to combine the desire or need to work with their child-rearing role or caring for the elderly and disabled (Allen and Truman, 1991; Carter and Cannon, 1992; Clark and James, 1992; Roberts-Reid and Curran, 1992). This may explain why around 50 per cent of women set up and run their businesses from home (Carter and Cannon, 1992; Clark and James, 1992; Roberts-Reid and Curran, 1992) and why they spend fewer hours in their businesses than men (Allen and Truman, 1991: p. 117). According to Price and Monroe (1992), studies indicate that women account for 70 per cent of all home-based sole proprietorships. Curran *et al.* (1987) found that over 80 per cent of male small business owners worked more than forty hours per week, compared to only 39 per cent of female business owners. Among the female self-employed, over 40 per cent worked less than twenty hours per week (Curran *et al.*, 1987: p. 43). According to the US Small Business Administration (USSBA) Report (1988) most women entrepreneurs run their businesses on a part-time basis. Older women, on the whole, work longer hours (Kaplan, 1988), reflecting the fact that they have fewer domestic responsibilities (Roberts-Reid and Curran, 1992). Another reason why many women run their businesses on a part-time basis is that they have second jobs. Curran *et al.* (1987) found that almost 13 per cent of the female small business owners reported having a second paid job, a figure over three times greater than that for male small business owners.

Yet again, however, these characteristics are not applicable to all women alike. Cromie and Hayes (1988), in their typology of female entrepreneurs, find that 'innovators' are usually single, without children and tend to reject conventional female roles. As a result, motivation for business ownership centres around career advancement, not accommodating a family. On the other hand, 'dualists' are usually married or divorced women with children, whose desires are to fulfil both roles – meeting the needs of their children and continuing some kind of paid employment. Business ownership is seen by such women as offering 'far more flexibility than conventional organisational careers' (Cromie and Hayes, 1988: p. 102). Nevertheless, women who make the decision to combine both roles often meet with severe problems which are discussed in section 1.3.3.

1.2.7   The desire to make money

Women are usually portrayed as placing less emphasis on making money than men (Cromie, 1987a; Carter and Cannon, 1992). Indeed, in a survey by Carter and Cannon (1992), no women stated 'earning a lot more money' as a reason for becoming self-employed. Similarly, the female business owners in Brown and Segal's study (1989) rated the desire to make money third compared to the male business owners who rated it first. However, when questioned further, both the men and the women were found to be equally driven by the desire to achieve success and both expressed 'success' in terms of increased sales (of at least 35 per cent) which implies a desire to grow and to make money. Hertz (1987) suggests that such contradictions lie in the fact that the desire to make money is not as 'romantic' a reason for starting a business as the desire for independence. Certain women may also feel that they are simply succumbing to what is perceived as a 'male' business objective in admitting that they are interested in money. As a result, there may be a tendency for women to underplay the desire for money and to overplay the desire for independence. Nevertheless, many women do recognise or admit the importance of making money in their business. For instance, one of the respondents in Hertz's study (1987) explained that 'the way you get independent is to have your own money' (p. 61).

Again, the desire to make money depends largely on the type of female entrepreneur and what she wants out of the business. Older female business owners tend to use entrepreneurship as a means to fulfil personal goals such as achievement and independence (Carter and Cannon, 1992). Younger women often have more business-oriented goals, such as profit, growth and diversification (Kaplan, 1988; Godfrey, 1992). The latter type of female entrepreneur will tend to show more interest in making money.

1.2.8   Environmental factors

Changes in the economic, political and social environment surrounding all actual or potential small business owners have had a number of important effects on the number of women starting their own businesses. First, the shift in the industrial structure of all industrialised countries, away from manufacturing and towards services, has been very important in facilitating both the growth of women's employment in general and also the growth of women's business ownership. While women are found to start businesses in sectors other than services (Hertz, 1987; Carter and Cannon, 1992), demonstrating that there is nothing inherent in women which confines them to occupations in the service sector, in reality women's businesses follow the traditional patterns of women's work and therefore female entrepreneurs have benefited from the growth of the service sector (Curran and Burrows, 1988: p. 56). It has provided opportunities for women to set up businesses in which they already have experience. Many service sector industries have traditionally employed women (Massey, 1984) and are relatively unattractive to men (Loscocco and Robinson, 1991). As indicated in section 1.2.2, increasing consumer affluence and a rise in the number of dual income households has also created niches for women to set up in businesses providing 'quasi-domestic' services (McDowell, 1991: p. 416).

Second, technological change (Rothwell, 1992) has reduced the cost and increased the ease of business start-up for everyone, including women (Batchelor, 1987). In particular, advances in telecommunications technology (e.g. telephone, computer, facsimile) have enabled work to be performed as quickly and professionally at home as in an office (Bacon, 1989). In turn, this has allowed many more women to run businesses from home, thus enabling them to combine work with their domestic commitments.

Third, would-be entrepreneurs of both sexes have benefited from the new enterprise ideology fostered by the Thatcher Government during the 1980s. There has been a continuing Government commitment to encourage new forms of economic enterprise to exploit the changes occurring in the economy. In particular small businesses have been encouraged because of their perceived potential contribution to the regeneration of the economy in terms of both job creation, increased competitiveness and innovation (Carter and Cannon, 1992). As part of this commitment, all entrepreneurs, including female entrepreneurs, have benefited from various financial aid packages for small firms such as the Loan Guarantee Scheme and the Enterprise Allowance Scheme (Chapman, 1987). For example, 38 per cent of those people starting on the Prince's Youth Business Trust Scheme (PYBT) between 1988 and 1991 were women (Dalgleish, 1993).

Many countries have also implemented specific policies to promote the creation of new ventures by women; however, the scope and focus of these vary widely. In Britain, women have benefited from a number of '*ad hoc*' schemes aimed at meeting the needs of those who might find it difficult to obtain start-up finance from conventional sources. For example, the London Business Incentive Scheme was established in order to provide financial support for 'minority' groups such as ethnic minorities, the disabled, the long-term unemployed and women. Sponsored by Greater London Enterprise, BP and Midland Bank, it provides unsecured loans of up to £5,000 for periods of up to 36 months (*Guardian*, 1991a: p. 16). The Women's Local Employment Initiatives (LEI) Programme, an initiative of the European Commission, is aimed at promoting female entrepreneurship in order to combat women's unemployment. Financial awards are made to new and young businesses started by women as long as at least two full-time jobs are created for women. There has also been an initiative run by the Women's Enterprise Forum. Set up in 1991, the Women's Enterprise Forum has been encouraging existing Enterprise Agencies to become more 'women-friendly'. As a result, Women's Enterprise Centres have been set up which offer advice and training specifically tailored to the needs of businesswomen.

Similar schemes have been set up in other countries. For example, in Australia there is the Victorian Women's Trust which offers financial assistance, advice and training to female entrepreneurs (LEDIS, 1989). In Sweden there are trade fairs and seminars to encourage women to start their own businesses, and the Swedish Development Fund offers special start-up grants just for women (Hisrich and Fan, 1991). Similarly, in the US, the Women's Economic Development Corporation (WEDCO) in St Paul, Minnesota, offers seminars, workshops and financial backing to women starting or growing businesses. Since 1983, WEDCO has assisted 3,700 women, 774 of whom have started businesses and 378 have expanded businesses. Of these enterprises, 87 per cent are still in business and provide, on average, three full-time and five part-time jobs. Since 1985, they have also made one or more loans to 135 businesses through their seed capital fund (Siegel, 1993). Other funds which have been set up in the US for women-owned businesses include Capital Rose, the Women's Equity Fund and Womensfund (*Entrepreneurial Woman*, 1993; *Inc.*, 1993). In Germany, a fund called Fonds Pour Femmes has been set up which encourages female investors to invest in German and international companies run by women (*Accountancy*, 1991).

Fourth, despite the fact that the growth of an 'enterprise culture' among the general population is open to question (Curran and Black-burn, 1991: p. 180), it is very likely that women have benefited from the shift in societal attitudes in favour of working women and the accept-ance of women running their own businesses (O'Hare and Larson, 1991), fuelled by increasing numbers of successful role models.

Fifth, female entrepreneurs have also benefited from better access to credit since the UK Sex Discrimination Act of 1975 (Chapman, 1976). The introduction of laws addressing inequalities in access to employ-ment opportunities (Malveaux, 1990) has also meant that women are entering more of the managerial positions within financial organisa-tions (Nelton, 1990) and are also reversing, to some extent, many of the stereotyped attitudes held by finance providers about women in business.

Sixth, increases in the number of women having access to education has, almost certainly, increased the numbers entering self-employment. Both O'Hare and Larson (1991) and Dolinsky *et al.* (1993) found that the likelihood of entering into self-employment for women clearly increased with increased levels of educational attainment. The reason for this is that educated women are more likely to have access to 'human' or 'intellectual' capital – the skills necessary to successfully start and run a business.

Finally, the large-scale down-sizing or 'right-sizing' of jobs in large companies, particularly during the 1990s, has led to persistently high levels of unemployment in many sectors of the economy in which women are concentrated, particularly in the service sector (Price and Monroe, 1992). Women have therefore been forced to consider self-employment and small business ownership out of economic necessity.

1.3   THE PROBLEMS FACED BY FEMALE ENTREPRENEURS

1.3.1   Introduction

Growth in the number and importance of women-owned businesses has been accompanied by a rapidly expanding literature on female entrepreneurship and business ownership. The need for research in this area was first recognised in the US during the early 1970s by Schreier and Komives (1973). Growing numbers of women-owned businesses and the prediction of continued growth in the future led to the realisation that existing research and models of entrepreneur-ship, based almost exclusively on male entrepreneurs, would not be sufficient. The first papers began to emerge in the US in the mid-1970s with a study by Schwartz (1976) of the characteristics of twenty female entrepreneurs. These studies tended to be largely descriptive and concentrated on the demographic characteristics of women-owned businesses and the background and psychology of female entrepreneurs (Bellu, 1993). However, it was not until the early 1980s that equivalent research was undertaken in the UK (Goffee and Scase, 1983; Watkins and Watkins, 1984). Subsequent studies of female entrepreneurship include work by Cromie and Hayes (1988), Carter and Cannon (1992), Allen and Truman (1993) and Rosa *et al.* (1994).

Existing research reveals that, despite the benefits of running a business, the reality of self-employment does not always conform to women's expectations. While there is a dark side to business ownership for both men and women, research suggests that some of the commonly shared problems (e.g. employing staff, getting business, late payment of bills, undercharging, cash-flow) appear to be exacerbated by gender for women (Simpson, 1991; Carter and Cannon, 1992). Indeed, Scottish Enterprise (1993b) argue that women have to work harder than men to achieve success in business. In most cases, the problems faced by women in business revolve around three main factors – their lack of management experience and training, conflicts associated with their roles in the home and at work, and discrimination and lack of credibility.

1.3.2   A lack of relevant education and experience

Studies indicate that the majority of female business owners have some form of further education qualification (Kaplan, 1988; Roberts-Reid and Curran, 1992; Dolinsky *et al.*, 1993). In the UK, Carter and Cannon (1992) found that 95 per cent of female entrepreneurs had further education qualifications. Some research has suggested that women business owners are better educated than their male counterparts (Schwartz, 1976; Smith, McCain and Warren, 1982; Watkins and Watkins, 1984; Welsch and Young, 1984; Curran and Burrows, 1988). However, Dolinsky *et al.* (1993) have argued that findings are inconsistent and equivocal. Nevertheless, women tend to have an educational background which is less relevant in preparing them for business ownership (Belcourt *et al.*, 1991). More women have training in 'non-practical', traditionally 'female' subjects such as the arts (Watkins and Watkins, 1984) and they lack the more directly relevant professional qualifications. Only 26 per cent of businesswomen in Watkins and Watkins's study had professional qualifications, compared to 62 per cent of businessmen (Watkins and Watkins, 1984).

Although businesswomen are often better educated than their male counterparts, they usually lack relevant managerial and entrepreneurial experience (Belcourt *et al.*, 1991; Kalleberg and Leicht, 1991; Fischer *et al.*, 1993; Barrett, 1995). Carter and Cannon (1992) found only 33 per cent of their sample of female entrepreneurs to have had any managerial experience and only 13 per cent had been small business owners before. Female entrepreneurs are also found to have less experience than their male counterparts (Barclays Bank, 1992; Scottish Enterprise, 1993b). Watkins and Watkins (1984) found that only 24 per cent of female business owners, compared to 72 per cent of male business owners, had any previous managerial experience. However, while Cromie (1987b) found that 66 per cent of female business owners had no founding experience, neither did 64 per cent of male business owners (p. 54).

Despite such contradictions, previous research generally indicates that women are unlikely to have had previous experience in areas which would help them to prepare for running their own businesses (Simpson, 1991). Female business owners are therefore more likely to suffer from problems doing their paperwork, marketing their business, raising finance, chasing bad debts or dealing with employees because of their lack of relevant experience and training. Financial management skills, in particular, are vitally important if a small business is to succeed (McMahon *et al.*, 1993).

1.3.3   Conflicts between work and domestic commitments

It has been suggested that many women enter self-employment to gain more control over their time and to achieve greater personal autonomy (Belcourt, 1991). However, it has been shown that business ownership can, in fact, bring irreconcilable demands for women. For all small business owners, running a business involves long hours, but because domestic duties and child-care are – frequently seen as a woman's responsibility, many businesswomen face conflicts in their roles as wife, mother and business owner (Stoner *et al.*, 1989; Lee-Gosselin and Grisé, 1990; Allen and Truman, 1991; Carter and Cannon, 1992; Davidson and Cooper, 1992; Jennings and Cohen, 1993).

It is common to find female business owners, particularly those who are mothers, displaying feelings of guilt because they do not fulfil the traditional female role (Cromie and Hayes, 1988). In addition, the 'support of the family is essential to entrepreneurial success' (Scottish

Enterprise 1993b: p. 15); however, female entrepreneurs often meet with 'doubts and disapproval' from their spouse or the rest of their family (Carter and Cannon, 1992: p. 138). Research undertaken by Scottish Enterprise (1993b) indicates that some husbands can be deliberately obstructive to the efforts of their entrepreneurial wives. When asked about her husband's attitude toward her business, one woman in a study by Goffee and Scase (1985) said that 'his attitude at the beginning was "well, as long as you're here and I have my dinner and the house runs, I don't mind"' (p. 48). Similarly, Scottish Enterprise (1993b) interviewed one female entrepreneur who had hidden the fact that she had left her former employer to start her own business from her husband for three months because she knew he would try to stop her.

Female business owners generally receive little or no help from their domestic partners to lighten the domestic work-load, unlike their male counterparts (Scase and Goffee, 1982). In Carter and Cannon' s study of female entrepreneurs, there were no examples of the spouse taking a leading role in running or managing the home (Carter and Cannon, 1992). However, even when male domestic partners do help out in the running of women-owned businesses, it is not always a successful 'partnership' (Carter and Cannon, 1992). Indeed, Carter and Cannon (1992) found that many female entrepreneurs felt it had been a catastrophic blow to their confidence and credibility, not least because their partners had 'taken over' and they no longer felt that it was *their* business. It is not unsurprising therefore that for some female business owners, business ownership has led to problems in their relationship with their spouse (Goffee and Scase, 1983). Although respondents in Carter and Cannon's survey felt that relations had not deteriorated, this was only because they had continued to give the family clear priority over the business (Carter and Cannon, 1992).

Domestic responsibilities may mean that the female entrepreneur faces problems allocating sufficient time to the business. The demands associated with running a business and a home may therefore restrict the growth and potential success of many women-owned businesses (Fischer *et al.*, 1993; Scottish Enterprise, 1993b; Srinivasan *et al.*, 1994). The need to accommodate domestic responsibilities such as child-care and caring for the disabled or elderly also means that many women run their businesses from home (see section 2.6.2). However, this can be problematical. First, there is the difficulty of separating the business and the home so that neither interferes with the other (Roberts-Reid and Curran, 1992). Second, problems associated with business credibility are often faced. Women need to get over the fact that many people regard a business run from home as 'a part-time business for a bored housewife with little interest in profits' (Carter and Cannon, 1992: p. 47). Third, the fact that women are more likely to run their businesses from home also means that they are more likely to suffer from feelings of isolation. Nevertheless, it has been suggested that running a business from home might give it an edge because it allows the owner to test the market before deciding to grow (Therrien *et al.*, 1986).

However, not all women business owners face work–home conflicts. For instance, 'achievement oriented' female entrepreneurs have fewer problems because, unlike 'returners', they do not organise their businesses around their family (Carter and Cannon, 1992: p. 73).

1.3.4 Discrimination and lack of credibility

Many women start their own businesses to avoid discrimination but continue to face it in self-employment (Belcourt *et al.*, 1991; Reuber *et al.*, 1991). The problem often stems from the fact that women generally lack credibility in the world of business ownership (Scottish Enterprise, 1993b). According to Harris (1994), men are often not convinced that a woman can run a small firm effectively. Many women feel that they are not taken seriously in business compared to male business owners and lack business credibility in the eyes of employees, customers, suppliers and financial institutions (Goffee and Scase, 1985; Hisrich, 1986; Clutterbuck and Devine, 1987; Miskin and Rose, 1990; Carter and Cannon, 1992; Carter, 1993). In particular, women have talked of 'an "assumed competence" which tends to be attributed to most men but not to most women' (Carter, 1993: p. 155). Even fathers are found to discriminate against their daughters by choosing sons to take over the family business more frequently (Belcourt, 1991).

Much of this problem has to do with traditionally defined notions of a woman's role in society, which is primarily the mother/homemaker (Goffee and Scase, 1983; Batchelor, 1987; Scottish Enterprise, 1993b). A woman who puts starting a business before domestic responsibilities may therefore be regarded by some as 'strange and exotic' (Clutterbuck and Devine, 1987: p. 131) or simply 'deviant' (Goffee and Scase, 1983: p. 640) because she does not adhere to male-defined notions of the female role. There is also a belief that women do not have the attributes of successful entrepreneurs (Buttner and Rosen, 1988a). Furthermore, the lack of relevant education and past experience frequently means that female business owners lack credibility in the world of business ownership.

Not being taken seriously can assume many forms. Some women have to contend with doubts and disapproval, others face downright negative and hostile attitudes. A good example of not being taken seriously is illustrated in the following comment made at a seminar run by the Women's Development Agency – 'a father of three children is considered to be stable and reliable; a mother with three children to look after is regarded as unstable and unreliable' (cited in a study by Scottish Enterprise, 1993b: p. 17).

As employers, female business owners often face problems in asserting their authority, particularly with their male employees, many of whom are unwilling to take orders from a woman (Carter and Cannon, 1992). It is well documented that some men are prejudiced against working for women (Kanter, 1981). In many cases, female business owners are forced to resort to delegating supervisory responsibilities for their male employees to a male intermediary (Carter and Cannon, 1992). Others will only employ females. Indeed, female business owners are found to use much more female labour than their male counterparts. In a study by Carter and Cannon (1992), over a third of female business owners stated a preference for employing females. This was not just because of the types of jobs being offered but also due to a belief that women are more adaptable, work harder and are less likely to be a challenge to their authority (p. 69). Research also indicates that female business owners feel they can communicate more effectively with female employees (Smith, Smits and Hoy, 1992). Another problem is that many businesswomen adopt a 'feminine' or 'matriarchal' management style, that is they are more 'people oriented' and 'less autocratic' than businessmen (Chaganti, 1986; Carter, 1993). However, despite the fact that a more egalitarian management style can create a relaxed, creative work atmosphere, not all employees are comfortable with such an approach. It is suggested that men have trouble adapting to this style of management because they 'want to know what their sphere of influence is' (Therrien *et al.*, 1986: p. 56).

Similarly, in dealing with customers and suppliers, female business owners face problems convincing them of their credibility. Many businesswomen are of the view that their gender is a barrier in getting new business (Carter and Cannon, 1992). Male customers, in particular, are often wary of businesses owned by women. According to one of the businesswomen interviewed by Goffee and Scase (1985), 'clients are very surprised when they find I'm a woman...when they find out I'm in charge. I think it puts them off for a little while...I guess they think I should be at home rearing children' (p. 48). While many female business owners have to put up with the annoyance of jokes and innuendoes from their male suppliers and customers, others face more serious problems when customers start questioning their ability to carry out a particular piece of work or suppliers refuse to extend them credit. One of the businesswomen in a study by Carter and Cannon (1992) believed that discrimination on the basis of both her gender and company structure (a co-operative) was responsible for her inability to secure a place on many tendering lists (p. 75). These problems can be even worse for women in non-traditional, male-dominated business sectors (Hisrich and O'Brien, 1981).

In the light of this discussion, it is not surprising to find that many businesswomen are found to lack confidence and have a low self-assessment (Hisrich and Brush, 1983; 1986; Honig-Haftel and Martin, 1986; Batchelor, 1987). In a study by Still and Guerin (1991), the most significant entry barrier to women starting their own businesses was found to be gaining the necessary confidence. Credibility is closely tied up with issues of self-confidence. According to one respondent in Carter and Cannon's study, 'there is only one real difference between men and women which shows itself and that is confidence' (Carter and Cannon, 1992: p. 76). The suggestion is that men succeed because they think they can. Men are also more used to feeling that they belong in the business world while women tend to be less sure of their role. According to one of the interviewees in an article by Therrien *et al.* (1986), the problem is that 'what girls are taught as acceptable behaviour is in the sharpest contrast to what you do in business' (p. 56). Women tend to be brought up to see themselves in a nurturing, supportive role, whereas successful entrepreneurs are aggressive, ruthless, tough, decisive and single-minded. In particular, risk-taking is crucial in running a small business but tends to be a more alien concept for women than for men (O'Hare and Larson, 1991).

A common problem linked to low levels of self-confidence and one which is frequently mentioned by women in business is that of under-charging (Carter and Cannon, 1992). While many women set up in highly competitive service sector businesses and therefore need to compete on price, it is often the case that, because women lack confidence and have an 'apologetic' approach to business (Carter and Cannon, 1992), many will not charge very much for their products or services because they do not have the confidence to regard them as being worth very much. Similarly, although the delayed payment of bills is a problem suffered by male and female business owners alike, many women lack the assertiveness to follow up bad debts (Carter and Cannon, 1992). Both of these factors are likely to constrain the growth opportunities of small women-owned businesses.

1.3.5 The problem of raising finance

A particular problem faced by female entrepreneurs, which is often discussed in relation to discrimination and lack of credibility, is that of raising finance (Carter and Cannon, 1992; Price and Monroe, 1992; Scottish Enterprise, 1993b). From the earliest studies of female entrepreneurship, dating back to the 1970s, raising finance has been identified as a particular problem for women in business. Indeed, in a review of the female entrepreneurship literature, Brush (1992) pointed out that the 'financial aspects of venture start-up and management are without a doubt the *biggest obstacles* for women' (p. 14 – emphasis added). Similarly, Stevenson (1986) argues that 'access to capital is a problem cited in *most* of the research studies on women entrepreneurs' (p. 35 – emphasis added). In particular, many businesswomen feel they are discriminated against by financial institutions, especially the banks. For example, in a study by Goffee and Scase (1985) most women described the reaction of their banks as 'generally unsympathetic and patronising' (p. 45). Although raising capital is a 'perennial problem for new and small businesses as a whole' (Jones *et al.*, 1992: p. 1), there is a widespread perception among female small business owners that their particular problems are, at least in part, a function of their gender (Schwartz, 1976; Goffee and Scase, 1985; Carter and Cannon, 1992).

1.4 SUMMARY, RESEARCH RATIONALE AND OVERVIEW

To summarise this chapter, it has been shown that since the 1970s, there has been a rapid growth in the number of women starting their own businesses. Female entrepreneurship offers women many opportunities: to escape the confines of a labour market that continues to discriminate against women; to gain independence; and to combine work with domestic commitments. In addition, women-owned businesses represent a growing source of employment and the money generated by women in business is helping to support many households where the male domestic partner is out of work or is under-paid. Furthermore, women-owned businesses account for one-third of the total small business population. Their success therefore has wide-ranging implications for the future success of the UK economy as a whole.

However, research suggests that many women face barriers in starting up and running their businesses, the greatest of which is that of raising finance. The ability to raise finance is one of the greatest challenges facing all small business owners and a critical factor in the formation and growth of small businesses (Harrison and Mason, 1986; Binks *et al.*, 1992; Sargent and Young, 1991). Without finance, it is impossible to start a business or to cover the initial loss making period which is experienced by most small firms (Scottish Enterprise, 1993a). Indeed, it is not surprising to find that the problem of under-capitalisation is one of the most common causes of small firm failure (McMahon *et al.*, 1993). According to Gould and Parzen (1990), 'capital cannot turn a weak business idea into a strong business, but lack of capital can derail a good business idea' (p. 89). Together, the amount, nature and cost of finance, especially at start-up, is therefore fundamental to the success of a small business enterprise (Scottish Enterprise, 1993a).

The fact that women are found to face barriers in their access to finance therefore has wide-ranging implications and the identification and examination of these barriers is therefore a research priority (Buttner and Rosen, 1988a; Carter and Rosa, 1995). In chapter two of this book, the full extent of existing knowledge on the financing of women-owned businesses is ascertained in an in-depth review of the literature. There is a strong suggestion running through many existing studies that women are discriminated against in their access to business finance because of their gender. However, despite evidence for the existence of gender-related discrimination in women's access to external finance, whether based on the perceptions of the female entrepreneurs involved (Schwartz, 1976; Goffee and Scase, 1985; Carter and Cannon, 1992), or on evidence from research into the behaviour of financial organisations (Buttner and Rosen, 1988a; Riding and Swift, 1990), many findings are found to be inconclusive or contradictory in nature. One of the major problems with existing research is the lack of an appropriate theoretical framework. Chapter 2 therefore explores 'gendered' small firm finance theory as a means to explore further some of the factors underlying the problems faced by women in the financing of their businesses which are identified in the literature.

However, the overall conclusion of chapter 2 is that, given the existing literature, it is far from clear as to whether, or to what extent, gender plays a role in the financing of small firms and how far difficulties faced by women in the financing of their businesses are caused by gender discrimination or are merely a function of the characteristics of the businesses and their owners. In chapter 3, it is demonstrated that this lack of clarity largely reflects the fragmentary nature and flawed methodologies of much of the existing research. In particular, studies in the UK have failed to compare the experiences of female business owners with those of similarly placed male business owners.

In the light of these findings it is therefore proposed that further research should be undertaken into the financing of women-owned businesses in the UK which seeks to clarify the role of gender and which overcomes the methodological problems of previous studies. In order to account for systematic differences between male and female business owners which may influence the financing of their businesses, a matched pairs methodology is adopted in order to undertake a comparative study of forty pairs of male and female business owners. The advantages and disadvantages of the survey method are outlined and chapter 3 concludes with an overview of the general character-istics of the sample of businesses included in the study.

In the remaining chapters, results from a study of forty matched pairs of female and male business owners are reported in an attempt to answer the main research questions posed at the end of chapter two. Chapter 4 seeks to discover whether matched pairs of male and female business owners differ in terms of the types and amounts of finance used, and the problems faced in the financing of their busi-nesses (as suggested in previous studies). Given the importance of banks as a source of small firm finance, chapter 5 goes on to explore and compare the banking relationships of male and female business owners in more detail and to investigate the allegations that banks sexually discriminate against women, which frequently occur in the female entrepreneurship literature. In chapter 6, a comparison is made between the men and women in terms of their access to sources of external advice and assistance which has important implications for the financing of their businesses.

Finally, chapter 7 puts forward a number of conclusions and impli-cations of the study findings and reviews the importance of this research in terms of both its contribution to existing academic debates and its relevance to female business owners, financial organisations and policy makers.

The overall aim of the research is therefore to provide the first, in-depth, comparative study of the experiences of female and male busi-ness owners in raising finance in the UK – the amount, nature and conditions of finance raised, attitudes towards the various sources of finance available to small business owners, and problems faced in the financing of their businesses.

2 The financing of women-owned businesses

An empirical overview and theoretical framework

2.1 PROBLEMS FACED BY WOMEN IN THE FINANCING OF THEIR BUSINESSES

From the earliest studies of female entrepreneurship, dating back to the 1970s, raising finance has been identified as a particular problem for women in business. Indeed, Schwartz (1976) found 'the initial and major barrier experienced by female entrepreneurs was felt to be credit discrimination during the capital formation stage' (p. 60). For many women, financing their business appears to be *the* major problem faced (Hisrich and O'Brien, 1982; Hisrich and Brush, 1983; 1984; 1985; 1987; Collerette and Aubry, 1990; Department of Industry, Technology and Commerce, 1991; Carter and Cannon, 1992). In Hisrich and O'Brien's study of female business owners, almost 45 per cent of respondents indicated that obtaining lines of credit was a significant problem (Hisrich and O'Brien, 1981). Studies suggest that businesswomen face greater difficulties obtaining capital than similarly placed men (Loscocco *et al.*, 1991; Carter and Cannon, 1992; Godfrey, 1992; Johnson and Storey, 1993; Koper, 1993). To quote Van der Meer (1986), 'women have greater difficulty than men in obtaining credit, whether from the banks or from the state, for the creation of a business'. In a study by Scott (1986), 44 of the 154 female entrepreneurs interviewed felt that they would find it easier to borrow money if they were men.

2.1.1 The treatment of female business owners by banks

Reasons why women feel that they face more problems in the financing of their businesses generally centre around the perception that banks are biased against female entrepreneurs (Hisrich and Brush, 1987) and that they are often 'unsympathetic and patronising' (Goffee and Scase, 1983: p. 636), basing their lending decisions on sexual stereotypes, rather than ability to control the business (Buttner and Rosen, 1988a). Indeed, banks 'have had a notorious reputation of failing to give women's businesses the credibility they deserve' (Allen and Truman, 1991: p. 122; Carter and Cannon, 1992). According to Hisrich and Brush (1986), 'few aspects of business present as great a problem for the woman entrepreneur as obtaining a bank loan' (p. 123). Bank managers have been accused of treating businesswomen with a condescending attitude and immediately assuming financial ignorance (Reilly, 1989; Still and Guerin, 1991; Fabowale *et al.*, 1993). According to a study by Goffee and Scase (1985), there is a 'general "biased" opinion of women's ability to own and control businesses' (p. 45). Women are frequently given the impression that banks think they lack the motivation and ambition necessary to start a business and that they are only doing it for 'pin money' (Kaur and Hayden, 1993). A typical example of such attitudes is that of Mrs Hardy Hall, reported in the *Observer* (1994a). When she approached her bank during start-up, 'the loans manager fired off a series of questions about what her husband does and how much he earned, rather than discussing her business plan' (p. 7). Indeed, she felt his whole attitude was 'go back and make jam, Mrs Hall'. According to a report by Therrien *et al.* (1986), banks generally see a woman's business as a hobby rather than a serious business venture.

During interviews with their bank manager, female entrepreneurs are often reported to have been asked questions which would not have been asked were they men. In the Netherlands, Koper (1989) found that the female business owners in the sample were asked different questions by their bank managers compared to their male counterparts, in particular questions about their plans for starting a family. Similarly, one of the businesswomen interviewed by Reilly (1989) complained that 'when I was starting out, bank managers only wanted to know how much I spent on clothes and when was I – a single professional women – going to start having babies' (p. 25).

It is not only the attitudes of bank managers towards their female business customers that appears to be problematic. Indeed, there is also evidence to suggest that the terms and conditions of bank finance are also less favourable for the female entrepreneur. Research suggests that female entrepreneurs are more likely to be asked to provide security or guarantees, either from their husband or their father (Clutterbuck and Devine, 1987; Carter and Cannon, 1992; Koper, 1993). In a study by Collerette and Aubry (1990), 35 per cent of female entrepreneurs who had borrowed money from a financial institution were asked to provide a co-signer. According to a parallel survey, these female entrepreneurs were asked to provide co-signers twice as often as their male counterparts. In one case, reported by Kaur and Hayden (1993), 'a woman was told by her bank manager that if all else failed [that is, if she were unable to raise finance for her business], she could always find herself a "sugar daddy"' (p. 103). In addition, women are often required to provide more security or collateral than would be required for the same loan to a man (Godfrey, 1992). Riding and Swift (1990), in a comparative study of male and female business owners in Canada, found that women were required to provide more collateral to secure a line of credit than their male counterparts.

In response to the problems outlined above, many female entrepreneurs are found to use 'straw men' (Hertz, 1987: p. 189) or male 'sleeping' partners (Goffee and Scase, 1985: p. 45) to give themselves added credibility when dealing with the banks, to negotiate credit on their behalf or to act as financial guarantors. These men generally 'perform no active, day-to-day function in the running of women's businesses [but] may, nevertheless, claim a significant share of the profits' in return for their involvement (Goffee and Scase, 1983: p. 636).

2.1.2   Explaining the differential treatment of female business owners by banks

A number of studies have been undertaken which seek to explore possible explanations for why banks might treat their female customers differently to their male customers. Two of the main studies are those of Buttner and Rosen (1988a; 1988b). The aim of their first study (Buttner and Rosen, 1988a) was to test whether loan officers in the South-East USA judge female entrepreneurs in terms of sex stereotypes, rather than on their actual accomplishments. Sixty male and forty-six female loan officers were selected from a medium-sized banking institution and asked to evaluate men and women on nine attributes of successful entrepreneurship (leadership, autonomy, propensity to take risk, readiness for change, endurance, lack of emotionalism, low need for support, low conformity and persuasiveness). Loan officers of both sexes were found to ascribe these characteristics more readily to men than women, although female loan officers indicated fewer differences. This finding raises serious implications for female business owners because it would appear that their loan applications are being judged by financial decision-makers with biased and stereotyped notions about women and their business abilities.

In a follow-up study, Buttner and Rosen (1988b) sought to assess the effects of the entrepreneur's sex, type of business and sex of decision-maker on decisions to provide new venture funding. A simulated study was set up using undergraduate business students to assess a hypothetical business plan and loan application presented by either a male or a female entrepreneur. It was found that male decision-makers were more supportive of female entrepreneurs seeking finance to start a traditionally 'female' business and more supportive of male entrepreneurs seeking to start a traditionally 'male' business. However, female decision-makers tended to support entrepreneurs of both sexes starting businesses in non-traditional sectors. Despite this being a simulated experiment, these findings have important implications for female entrepreneurs. In particular, those women seeking funds for what are perceived as 'male-oriented' ventures are at a disadvantage because they have to overcome scepticism by male financial decision-makers about their abilities to run businesses in traditionally male domains. According to the authors, the best hope for such women is to find a female bank manager, or venture capitalist.

Fay and Williams (1991), again using a hypothetical business plan approach, mailed scenarios of an application for loan finance to loan officers in 200 branches of the four major trading banks operating in New Zealand. The scenarios were identical in all respects except that half were from a male entrepreneur and half from a female entrepreneur. To emphasise this point, the loan applications incorporated photographs of a either a man or a woman. Loan officers were asked whether or not they would approve the loan and to indicate factors that were important in their decision. It was found that loan officers were less likely to recommend a loan for the female applicant than they were for the male applicant. More reasons were given for declining the loan of the female applicant. These generally included inadequacy of available equity and security. However, in a follow-up study, Fay and Williams (1993) found that the situation was complicated by the level of the entrepreneur's education. When both the hypothetical male and female entrepreneurs were described as having a university level of education, they were both equally likely to be granted the loan. When both entrepreneurs were attributed with a lower education level, female entrepreneurs were less likely to be granted the loan. Similarly, Bowman-Upton *et al.* (1987) found that female entrepreneurs with a high school diploma or higher education found financial institutions to be more co-operative. These findings are not surprising because '(t)he level of education of the entrepreneur, like experience, should be considered a positive predictor of new venture success and therefore positively accepted by the lending agency' (Bowman-Upton *et al.*, 1987: p. 6; Berry *et al.*, 1993)

2.1.3   The banks and women-owned businesses: contradictory evidence

Although there is a substantial body of research which suggests that women business owners face particular problems in raising finance, it is important to note that there is also a smaller body of contradictory evidence. For example, a number of studies have found that raising finance is not a significant problem for women in business (Stevenson, 1983; Hertz, 1987; Department of Alberta, 1990). Carter and Rosa (1995) could find no evidence to suggest that female business owners are refused finance more than their male counterparts. Similarly, Johnson and Storey (1993) could find no evidence to suggest that female business owners attempted and failed to obtain finance at start-up more than their male counterparts and both Wynant and Hatch (1990) and Rosa *et al.* (1994) found comparable levels of satisfaction with the banking relationship between male and female small business customers. In a recent Canadian study (Fabowale *et al.*, 1993), no evidence could be found to suggest that the gender of the business owner was significant in explaining differences in the terms of credit[1] offered to small businesses by the banks. Carter and Rosa (1995) have also found that gender does not account for differences between male and female business owners in either the requirement for or usage of financial guarantors.

On the supply side, Wynant and Hatch (1990) found no significant differences between female and male business owners in the borrower ratings assigned to them by lending officers, nor in the rejection rates for loans. In fact, similarities were found in both loan cost, type, amount of collateral required, repayment provisions and the frequency of spousal guarantees being required. By way of an explanation, businesswomen in a study by Hertz (1987) describe banks as not having 'a bias against or for businesswomen', rather 'a bias against people generally' (p. 188). Gumpert (1985) also found bankers and investors to be 'equally uncompromising for men and women'.

Inconsistencies and contradictions have also been found within research by the same authors. Paradoxically, while Buttner and Rosen (1988a; 1988b) found that loan officers of both sexes ascribe the characteristics of successful entrepreneurs more readily to men than to women and that male financial decision-makers tend to be more sceptical about a woman's ability to run a business in a traditionally male domain, in a later study they found loan officers to be equally likely to approve the loan applications of male and female entrepreneurs and equally likely to make a counteroffer to both sexes (Buttner and Rosen, 1989). Similarly, Koper (1989) found that female business owners are asked different questions by their bank managers compared to their male counterparts. Koper (1993), however, found no differences in the characteristics ascribed by the bank lenders to male and female entrepreneurs. Nevertheless, it must be borne in mind that these discrepancies may simply be a reflection of the fact that later studies adopted different and more sophisticated methodologies.

To summarise, there appears to be a paradox within the existing female entrepreneurship literature. On the one hand there is copious evidence, particularly of an anecdotal nature, to suggest that female entrepreneurs face greater difficulties than male entrepreneurs in financing their businesses, particularly sexual discrimination. On the other hand, there is also empirical evidence to suggest that male and female business owners are not treated differently by finance providers and are offered the same terms of credit. In an attempt to reconcile this paradox, Buttner and Rosen (1989) made three suggestions as to why this might be the case. First, that female entrepreneurs are more likely to underestimate the difficulties associated with raising finance, primarily because they lack experience of raising finance. Second, that they are more likely to attribute the bank's rejection of their proposal to gender bias. Third, that male owners are more active in their search for alternative sources of finance if they are faced with problems raising bank finance. However, in a follow-up survey to test these hypotheses, Buttner and Rosen (1992) could find no supporting evidence.

2.2 THE FINANCING OF WOMEN-OWNED BUSINESSES: A THEORETICAL FRAMEWORK

2.2.1 Introduction

One of the main problems of existing research is that it is very difficult to compare the results of previous studies, not least because most of them have been carried out in the absence of a theoretical framework. Indeed, according to Fischer *et al.* (1993),

> research on sex and gender differences in entrepreneurship needs ... a theoretical overview if future studies are to be reconciled with previous ones, and if progress is to be made in understanding the extent to which relevant differences exist and what, if anything should be done to address them.
>
> (Fischer *et al.*, 1993: p. 153)

The advantage of working within a theoretical framework is that it allows for better interpretation of complex findings and for highly disparate empirical findings to be reconciled in a more coherent and meaningful way (Fischer *et al.*, 1993). The aim of this section is therefore to develop the most appropriate theoretical framework within which to explore the financing of women-owned businesses.

2.2.2 Choosing the appropriate theoretical framework

Theoretical frameworks adopted in previous research

Existing research on female entrepreneurship has been approached from a number of different perspectives, reflecting the variety of different disciplines from within which the subject has been studied. In a review of fifty-seven empirical articles on female business owner-ship, Brush (1992) found that most studies with a named theoretical base originate from the discipline of Psychology (e.g. Sexton and Bowman, 1986) and Sociology (e.g. Aldrich *et al.*, 1989) (Table 2.1). However, Table 2.1 also shows that more than a third of studies neither explicitly state that the research is connected to a theory base, nor indicate whether they are exploratory in nature or designed to generate theory (Brush, 1992). To date, most of the studies which have concentrated on the financing of women-owned businesses also appear to lack a theoretical base.

The call for more theory-driven research has already been heard from the broader entrepreneurship literature. Indeed, in 1991 there was a conference[2] held at the University of Illinois devoted entirely to discussing existing theories and formulating new ones, papers from

Table 2.1 Theory bases used in research on female business owners

Stated theory base	Number	%
None stated[a]	22	39
Psychology (i.e. trait, psychoanalytic)	15	26
Sociology (i.e. network, social interaction)	10	17
Exploratory (grounded theory)	6	11
Business strategy and policy (problem-solving, decision-making)	4	7
Total	57	100

Source: Brush, 1992: p. 11
Note: [a] Many articles did not explicitly link the empirical study to a theory. Instead, the research was frequently justified by a 'lack of information about women business owners'. It is these studies that are in this category.

which were subsequently published in a special issue of *The Journal of Business Venturing* (1993). The same call for theory is now being heard from the female entrepreneurship literature. Fischer *et al.* (1993), for example, point out that there is a need to articulate and test theories rather than 'merely accumulating empirical findings' so that knowledge might be more systematically developed (p. 153). The argument for the development of a more adequate theoretical model of female entrepreneurship is also taken up by Allen and Truman (1988: p. 13). The question is, which theoretical framework is most relevant for a study of the financing of women-owned businesses? In the remainder of this section, a number of theoretical approaches are critically evaluated.

Modern finance theory (agency theory)

The most common perspective from which research into the financing of small businesses has been undertaken is that of modern finance theory. To summarise its basic concepts, 'modern finance theory directs scholarly attention to the way in which the capital market enables allocation of scarce financial resources between individuals and business enterprises over time' (McMahon *et al.*, 1993: p. 69). Although in its early development small firms were largely ignored (Ang, 1991), modern finance theory has been used by a growing number of researchers in recent years as a framework for studying the financing of small businesses. A theoretical perspective which has contributed significantly to modern finance theory in its recent development is that of agency theory (McMahon *et al.*, 1993).

In general, agency theory 'considers a business enterprise from the viewpoint of the various stakeholders it might have and explores how their financial interests are furthered and protected in their dealings with each other' (McMahon *et al.*, 1993: p. 80). Stakeholders might include business owners or managers, creditors, customers, employees, family members and the general community. A particularly valuable contribution by agency theory has been to examine the relationship between small firms and their finance providers (Hand *et al.*, 1982; Pettit and Singer, 1985; Ang, 1991). For example, Landström (1992) adopted agency theory as a framework to explain the interaction between private investors and entrepreneurs. Similarly, Sapienza (1989) used an agency theory perspective to explain the relationship between formal venture capitalists and entrepreneurs. Deakins and Hussain (1992) also used agency theory to explore small firm–banking relations.

The agency relationship is based around the concept of 'agents' who exercise control on behalf of stakeholders or 'principals' (Jensen and Meckling, 1976). In the case of small firm finance, the agent is typically an owner-manager of a small firm and the principal is the supplier of external finance. According to agency theory, the agency relationship is inherently problematical. The 'principle of self-interested behaviour' explains that both principals and agents act in an economically rational manner, thus both parties will act in their own best interests (McMahon *et al.*, 1993: p. 81) even if their actions are detrimental to achieving common objectives (Hand *et al.*, 1982). Both parties usually have different goals and it is this incongruity which ultimately leads to conflict within the relationship. The problems inherent in all agency relationships are likely to be most significant when the business is small (Hand *et al.*, 1982) because day-to-day control of the small firm is typically in the hands of just one owner-manager who often has a major personal stake in the business. Any business risks taken are therefore likely to represent personal risks for the owner-manager. This will lead many owner-managers into taking financial decisions which minimise the level of personal risk rather than those which might be more beneficial to the finance provider. In addition to this central issue, there are a number of other problems which frequently arise in the agency relationship between small business enterprises and their finance providers.

First, as Barnea *et al.* (1981) point out, agency problems often arise in the financing of small firms because of the level of *asymmetric information*. The term asymmetric information refers to the situation in which the agent tends to have more information on the financial circumstances and prospects of the business than the principal (McMahon *et al.*, 1993). In the case of small firms, such information asymmetries are exacerbated as information on small firms is less readily available (Storey, 1994), less subject to control, and relatively more expensive to supply and obtain than is the case for larger firms (Pettit and Singer, 1985). There are few incentives for a third party, such as an outside analyst, to collect information on small firms because the market for such information is so small (Ang, 1991). The data generated by the small business owners themselves may be fairly poor in quality because many lack the skills to come up with the most relevant and useful data. In addition, small business owners are under no constraint to produce verifiable information as they tend not to have any publicly traded securities (Ang, 1991). Furthermore, many small firm owners lack the motivation to disclose such information for fear that it might be used against them, an issue which is referred to as 'information impactedness' (Kaplan and Atkinson, 1989). The small firm owner-manager therefore tends to be much more highly informed than any external finance provider.

However, it has been argued that the seriousness of information asymmetries varies according to the type of small business involved. For example, the owner-manager of a wholly new firm or business start-up may, in fact, have a highly imperfect idea of whether or not they will be successful, while their bank manager may have a much better idea because they have had previous experience of similar businesses at similar stages of development (Storey, 1994). Similarly, in the case of small businesses which are reliant on their local market and which have an account with a local bank, it may often be the bank manager who has a superior knowledge of the local business conditions. In such cases, information asymmetries may therefore be less pronounced. However, in the case of very small or young firms, particularly in dynamic industries such as high-tech firms, information asymmetries may be more pronounced than usual. Owner-managers of these sorts of firms often have a far greater level of knowledge of the business than any external finance provider and may be the only experts in a narrow field (Ang, 1992). These types of owner-managers, in particular, may not be able to communicate their knowledge of the firm very easily to external finance providers (Mason and Harrison, 1991).

Second, the agency relationship may suffer from problems associated with *moral hazard*. This refers to the situation in which an agent does not act in a manner consistent with the contract they have with the principal or in the principal's best interests. For example, the agent might deliberately take advantage of information asymmetries to redistribute wealth to him- or herself or might not invest the finance in the ways agreed upon in the financial contract. As Keasey and Watson (1993a) have argued, 'agents do not give up their own self-interests just because they have entered into an economic relationship' (p. 24). They may therefore attempt to deceive the principal to further their own interests. Small firms in particular present a high risk of moral hazard. Because they tend to have a 'close' company status, that is they rarely have shareholders and the owner-manager holds 100 per cent of the equity, they are in a much stronger position to exploit information asymmetries and to act in their own interests. Furthermore, it is usually the case that small firms will be financed mainly by external debt finance. Their borrowing will therefore require regular repayment of the debt plus interest, irrespective of how well or badly they are performing. If the small business has limited liability status, and finance is not secured on personal assets or collateral, the costs of a bad debt will not fall on the owner-manager but on the creditor. In the light of these two factors, many owner-managers are therefore tempted to take on increasingly risky projects since they will benefit from any of the up-side gains but bear none of the down-side risks (Keasey and Watson, 1993a).

A third problem in the agency relationship from the principal's point of view is that of *adverse selection*. This refers to the situation in which an external finance provider is unable to distinguish between good and bad projects. Work by Deakins and Hussain (1992) highlights two types of lending errors: TYPE I errors (turning away future successes); and TYPE II errors (taking on future failures). Central to this problem is the fact that finance providers have to make decisions based on their knowledge of the agent's skills and competencies. In the case of making decisions on small business owners, this knowledge is frequently incomplete and therefore finance providers are often in no position to judge whether an owner-manager actually possesses the competencies required. By exploiting information asymmetries, an owner-manager is also in a good position to misrepresent the skills or abilities they bring to an enterprise (McMahon *et al.*, 1993). Another adverse selection problem is that the finance provider may also choose to use selective subsets of information that are inappropriate for assessing the risk of small businesses (Deakins and Hussain, 1992: p. 3).

Because of the increased risk and severity of problems (e.g. information asymmetries, moral hazard and adverse selection) associated with the financing of small businesses, it is not surprising that the costs of maintaining such an agency relationship are high (McMahon *et al.*, 1993). Agency costs involve both *monitoring* and *information costs*. The principal incurs monitoring costs in attempting to overcome problems associated with moral hazard. These costs are usually associated with setting up bonding arrangements, in other words, contracts which formally bind the agent to 'agreed types of behaviour and provide for sanctions should actual behaviour deviate from that specified in the contract' (McMahon *et al.*, 1993: p. 82). In the case of small firm financing, especially bank financing, these contracts usually take the form of loan or overdraft agreements – contracts whereby small firms face penalties if they do not comply to the stated terms and conditions, notably repayment within an agreed length of time. Sanctions might include higher interest rates, larger fees or withdrawal of the facility. Another bonding arrangement is through the provision of incentives which encourage small business owners to behave in a manner which is consistent with the contract. These might include favourable interest rates, waiving of fees or repayment holidays. Again, the costs are incurred by the finance provider. Information costs arise from the information asymmetries which are generally associated with transactions involving small businesses. Finance providers therefore may incur costs in improving their access to more reliable facts and figures which would allow them to judge more accurately the performance of the small business (McMahon *et al.*, 1993: p. 82).

Agency costs may also be high for the small firm itself. The finance provider may require the small business owner to provide financial statements or to undertake audits conducted by independent agents on a regular basis. The fixed cost of any monitoring system, for example an accounting or auditing system, is not proportional to the size of the firm (Pettit and Singer, 1985), therefore small firms may pay relatively more agency costs than a large firm.

In order to cover the risks inherent in the agency relationship, banks often demand higher levels of interest from their small business customers, primarily to compensate for the greater possibility of wealth expropriation (Pettit and Singer, 1985). The banks also want to ensure that, in the event of the small business defaulting on the loan, their investment will be secured. The small business owner may therefore be required to provide a guarantee and/or security on loans or overdrafts (Cosh and Hughes, 1994). In the face of increased levels of uncertainty surrounding the financing of small firms, securities and guarantees also act as *signals* to finance providers that the owner-manager is committed to the business. Banks are interested in identifying firms with a low risk of defaulting on their loans. In particular, because banks do not share in the up-side gains of lending to small businesses but bear the down-side losses, they are more concerned about minimising their exposure to TYPE II lending errors (taking on future failures) rather than TYPE I errors (turning away future successes) (Deakins and Hussain, 1992). Small business securities are usually preferred in the form of personal guarantees or assets such as the owner's home. Those owner-managers who are prepared to put up their home as collateral on a loan signal to their creditors that they are committed and confident in its success. However, Ang (1991) suggests that a reliance on personal security by the banks will lead many owner-managers to make business decisions which result in fewer risks but also provide lower business returns in order to guarantee paying off their debts and therefore not to lose their home.

The contextual approach

While it is evident that modern finance theory has been modified and extended 'to accommodate the unique characteristics of small enterprises' and therefore goes a long way towards explaining the processes underlying the financing of small businesses more generally (McMahon *et al.*, 1993: p. 95), it fails to consider the role of characteristics such as the sex of the business owner in these processes. The problem is that modern finance theory represents just one element of the small firm financing issue, that is, the traditional economic view of small firm financing. Economic theories have tended to concentrate on concepts of project viability, efficient markets and the rational allocation of resources. However, Sargent and Young (1991) argue that these assumptions do not fully explain the flow of capital and that there is a need to integrate the 'economic' with concepts about social processes. For instance, other factors which are of great importance in the process of procuring capital include the *past context* of both the entrepreneur and the investor (education, background and experience), the *current opportunities* (and constraints) and *individual characteristics* (personality and competencies).

The contextual approach, put forward by Sargent and Young (1991), acknowledges the fact that raising finance is a complex and dynamic process and may be affected by a number of different factors, both economic and social (Buttner and Rosen, 1989; Moore *et al.*, 1992) (Figure 2.1). The 'context' of both the entrepreneur and the lender/investor will impinge on the financing of a small business. Perceptions also play a major role, not just those of the lender/investor but also those of the entrepreneur. How both parties perceive each other will ultimately shape the funding outcome. The financing relationship therefore incorporates a level of social interaction based on the expectations and interpretations of both parties involved (Koper, 1993). Such an approach recognises that entrepreneurs with 'different occupational, social, and educational experiences' may well follow different approaches to venture creation which may result in 'different problems, and different business outcomes' (Brush, 1992: p. 15).

This perspective has important implications for a study of the financing of women-owned businesses. As the relationship between small business owners and the financial community is not purely an economic one and small business finance is highly integrated into the context of the owner's whole life situation, it is therefore necessary to integrate an understanding of the 'economics' of small firm financing with an understanding of the female 'context' of business ownership.

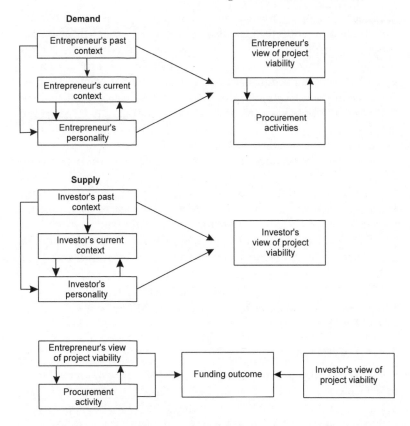

Figure 2.1 The entrepreneur's search for and acquisition of capital (proposed relationships between variables)
Source: Sargent and Young, 1991 (p. 245)

An approach which has recently been discussed and which helps to develop such concepts is the Integrated Perspective (Brush, 1992). The foundations of the Integrated Perspective are rooted in Psychology and Sociology. Psychological research has found women to have a different personal 'reality' than men, characterised by 'connectedness' and relationships rather than autonomy and logic which appear to be more typical of men's reality (Gilligan, 1982). Meanwhile, sociological research has identified the fact that women in business view their social relationships in a different way to men and have different social networks (Aldrich, 1989). Women's perspectives on entrepreneurship and business ownership are therefore found to be very different to those of men (Reilly, 1989: p. 25; Koper, 1993: p. 67). An integrated approach recognises that women perceive and experience business ownership differently to men (Brush, 1992) and argues that attempts to separate the female entrepreneur from her wider contextual setting is both misleading and distorts the wider picture. Similarly, Carter and Cannon (1992) point out that it is futile to extract a woman from her social context and Jennings and Cohen (1993) have argued that 'the reality of life for a woman entrepreneur therefore, has to be considered against the background of women's wider role in society and in the workforce in general' (p. 21).

By adopting a broader, more holistic approach which recognises and incorporates the 'context' of female entrepreneurship within traditional economic thinking on small firm financing, a valuable framework is created within which to study the financing of women-owned businesses. In the remainder of this chapter, the aim is to consider possible explanations for the findings of existing research into the financing of women-owned businesses using such a framework.

2.3   EXPLAINING THE PROBLEMS FACED IN THE FINANCING OF WOMEN-OWNED BUSINESSES: A CONTEXTUAL APPROACH

2.3.1   Introduction

As illustrated by Sargent and Young (1991) (Figure 2.1), factors influencing the process of acquiring business capital can be viewed in terms of a 'supply' and 'demand' relationship. On the supply side of the relationship are factors associated with the policies and practices of the financial organisation, in particular the criteria with which they assess small businesses, and the characteristics of the individual lenders/investors which shape the decision to supply finance. On the demand side of the relationship are factors associated with the characteristics of the business owner which determine the financial choices they make and how they are perceived by financial institutions. In the remainder of this section, both supply- and demand-side perspectives on the financing of women-owned businesses will be examined.

2.3.2   The small firm finance relationship: supply-side factors

The impact of investment/lending criteria on the financing of women-owned businesses

In order to minimise the risks and costs associated with lending to or investing in small businesses, many lenders/investors base their decisions on a set of general criteria that they use to assess all small business propositions (Deakins and Hussain, 1991; Fletcher, 1995). These criteria are generally objective in nature and are concerned with specific information on the business (e.g. sector and profitability) and the personal characteristics of the entrepreneur (e.g. age, experience, education, capital). However, the female entrepreneurship literature reveals that female-owned businesses have different characteristics to male-owned businesses. The question therefore remains as to how far systematic differences in the characteristics of women-owned businesses account for differences in their access to credit. The remainder of this section seeks to explore this question further. As small firms tend to rely on debt finance from the major clearing banks, attention will be focused on the lending criteria adopted by the banks for assessing small firms.

As suggested by agency theory, one of the most important criteria for banks when deciding to finance a small business is whether the entrepreneur is able to provide a guarantee or collateral on the finance required. Indeed, Deakins and Hussain (1992) found that the ability to provide security and personal collateral is given disproportionately more importance than managerial attributes when analysing the risk of new ventures. This is particularly true during times of recession when banks are under pressure to avoid bad debts. As outlined in section 2.2.2, guarantees and collateral are important for three main reasons (McMahon *et al.*, 1993). First, in the light of the risks associated with adverse selection, which are particularly acute in the case of small businesses because of larger information asymmetries, banks are looking to limit potential down-side losses by providing themselves with an asset to fall back on in the event of a default. Second, collateral based on personal assets provides the entrepreneur with an incentive to commit him- or herself to the project, thus reducing the risks associated with moral hazard. Third, collateral may be used by the bank as a 'signal' of the owner-manager's commitment to the business.

However, because many female business owners come from low-paid employment backgrounds or from 'dependent' domestic situations, they lack the sound basis on which to have accumulated cash savings or collateral (Riding and Swift, 1990; Simpson, 1991; Thomas, 1991; Kaur and Hayden, 1993; Carter and Rosa, 1995). In this respect, there are many similarities with ethnic minority business owners (Jones *et al.*, 1992). Married women in particular are less likely to own personal assets outright, sharing control of assets such as the house or car (Fabowale *et al.*, 1993) and shared assets may have already been used by the domestic partner as security or collateral on some other form of finance (Brush, 1990). The fact that many female business owners share control of personal assets may explain why they are required to provide co-signatures for bank finance more often than male business owners (Fabowale *et al.*, 1993). There is evidence to suggest that some banks are more co-operative towards married businesswomen because they have access to joint financial resources, in particular, a second income (Bowman-Upton *et al.*, 1987; Price and Monroe, 1993). Nevertheless, it has also been found that some banks are wary of funding business partnerships involving both domestic partners, first, because independent partners may have even greater access to collateral and security because it is not shared, and second, because there is a risk that domestic problems may interfere with the successful running of the business (Clutterbuck and Devine, 1987). Even when female business owners have access to personal assets to use as collateral, they are often less prepared than male business owners to risk such important personal and family resources (e.g. the family home) on the business venture (Brush, 1992; Koper, 1993; Carter and Rosa, 1995).

In order for the banks to reduce the risks associated with adverse selection even further, another important criterion on which they make lending decisions is whether the business owner will be able to repay the loan or overdraft facility. One of the most important factors taken into consideration when assessing this criterion is whether the entrepreneur has a reliable financial track record. This usually involves an analysis of their personal financial background and personal credit ratings. However, it is often the case that women lack a full financial track record. Most financial organisations base their track record requirements on the 'typical male pattern of uninterrupted work experience' (Clutterbuck and Devine, 1987: p. 138). However, many women, particularly those with families, have an interrupted career pattern (Buttner and Rosen, 1989) and according to one of the respondents in a study by Godfrey (1992), this might be interpreted by a lender/investor as 'a sign of instability' (p. 131). In addition, married women frequently do not have an individual credit rating on which to borrow money because they share a joint bank account (Hisrich and Brush, 1986). The shorter financial track record can therefore make raising capital a more acute problem for the female business owner (Hisrich and Brush, 1984; 1987; Hisrich, 1985; Buttner and Rosen, 1989; Carter and Cannon, 1992).

Another factor which lenders judge when assessing small business risk is whether the business has a strong potential for survival and growth so that the terms of the financial contract can be adhered to, in other words, whether the business will survive to pay back the finance with interest. While both men and women starting new businesses are perceived as 'risky' lending prospects, many bank managers perceive women to be poorer business risks because of household and domestic commitments, especially those women who are single parents (Brush, 1990: p. 50). Many lenders feel that these commitments will impinge on the survival and success of the business and hence their ability to pay back any finance. However, being a single businesswoman with-out children appears to offer no better solution as many financial organisations see such women as being 'at risk' of marrying or having children, so jeopardising future business success (Kryzanowski and Bertin-Boussu, 1984). Young women in particular are often perceived by financial organisations as merely 'marking time as wage earners' before starting a family (Kryzanowski and Bertin-Boussu, 1984: p. 229). Indeed, over half of their survey of Canadian credit officers felt it to be acceptable to apply stricter standards to younger women for this reason (Kryzanowski and Bertin-Boussu, 1984).

In the case of investors in small businesses, whether private or institutional, the growth objectives of the owner-manager are also of particular concern. A study undertaken by Cousins Stephens Associ-ates for the DTI (1991) identified two types of small business reflect-ing fundamental differences in management objectives. 'Proprietorial' firms are 'normally led by individuals whose main concern is to establish and sustain a particular lifestyle. The individuals do not seek to expand the management team and are unhappy at the prospect of relinquishing any control of the business in pursuit of growth' (DTI 1991: p. 95). In contrast, 'corporate' firms 'seek to put in place a management team of sufficient strength and experience to generate and sustain growth of the business over an extended period' (DTI, 1991: p. 95). Although friends and family may be prepared to invest in a business venture 'driven by faith in the principal entrepreneurs involved' (Brophy, 1989: p. 61), external investors are generally more rational in their analysis. Investors are generally most concerned about whether the business will yield appropriate levels of financial return on their investments, particularly as agency relationships with small firms tend to be more expensive because of higher transaction and monitoring costs. The objectives of the entrepreneur, for example, whether their plan is for a 'lifestyle', 'low-growth' or a 'high-growth' venture is therefore of utmost importance (Brophy, 1989). Because small firm investors, particularly venture capital companies, and also informal venture capital investors tend to make high risk investments, they are looking for high rates of return and high growth ventures (Brophy, 1989). They therefore tend to finance 'corporate' style businesses more readily than 'proprietorial' ones (DTI, 1991: p. 115).

Many women-owned businesses, however, cannot or choose not to follow a high growth strategy and their businesses tend to be more 'proprietorial' in nature. A study by Godfrey (1992) suggests that most women do not grow their businesses as aggressively as investors like. Many women have domestic commitments and deliberately mute the growth of their businesses to incorporate these (Lee-Gosselin and Grisé, 1990; Clark and James, 1992), thus seriously reducing access to venture and equity finance. Others are in the 'impossible bind' described by Godfrey (1992), whereby they are expected to prove themselves in the marketplace before being 'worthy' of investment capital but without the capital cannot show the aggressive growth needed for investors to become interested. In addition, some women choose to pursue goals other than growth and performance (Brush, 1992) such as combining work with a family or job satisfaction (Brush, 1990). In general, it would appear that businesswomen place less emphasis on making money than men (Cromie, 1987a; Carter and Cannon, 1992). Gregg (1985) argues that 'men become entrepreneurs to create wealth; women become entrepreneurs to create income' (p. 12). Nevertheless, there is a certain amount of contradiction within the female entrepreneurship literature on this issue. For example, Fischer *et al.* (1993) have found that female entrepreneurs are significantly more financially motivated than male entrepreneurs.

Smaller firms also receive credit from bank lenders on more severe terms than larger firms because they are perceived as being more risky and do not offer the bank any benefits from economies of scale (Koper, 1993; Orser *et al.*, 1993). Small businesses tend to require smaller amounts of loan or overdraft finance than large firms, yet the administrative costs incurred by the bank to set up a loan or overdraft facility remain the same and the extra time small requests take to process is not justified financially by the profit they make for the bank (Koper, 1993). However, existing research shows that women in business borrow much smaller amounts from the bank than their male counterparts (Hisrich, 1985; Brush, 1992; Koper, 1993; Carter and Rosa, 1995). In addition, the perceived capacity of a small firm to repay or service a bank loan is also much lower when the firm has low sales (Fabowale *et al.*, 1993). However, profits, sales and business receipts tend to be lower for women-owned businesses than for male-owned businesses (Riding and Swift, 1990; Fabowale *et al.*, 1993). Indeed, Riding and Swift (1990) found 70 per cent of their sample of female-owned firms had gross annual sales of less than $500,000 compared to only 35 per cent of the men-owned businesses.

Education, general business experience and particularly managerial experience is also regarded by both lenders and investors as critically important when evaluating start-up companies (Brophy, 1989; Berry *et al.*, 1993). In order to avoid the problems associated with adverse selection, lenders/investors want to see a connection between past experience and the skills required to start a new business in order that the business will not be mismanaged (Berry *et al.*, 1993). However, as pointed out in chapter 1, female business owners are generally found to have an educational background which is less relevant in preparing them for business ownership (Belcourt *et al.*, 1991). They are also found to lack relevant managerial, industry and entrepreneurial experience (Belcourt *et al.*, 1991; Kalleberg and Leicht, 1991; Carter and Cannon, 1992; Fay and Williams, 1993; Fischer *et al.*, 1993; Barrett, 1995) and generally have much less managerial experience than male business owners (Watkins and Watkins, 1984; Welsh and Young, 1984; Hisrich and Brush, 1987; Simpson, 1991; Barclays Bank, 1992; Fabowale *et al.*, 1993; Scottish Enterprise, 1993b; Barrett, 1995). Particular skill weaknesses for female entrepreneurs appear to be in financial planning, accounting and marketing (Sexton and Bowman-Upton, 1991a).

Lenders/investors will also tend to finance certain types of small businesses. Service sector start-ups are often perceived as being particularly risky. Ease of entry into service sector industries, because of low capital requirements, results in high exit rates through displacement. This is because low barriers to entry within a particular sector generally result in high competition within that sector (Fothergill and Gudgin, 1982). Smallbone (1990) found small businesses with the shortest life-spans (6–9 months) to be concentrated in services, particularly wholesaling and retailing. The financing of on-going ventures is also sector-dependent. In the case of banks, it has already been noted that, because of their need to counteract the problems associated with moral hazard and to provide security in the face of adverse selection, they generally prefer to lend on tangible, hard assets such as plant and equipment (Loscocco and Robinson, 1991). For this reason, service sector businesses often receive less favourable terms of credit than manufacturing (Therrien *et al.*, 1986; Riding and Swift, 1990) because they lack tangible, pledgeable assets and have a low resale value in the event of the business being liquidated (Fabowale *et al.*, 1993). In the light of these factors, it may be speculated that the problems faced by many women in raising finance for their businesses are related, in part, to the fact that their businesses tend to be concentrated in the retail and service sectors (Brush, 1990; Fabowale *et al.*, 1993).

Finally, many lenders/investors are reluctant to put finance into new start-up companies because young firms suffer from high start-up costs, inexperience and lack of track record and are therefore likely to be perceived as more risky. Furthermore, information asymmetries in the agency relationship between younger firms and investors/lenders tend to be much higher because new firms do not have a track record and the owner-manager is likely to be new to business ownership (Wynant and Hatch, 1990). It is therefore not surprising to find that the likelihood of a loan being rejected is highest for young firms (Fabowale *et al.*, 1993; Carter and Rosa, 1995). While this problem is true of young businesses owned by women or men, research indicates that the general population of women-owned businesses is younger than that of men-owned businesses, primarily because female entrepreneurship is a relatively recent phenomenon (Riding and Swift, 1990; Clark and James, 1992; Smith, Smits and Hoy, 1992). It is therefore suggested that the relative youth of the female business population may account for the finding that women face more problems raising finance (Riding and Swift, 1990).

In summary, many of the objective criteria used by banks and other finance providers to assess small businesses have the potential to discriminate against women, primarily because the characteristics of women-owned businesses frequently do not correspond to these criteria (Orser and Foster, 1992). It is therefore suggested that many of the barriers faced by female business owners in the financing of their businesses are not due to direct discrimination but to the 'law codes and the structures of economic and financial institutions' which indirectly discriminate against them (Moore *et al.*, 1992: p. 90). However, these findings still do not explain fully why so many women feel that they are not treated seriously by the financial community and why women are frequently given the impression that banks think they lack the motivation and ambition necessary to start and run a business successfully (Kaur and Hayden, 1993). To explore these issues further, the following section considers factors which may influence the 'interpersonal' dimension of the relationship between female entrepreneurs and their finance providers.

The impact of lender/investor characteristics on the financing of women-owned businesses

In addition to the objective criteria adopted by financial institutions, women business owners are also subject to evaluation on a number of subjective criteria adopted by the individual lender or investor. When dealing with small businesses, which are frequently run by a single owner-manager, finance providers are often seen, or see themselves as lending to the 'person', rather than to the business (Berry *et al.*, 1993). In these situations, more subjective criteria are likely to come into play. These sorts of criteria are often referred to as 'gut feeling' (Berry *et al.*, 1993: p. 129) and it is widely accepted that both lenders and investors will make decisions to supply finance to small businesses based on 'gut feeling' as well as on more formal criteria. The subjective criteria that make up a 'gut feeling' tend to include opinions, interpretations, personal evaluations of objective criteria and stereotypes (Koper, 1989).

In the case of bank finance, although the lending decision is based on the formal lending criteria of the bank, the individual bank manager's personal assessment of a client usually – perhaps inevitably – supplements the formal appraisal recommending acceptance of a project to the bank's head office (DTI, 1991). Thus, financial loan practices are likely to vary to a certain extent within and between individual banks (Kryzanowski and Bertin-Boussu, 1984), depending largely on the particular manager in charge of interviewing the prospective client and his or her previous experience, attitudes and beliefs (Sargent and Young, 1991).

Direct discrimination against women by individuals within a financial organisation, such as a bank, is illegal but every female business owner is 'prey to her own bank manager's particular image of women' (Hertz, 1987: p. 190). A bank manager may well be unaware that he or she has stereotyped views about women because these views are often deeply embedded in cultural attitudes (Hertz, 1987: p. 188). Evidence exists to suggest that some bank managers, particularly male bank managers, see business ownership among women as socially inappropriate (Loscocco and Robinson, 1991: p. 524), a fact which may have an important impact on their success in raising finance. This type of sex-related bias can be viewed in terms of a mismatch between a particular situation/context and certain sex-role expectations that exist (Nieva and Gutek, 1980). According to Nieva and Gutek (1980), 'behaviours that violate societal sex-role expectations tend to be negatively regarded' (p. 271). In other words, a woman running her own business may be regarded as going against what is expected of her role in society. Research such as that undertaken by Buttner and Rosen (1988a) indicates that there can be a mismatch in the minds of finance providers between the characteristics associated with running a business (e.g. propensity to take risk, readiness for change, endurance, lack of emotionalism, low need for support, low conformity and persuasiveness) and the expected role/characteristics of women (e.g. domestically oriented, nurturing). Indeed, as highlighted in chapter 1, the rise in numbers of women-owned businesses can be seen as part of a movement to undermine 'conventional and stereotyped notions of a woman's place' (Goffee and Scase, 1983: p. 627).

Such perceptions have important implications for the financing of women-owned businesses, particularly for those in non-traditional business sectors which 'violate societal sex-role expectations' even further. Hisrich and O'Brien (1982) found that businesswomen operating in non-traditional or male-dominated sectors such as manufacturing faced more problems obtaining lines of credit than women in traditional 'female' sectors such as retailing and services. Buttner and Rosen (1988b) also found male loan officers to be more supportive of women initiating traditionally 'female' businesses but less supportive of women starting non-traditional, 'male' businesses. According to one businesswoman in a study by Charbonneau (1981), 'their justification for turning me down was that I was a woman going into a man's field' (p. 23). Businesswomen are often perceived as not having the necessary skills or managerial strengths to compete successfully in traditionally 'male' industries. As a result, these sectors tend to lack examples of other successful female business owners with which to reassure the investor/lender that they can succeed (Clutterbuck and Devine, 1987: p. 136). However, women running traditionally 'female' businesses may also face problems in that many male bank managers will be unfamiliar with the products and services they provide (Summers, 1992). These factors have important implications for the financing of women-owned businesses because it has been found that sexual stereotyping often results from a lack of understanding of the unknown (Sexton and Bowman-Upton, 1988).

As well as the widespread perception that women do not possess the skills or characteristics required to run a small business, the success of a female business owner in raising finance may also be influenced by the perceptions of lenders/investors with regard to the likelihood of her business surviving and growing. Indeed, it is commonly perceived that businesses run by men are more likely to survive and grow than those run by women (Aldrich, 1989; O'Hare and Larson, 1991; Price and Monroe, 1992; Srinivasan *et al.*, 1994). However, Kalleberg and Leicht (1991) found that 'businesses headed by women are not more likely to go out of business, nor to be less successful than those headed by men' (p. 136). Similarly, it is often assumed that women cannot manage money successfully (Brush, 1990) although there is no empirical evidence to suggest that, in reality, this is true.

Female business owners may also face problems with finance providers because they manage their businesses differently to men. For instance, Chaganti (1986) found that female business owners prefer to adopt a management style which is less formal, 'less autocratic' and more 'people oriented' than male business owners (p. 28). However, as pointed out by Fischer *et al.* (1993), when the bank manager has little evidence to go on, other than gut feeling, in assessing whether a female-owned business will be run in a different but equally effective way, there is more scope for subjective criteria to be employed, which may incorporate discriminatory attitudes.

Lender/investor attitudes and perceptions are shaped by a variety of factors. In particular, exposure to women in positions of responsibility can be highly influential in shaping lender attitudes towards female business owners. Indeed, Fandt and Stevens (1991) suggest that 'early exposure to women in positions of responsibility may reduce stereotypical attitudes regarding women's ability to function effectively in non-traditional roles' (p. 474). Students in their sample assigned higher evaluation ratings to male than female professors, unless they had previously been taught by a female member of the department. These findings have important implications for the evaluation of female entrepreneurs because there are few female managers in most lending organisations. Indeed, it has been claimed that 'the biggest obstacle women entrepreneurs face is dealing with a 99 per cent male banking and financial community' (Charbonneau, 1981: p. 22). In the US, for example, 63 per cent of loan officers are male (Buttner and Rosen, 1988a). In the Netherlands there is a similar 'male-dominated bank culture' (Koper, 1989: p. 13). In the UK, until more recently, women have tended to be recruited to the lower level, clerical positions in banks, rather than managerial positions (Crompton, 1989) and are rarely concerned with credit granting to entrepreneurs. Therefore, many male bank managers are unlikely to have been exposed to women in positions of responsibility and are more likely to hold 'traditional' views about the role of women which stem from a 'highly paternalistic banking culture' (Collinson, 1987: p. 13).

Having considered ways in which the characteristics of financial institutions, their lending/investment criteria and the attitudes and characteristics of individual lenders/investors managers might impinge on the financing of women-owned businesses, attention is now turned to the ways in which the characteristics and attitudes of the female entrepreneurs themselves might shape the relationship further.

2.3.3   The small firm finance relationship: demand-side factors

The individual characteristics and attitudes of the small business owner are very important factors in the acquisition of business capital but are often neglected in research on the 'finance gap'[3] (Holmes and Kent, 1991; Landström and Winborg, 1995). Characteristics such as personality, background, education and experience will all impinge on the financial decisions made by a business owner and how they will be perceived by external lenders/investors.

It is the aim of this section to consider how the characteristics of female business owners might have an impact on three of the key demand-side factors which shape the process of small firm financing – the *personal choices* made by the owner-manager, the *need* for external finance, and the owner-manager's *awareness* (of need, of the sources of finance available and of how to successfully present a case to finance providers).

The importance of personal choice in the financing of women-owned businesses

The use of a particular source of finance is not shaped purely by the small business owner's access to the sources on offer, but also by the wishes of the entrepreneur or entrepreneurial team. Indeed, it has been suggested that the financial structure of small firms reflects the desires of their owners as much as constraints by the suppliers of finance (Hughes and Storey, 1994: p. 4).

Many business owners are found to operate their businesses in such a way as to minimise their need for external finance. One of the main reasons for this is the desire to avoid external interference and to maintain independence. This is to be expected given the fact that 'in many cases the entrepreneur has established a small firm to become self-employed and to avoid the control of outside directors' (Walker, 1989: p. 290; Bolton Report, 1971; Kets de Vries, 1977; Goffee and Scase, 1985). Ownership and management are also more closely linked in small firms and small firm owner-managers usually have a high personal financial stake in the business. They therefore tend to have a particular desire not to dilute ownership or control over the business and its assets. Indeed, for many small business owners, the desire to retain control of their business is so strong that they will protect it at any cost.

In an attempt to explain the financial structure of small and large enterprises, the Pecking Order Hypothesis (POH) explores the role of managerial preferences towards the various sources of finance on offer. While Myers (1984) used the POH in relation to listed companies, it is argued that the findings of studies which identify a finance gap for small firms (e.g. Norton, 1991a; 1991b; Scherr *et al.*, 1993; Landström and Winborg, 1995) are consistent with the concepts of the POH and that the POH is equally applicable to small unlisted companies which cannot raise additional funding through the issuing of equity to the public (Holmes and Kent, 1991).

The POH suggests that, because small business owners want to minimise external interference and ownership dilution, they will prefer 'internal to external financing, and debt to equity' (Myers, 1984: p. 576; Cosh and Hughes, 1994). Small business owners therefore have a hierarchical ranking by which they choose sources of finance. They tend to start with their own personal savings, move on to debt finance if the need arises and finally consider the least preferable option – the relinquishing of equity to outsiders – as a 'last resort' (Myers, 1984: p. 581) (Figure 2.2). As a result, small firms tend to be closely held, that is, their equity is held entirely or almost entirely by the owner-manager/s rather than external investors. An analysis of share ownership characteristics among UK businesses, undertaken as part of the Cambridge Study (SBRC, 1992), revealed that over 80 per cent of all boards of companies employing less than 100 people held 100 per cent of shares. Furthermore, the largest shareholders in businesses of under 100 employees tend to be individuals rather than other companies or

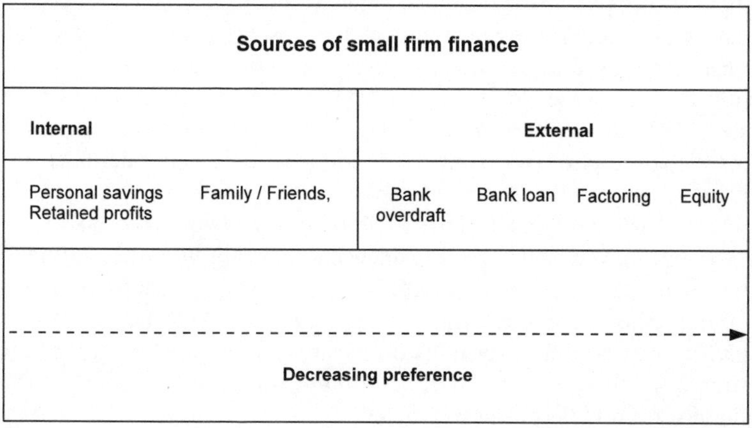

Figure 2.2 Diagrammatic representation of the Pecking Order Hypothesis applied to sources of small firm finance

financial organisations. The smaller and the younger the firm, the more closely held it tends to be (Cosh and Hughes, 1994: p. 25). The POH may therefore explain why only 2 per cent of 'micro' businesses and 7 per cent of 'small' businesses in the Cambridge Study (SBRC, 1992) had obtained venture capital, in addition to the fact that micro-businesses are not attractive venture capital investment prospects (Mason and Harrison, 1990; 1994; Murray, 1990; 1993; Storey, 1994).

When external finance is required, debt is favoured over equity because it involves fewer constraints in the management of the business and debt finance from the bank is generally sought above any other source (Binks, 1993; McMahon *et al.*, 1993). According to the POH, this is because bank finance results in no loss of equity and little dilution of ownership control. However, Cressy (1992) found that small firm bank borrowers often prefer to substitute their own funds for borrowed funds as business wealth increases, in order to reduce perceived bank control over their affairs (p. 196).

While these characteristics are true of all small business owners, regardless of their sex, it is possible that women exhibit a more extreme version of the POH for a number of reasons. First, as noted in chapter 1, women are driven by similar factors to men when starting a business, in particular the need for independence (Schwartz, 1976; Hisrich and O'Brien, 1981; Stevenson, 1983; Watkins and Watkins, 1984; Hertz, 1987; Cromie, 1987a). Nevertheless, a woman's need for independence is very often provoked by specific problems which she has faced in the labour market. These problems might include blocked career promotion due to the 'glass ceiling', frustration over labour market segregation which keeps women in the lower-paid, unskilled jobs, and the desire to escape economic dependency on men (Goffee and Scase, 1983; Cromie, 1987a). Female entrepreneurs with such motives for start-up are likely to be even more keen than their male counterparts to retain their independence and therefore may have an even greater desire to prevent the involvement of external finance providers, particularly male finance providers.

Second, given that there is evidence in existing literature to suggest that female business owners frequently encounter problems of discrimination when raising external finance, it is likely that female business owners will exhibit an even greater desire to rely on their own internal sources of finance and will be even more wary about raising external finance than male business owners.

Third, the banks are well known for requiring small business owners to provide security on debt finance, particularly security based on personal assets. In accordance with the POH, many small business owners will avoid bank finance because they do not want to give away control of their personal assets. In addition to the control aspect, many small business owners are reluctant to risk personal assets, particularly their homes. Others will not have any collateral available to them. The implication of these factors for the woman-owned business are two-fold. As indicated in section 2.3.2, female business owners are less likely than male business owners to have access to sources of collateral to offer as security. In addition, the female entrepreneurship literature also finds that women are less inclined to take risks in their businesses than men (Therrien *et al.*, 1986; Sexton and Bowman-Upton, 1988; O'Hare and Larson, 1991), particularly risks which might impinge on personal or family well-being. In this way, even those businesswomen in the position to put up collateral on bank finance may decide to rely upon internal sources rather than risk personal assets that might be detrimental to the family (Brush, 1992; Koper, 1993). Indeed, Brown and Segal (1989) argue that the desire not to jeopardise the family home may explain why women tend to be more cautious about bank borrowing (Carter and Cannon, 1992).

Fourth, the aversion to risk exhibited by female business owners is likely to be exacerbated by the finding that women lack self-confidence. An important factor shaping the business owner's personal assessment of whether they will be successful in raising external finance is self-confidence. It is therefore suggested that many women will not choose to seek external finance for their businesses because they lack confidence and have a lower self-assessment than men (Hisrich and Brush, 1983; 1986; Honig-Haftel and Martin, 1986; Batchelor, 1987; Still and Guerin, 1991). In particular, women are more frequently conditioned by society to regard themselves as weaker in areas such as finance and business operations, regarding these as 'male' attributes (Hisrich and Brush, 1984; Hisrich and Brush, 1985; Chaganti, 1986). As a result, they see the world of 'business' as a 'male world of employees, bankers and everything' (Goffee and Scase, 1985: p. 105) and this might, in turn, lead to cautious borrowing (Carter and Canon, 1992). According to one respondent in a study by Carter and Cannon (1992), 'there is only one real difference between men and women which shows itself and that is confidence' (p. 76). Therefore, female business owners may lack the confidence to approach potential formal and informal lenders and investors (OECD, 1986). Female business owners are also found to have less management experience than men and have fewer skills in areas relevant to running a business, in particular financial skills (Hisrich and Brush, 1983; Watkins and

Watkins, 1984). With such a background, many more women than men will be unfamiliar with the requirements of financial institutions and this unfamiliarity might make raising external finance appear even more risky to the female entrepreneur, again leading her to rely on her own personal sources of finance.

The importance of 'need' in the financing of women-owned businesses

Of course, many small business owners will choose to finance their businesses internally because the *need* for external finance does not actually exist. Many small firms do not require significant amounts of additional finance because they are able to meet their on-going requirements with self-generated finance (Mason and Harrison, 1994). The need for external finance is shaped by a number of factors.

First, financing requirements vary by sector. In a survey of entrepreneurs in high technology enterprises, Roberts (1991) found that financing requirements were smallest in consultancy and software and highest in biotechnology. Manufacturing firms generally require a higher input of finance than service sector firms because they require more equipment, have higher working capital requirements and higher overheads. However, women tend to start businesses in low-capital sectors such as services which may serve a limited local market (Brush, 1990). This may therefore explain why female business owners rely more on their own internal sources of finance rather than external sources of finance and are found to start their businesses with less capital than men (Brush, 1990; Collerette and Aubry, 1990).

Nevertheless, it is important to note that female entrepreneurs, as with all entrepreneurs, are not a homogenous group. Different types of female entrepreneur will have different capital requirements. For example, Goffee and Scase (1985), in their typology of female entrepreneurs, found that 'innovative' female business owners, who have a high attachment to entrepreneurial ideals and a low attachment to conventional gender roles, tend to set up in non-traditional business sectors such as manufacturing and therefore require a high level of start-up capital. In comparison, 'domestic' business owners, who have a low attachment to entrepreneurial ideals but a high attachment to conventional gender roles, tend to run traditionally 'female', service sector firms from home and therefore require much less finance.

Second, it is usually the case that, the smaller the scale of the business enterprise, the less finance, particularly external finance, is required. For instance, a business run from rented premises and employing a number of staff will have higher overheads and therefore require more finance than one run from home with no employees. Indeed, research by Curran and Roberts (1989) found that one-person enterprises, which tend to be run from home, find raising finance less of a problem. This is primarily because they have low start-up costs and many of them are in the service sector. These findings are of great importance given the fact that female-owned businesses tend to be smaller than male-owned businesses, they have few, if any employees (Goffee and Scase, 1983; Kaplan, 1988; Clark and James, 1992), their profits, sales and business receipts also tend to be lower than for male-owned businesses (Riding and Swift, 1990), around 50 per cent of women are found to set up and run their businesses from home (Carter and Cannon, 1992; Clark and James, 1992; Price and Monroe, 1992; Roberts-Reid and Curran, 1992), and women are concentrated in one-person enterprises (Roberts-Reid and Curran, 1992). They therefore tend to have lower overheads and subsequently, lower external financial requirements.

Third, the need for different sources of finance changes according to age and the small firm's stage of development in the financial life-cycle (Churchill and Lewis, 1983; Hutchinson and Ray, 1986; Brophy, 1989). As illustrated in Table 2.2, it is only during the later growth phases that more diverse sources of finance are needed and used. While this is true of businesses owned by women or men, research indicates that the age distribution of the population of women-owned businesses is skewed towards the younger age categories. Indeed, as outlined in section 2.3.2, the general population of female-owned

Table 2.2 The traditional view of the financial life-cycle of the firm

Stage	Source of finance	Potential stress factors
Inception	Owners' resources	Undercapitalisation
Growth I	As above plus: retained profits, trade credit, bank loans and overdrafts, hire purchase, leasing	'Over-trading' Liquidity crises
Growth II	As above plus: longer-term finance from financial institutions, e.g. ICFC	Finance gap
Growth III	As above plus: new issue market	Loss of control
Maturity	All sources available	Maintaining ROI[a]
Decline	Withdrawal of finance, firm taken over, share repurchase, liquidation	Falling ROI

Source: Hutchinson and Ray, 1986: p. 55
Note: [a] ROI = return on investment

businesses is younger than that of male-owned businesses. Women business owners are therefore more likely to be in the earlier stages of development and thus more reliant on the resources of the owner.

Fourth, the need for finance is also linked to the growth objectives of the owner-manager. The characteristics of owner-managers can have a considerable impact on their objectives (Cosh and Hughes, 1994). As outlined in section 2.3.2, businesses can be categorised by the objectives of their manager or management team (DTI, 1991). 'Corporate' firms which have higher growth objectives than 'proprietorial' firms will tend to require more external finance to fuel this growth. However, as has already been pointed out, many more female business owners than male business owners cannot or choose not to follow a high growth strategy because of domestic commitments. Their businesses therefore tend to be more 'proprietorial' in character (Lee-Gosselin and Grisé, 1990; Clark and James, 1992). As a result, they will tend not to require as much external finance.

The importance of 'awareness' in the financing of women-owned businesses

As outlined at the beginning of this section, the finance gap cannot be viewed simply as a supply gap. According to Holmes and Kent (1991) it is also the result of limited awareness among many small business owners of the appropriate sources of small business finance and their relative advantages and disadvantages (McMahon *et al.*, 1993; Scottish Enterprise, 1993a). In other words, a significant number of businesses that need external finance do not seek it because the business owner lacks awareness of:

1 the financial needs of their business;
2 the sources of finance available to small firms;
3 how to successfully present themselves to potential sources of finance.

An issue which has been discussed throughout this chapter is that the problems faced by women in raising finance may often be exacerbated by their inexperience, especially with financial matters (Brush, 1992). Without financial skills and experience, many female business owners are unable to asses adequately the financial needs of their business, handle their business finances or successfully negotiate financial deals (Therrien *et al.*, 1986). Therefore, according to Hisrich and Brush (1987) 'it is not so much the availability of credit that is the financial obstacle' for businesswomen, 'rather, difficulties in managing the capital resources of the enterprise' (p. 196). Schwartz (1976) found that female entrepreneurs often underestimate the cost of operating and marketing a product or service. Similarly, Chapman (1987) notes that 'a common error' among businesswomen 'is not having enough money to start up with but going ahead anyway' (p. 89).

A lack of experience may also mean that many female entrepreneurs are unable to identify potential funding opportunities (Sargent and Young, 1991). For example, certain social situations hold the potential for funding opportunities but it takes experience to recognise this (Sargent and Young, 1991). A lack of relevant past experience also means that many female business owners may have little knowledge as to what exactly financial organisations require of them (Schwartz, 1976; Moore *et al.*, 1992) and how to communicate their own requirements (Moore *et al.*, 1992). Female business owners also lack experience in negotiating financial matters (Schwartz, 1976; Moore *et al.*, 1992) and may therefore be uncertain as to how to present their case. They are further hindered by inadequate communication on the part of many financial organisations regarding their requirements for loan acceptance (Moore *et al.*, 1992). If, because of their relative lack of experience, women have inflated expectations of how successful they will be in the loan application process (Chaston, 1993), it is possible that the bewilderment of having their finance proposal rejected, coupled with the fact that the bank may not have adequately explained reasons for the rejection, may lead some women to believe they have been discriminated against (Buttner and Rosen, 1989; 1992). In addition, Truman (1993) has pointed out that, because female business owners frequently lack self-confidence, they may not go back to a bank manager who has turned down their proposal and demand to know the reasons for the rejection. As a result, many female business owners may blame 'discrimination' because they do not know the real reason behind their application being turned down.

Previous research has also suggested that one of the main reasons why female business owners fail to raise adequate business finance is because of their inability to access informal networks (Olm *et al.*, 1988; Riding and Swift, 1990; O'Hare and Larson, 1991; Carter and Rosa, 1995). Networking is important for raising the small business owner's awareness of the financial sources available to them and provides business owners with greater access to important sources of financial information and advice, assistance in financial decision-making, assistance in actually raising finance, and even access to sources of finance (Birley, 1985; Hisrich and Brush, 1986; Olm *et al.*, 1988; Moore *et al.*, 1992). For example, Olm *et al.* (1988) found that access to a network of contacts gives the female entrepreneur greater access to more formal sources of capital. Carter and Rosa (1995) found that male and female business owners were more likely to be refused finance from the banks if they were not members of The Rotary Club or similar organisations.

Reasons why women find it very difficult to gain access to business networks include the fact that most of the traditional, well-established business networks are male-dominated (e.g. The Rotary, The Masons) (Smeltzer and Fann, 1989). As well as experiencing difficulty in gaining access, Therrien *et al.* (1986) suggest that many women will shun such business groups because they are male-dominated. Aldrich (1989) has also suggested that many women lack the necessary experience and skills with which to undertake networking activity. Whatever the cause, women are less likely than their male counterparts to benefit from access to sources of finance and advice on raising finance because of networking difficulties (Moore *et al.*, 1992; Rees, 1992).

Preparation is one of the most important parts of the loan application process. Loan applications are rarely considered without a well-formulated and well-presented business plan (Deakins and Hussain, 1991; Berry *et al.*, 1993; Carty, 1994). Business plans are used by the banks to evaluate the ability of a small business to repay finance. They also give the small business owner an opportunity to demonstrate his or her skills and experience. Business plans are even more important for a woman in business because sound financial data has been shown to outweigh other factors such as gender (Hertz, 1987; Buttner and Rosen, 1989). Thorough preparation and a comprehensive business plan can 'de-personalise' the loan application, thus eliminating the effect of gender (Carter and Cannon, 1992). Furthermore, if full information is provided, it avoids the lender/investor having to make inferences about the business, a factor which has also been found to contribute towards sex-related bias – 'the greater the amount of inference required in the evaluation situation, the more likely it is that evaluation bias will be found' (Nieva and Gutek, 1980: p. 270). Businesswomen, however, often lack the experience or financial skills to either recognise the need for a business plan or to be able to prepare an adequate business plan (Charbonneau, 1981). Many women who run their own business also have to run a home, bring up a family or care for elderly or disabled family members at the same time. Such demands may mean less time is devoted to a well-planned loan application or a well-devised strategy to seek out new sources of finance.

Knowing how to present a business plan is also vital to the small business owner (Berry *et al.*, 1993). An important factor when presenting a loan application is the need to show confidence in one's own managerial skills and in the proposed venture (Hisrich and Brush, 1986; Berry *et al.*, 1993). It is a problem for all entrepreneurs convincing an investor 'that the proposed venture is economically feasible and capable of producing a rate of return acceptable in light of the risk involved' (Brophy, 1989: p. 61). However, as explained earlier in the chapter, businesswomen tend to lack the necessary business confidence (Carter and Cannon, 1992; Miskin and Rose, 1990; Jennings and Cohen, 1993), often because they lack business experience. Self-doubts, if conveyed to the investor, may be translated as a lending risk (Nieva and Gutek, 1980; Fertuck, 1982; Hisrich, 1985; Deakins and Hussain, 1991). Sargent and Young (1991) found self-esteem to be a very important influence on the successful acquisition of capital because high self-esteem usually accompanies self-confidence, thus encouraging a positive response from the investor. In a survey by Thomas (1991), one female business owner explained how her body language had 'given her away' at a meeting with her bank manager – 'despite what I said, my body language was telling him I wasn't sure about myself and I could see that he saw that'. She did not get the extension to her overdraft.

Another reason why businesswomen may be less successful in presenting their case lies in the nature of the loan interview itself. Loan application panels tend to be all-male and the interview based on the 'big mahogany desk carry-on designed to intimidate' (Summers, 1992: p. 9). This tends to represent a way of doing business which most businesswomen are unfamiliar with. Similarly, there is also an accepted 'language' used by financial organisations when discussing loan applications (Berry *et al.*, 1993). Again, women, often through lack of experience, are not familiar with the language of finance. Factors such as these may jeopardise their chances of raising finance.

A final area which may influence or improve the chances of a businesswoman to acquire business capital is that of dress code. Scherbaum and Shephard (1987) have found that, for business interviews, a male or female wearing blue or a jacket (the traditional male business uniform) is perceived as being more competent and properly dressed than someone wearing red or no jacket. Thus a woman may be more successful if she adopts a more masculine business dress code.

2.4 CONCLUSION AND RESEARCH AGENDA

The main aim of this chapter has been to give an in-depth insight into the current state of knowledge on the financing of women-owned businesses. An analysis of existing demand-side and supply-side studies shows that there is both research and anecdotal evidence to suggest that female business owners are treated differently by the financial community, in particular the banks. Female business owners are found to face more or different problems in raising finance than male business owners and receive, or feel that they receive, unequal treatment when dealing with the banks. There is also evidence to suggest that bank managers ascribe different characteristics to male and female business owners and that they assess male- and female-owned business proposals in different ways. However, the existing literature is far from consistent in its findings, with other studies providing no evidence to support the suggestion that female business owners are refused finance more than their male counterparts, that they are less satisfied with the banking relationship, or that they are treated differently by the banks.

One of the main problems with much of the existing literature is that it lacks a sound theoretical framework. By adopting a theoretical approach which allows traditional economic thinking on small firm financing to be integrated with concepts relating to social processes, a valuable framework has been suggested within which to study the financing of women-owned businesses – one which recognises the importance and incorporates the role of individuals and their interactions with each other. By adopting such a framework, this chapter has highlighted the complexity of issues surrounding the financing of women-owned businesses. In particular, it highlights the fact that the financing of women-owned businesses is influenced by a combination of factors which include the criteria adopted by financial organisations and the characteristics of individual lenders/investors, female owner-managers, and women-owned businesses. While many of these factors are not gender-specific, many have an important gender dimension (Jennings and Cohen, 1993).

However, the overall conclusion to be put forward in the light of this chapter is that popular wisdom, public press and academic research continue to cite greater difficulties for female entrepreneurs in the financing of their businesses, but that 'what is not substantiated is the cause of this difficulty' (Sexton and Bowman-Upton, 1991a: p. 291). In particular, it is far from clear as to whether gender plays a role in the problems faced by female business owners, how far difficulties are caused by discrimination, or whether they are merely a function of the characteristics of female business owners or of women-owned businesses. This lack of clarity largely reflects the fragmentary nature and flawed methodologies of much of the existing research (to be discussed in chapter 3).

The lack of clear understanding about these issues has some important implications. If female entrepreneurs do face particular problems in their access to small business finance, public policy makers need guidance as to whether businesswomen require specific training and support. However, as pointed out by Sexton and Bowman-Upton (1991a) 'present data regarding women-owned businesses are inadequate to assist public policy makers in dealing with problems faced by women business owners' (p. 286). There also needs to be a better understanding of the relationship between female business owners and finance providers in order that financial institutions such as banks can appraise their equal opportunities policies and so that they do not lose a growing source of new customers.

Consequently there is a clear need for research which establishes the extent to which gender affects the financing of small businesses. A research agenda for the financing of women-owned businesses in the UK is therefore required to answer a number of key questions:

1 First, how do women finance their businesses and does this differ from the way in which men finance their businesses?
2 Second, what problems do female entrepreneurs face in the financing of their businesses and how do these compare with the problems faced by male entrepreneurs?
3 Third, what kind of relationship do female business owners have with their banks? Is it different to the relationship male business owners have with their banks?
4 Fourth, is there any evidence to suggest women feel discriminated against in the banking relationship because of their gender?
5 Fifth, do female entrepreneurs have a similar level of access to sources of advice and assistance in raising finance, compared with their male counterparts?

The study for which this chapter has set the context will address this research agenda and in doing so, will also provide the first empirical study specifically on the financing of women-owned business to be undertaken in the United Kingdom. In the following chapter, a research methodology is put forward with which to carry out this project.

3 Research into the financing of women-owned businesses
Methodological considerations

3.1 INTRODUCTION

One of the principal motivating factors behind the book is the fact that, despite the large and growing body of literature which has identified various problems associated with the financing of women-owned businesses, our understanding of the underlying issues is far from clear and many of the research findings are fraught with inconsistencies and contradictions (see chapter 2). One of the key factors responsible for this situation has been the lack of methodological rigour in previous studies (Carter and Cannon, 1992; Fay and Williams, 1993; Read, 1994; Rosa *et al.*, 1994) and it has been argued that it is these 'methodological challenges [that] have limited our understanding of the relationship among measures of business risk, gender of owner, and credit terms' (Fabowale *et al.*, 1993: p. 2). Fabowale *et al.* (1993) also suggest that there has been such a variety of different methodologies employed that 'findings sometimes appear to be methodology-dependent' (p. 4). In the following section, a number of the most common of these methodological flaws are explored in more detail.

3.2 THE METHODOLOGICAL SHORTCOMINGS OF EXISTING RESEARCH

The methodological shortcomings of existing research into the financing of women-owned businesses can be divided into eight main categories. First, there are relatively few studies which have concentrated specifically on the issue of gender and small firm financing and those that have are generally based on the North American experience (e.g. Buttner and Rosen, 1988a; 1988b; 1989; 1992; Riding and Swift, 1990; Fabowale *et al.*, 1993). Our understanding of the situation in the

United Kingdom is limited to findings from more general surveys of
the characteristics and problems faced by female entrepreneurs (Watkins and Watkins, 1984; Goffee and Scase, 1983; Carter and Cannon,
1992; Rosa *et al.*, 1994).

Second, there has been a reliance upon poor sampling frameworks.
It is acknowledged that a major barrier to any research on women-
owned businesses is that the businesses themselves are very difficult to
find, primarily because of the lack of an appropriate national database
of women in business which 'limits our knowledge of women in
business and makes the construction of representative samples impossible' (Carter and Cannon, 1992: p. 6). In addition, many women run
their businesses from home, on a small scale and thus remain largely
'invisible' to official statistics. Many researchers in the field of female
entrepreneurship have therefore resorted to drawing samples on the
basis of 'convenience rather than design' (Carter and Rosa, 1995: p. 4;
Brush, 1992). This, again, has led to concerns over how representative
many of the findings are to the population of women-owned businesses as a whole (Allen and Truman, 1991).

Third, many studies have used fairly small sample sizes. Therefore,
the extent to which generalisations can be made is limited, as is the
extent to which statistically rigorous analyses can be employed
(Fabowale *et al.*, 1993). For example, it is argued that

> (t)he work of Riding and Swift (1990) would have been strength-
> ened had multivariate analysis been used. However, the sample
> available to Riding and Swift included too few women business
> owners to permit the use of multivariate analyses.
>
> (Fabowale *et al.*, 1993: pp. 4–5)

A fourth problem has been the tendency in many studies to sensitise
respondents to the issue of gender and discrimination. Many researchers have asked leading questions. For example, Wynant and Hatch
(1990) asked female business owners if they felt that being a woman
had been problematical in running a business (p. 97). The danger of
such an approach is that respondents will be led into giving the
'desired' answer (Riding and Swift, 1990). It might also alert respondents to the possibility that their experiences in raising finance have
been gender-related. Similar problems are also true of studies looking
at the supply-side of the issue. For example, when exploring sex-
discrimination within financial organisations, it is important to remember that this type of behaviour is not only socially unacceptable,
counter to organisational policy but most importantly, is illegal. As a
result, any 'investigation of discriminatory behaviour on the basis of a

person's gender is constrained by these . . . factors, and by the possibility that the actions may be "unconscious"' (Fay and Williams, 1993: p. 365).

Therefore, any study which asks lenders to consider their own level of gender discrimination or which sensitises them to this issue may yield invalid results. Kryzanowski and Bertin-Boussu (1984), for example, undertook a survey of lender attitudes towards an applicant's sex and marital status and asked credit officers to rate their agreement with statements such as 'men are better credit risks than women'. Such a method can be seen as merely collecting 'socially acceptable responses' (Fay and Williams, 1993: p. 365). Similarly, research undertaken by Buttner and Rosen (1988a) may have sensitised bank loan officers to the issue of gender by asking them to evaluate male and female entrepreneurs on attributes of successful entrepreneurship.

A fifth problem, and one which is related to the previous problem, is that of 'androcentrism' in the construction of the questionnaires (Hamilton *et al.*, unpublished). By this the authors mean that the way in which the questions are constructed is often based on stereotypical values and therefore the study

> may involve analysing how gender is traditionally perceived to impinge on the management process, rather than how it actually may do so. For example, androcentric bias may be responsible for the fact that male owner managers are seldom asked whether they feel confident or assertive when negotiating finance with bank managers. They are just assumed as a sex to be strong and confident. Women, however, assumed to be a more timid sex, are invariably asked about issues such as self-confidence.
>
> (Hamilton *et al.*, unpublished: pp. 2–3)

In this way, it is suggested that studies which find evidence of discrimination against women in business may do so because of the way in which the questions have been constructed – with the view that gender differences are pervasive and invariably operate to the disadvantage of women (Hamilton *et al.*, undated). For example, by asking the question, 'in your opinion, have you personally encountered any problems with your bank as a consequence of being a female?', Wynant and Hatch (1990: p. 97) are assuming that women *do* face a problematical relationship with their banks and may simply be perpetuating stereotypical beliefs. As pointed out by Eichler (1988), in order for research to be non-sexist, the questions asked have to be the same for both sexes.

A sixth methodological problem in existing studies centres around the over-reliance on subjective, perceptual data and anecdotal evidence of discrimination, without reference to any empirical data or objective evidence to reinforce it (Riding and Swift, 1990: p. 329). The effects of this problem have been exacerbated in the existing literature because 'the line between empirical data and statements which are based on more subjective criteria' has frequently been obscured (Department of Alberta, 1990: p. 27) and feelings/perceptions about discrimination have been manipulated to become evidence of discriminatory behaviour. While it is vital that qualitative material should be collected in order to explore underlying processes, Carter and Cannon (1992) believe that the failure to collect more quantifiable measures has resulted in a lack of replicable and verifiable studies of female entrepreneurship. For the same reasons, while much of the existing research has demonstrated that female entrepreneurs do face distinctive problems, the 'extent to which these are either caused or exacerbated by gender is difficult to quantify' (Carter and Cannon, 1992: p. 13) because of an almost total reliance on verbal reports and individual explanations, particularly when exploring business-related problems. In addition, it is often difficult to distinguish between 'perceived' problems and 'real' problems (Carter and Cannon, 1992: p. 7). While many women perceive that they have experienced what they believe to be gender-related problems, others will not have recognised the same problems as having a gender dimension. The social and political backgrounds of interviewees often determine whether discrimination is perceived or recognised as such. Nevertheless, as Carter and Cannon (1992) point out, 'whether these problems are real or based on misconceptions is of little consequence, the perception of a problem, in many cases, is as valid as a "real" problem' (p. 14).

Seventh, one of the biggest problems in any study attempting to look at the relationship between gender and small business financing is the complexity of the subject and the fact that the financing of small businesses may be affected by many factors other than gender. As Carter and Rosa (1995) have pointed out,

(e)ven the apparently simple task of describing how male and female entrepreneurs access and use different types of finance is a significant task when broken down into a large diversity of relevant and potentially relevant categories (for example, age, education, sector, capital resources and guarantees, start up, business age, size of the business, social networks, patterns of ownership, type of business organisation, personal goals, motivations and so on).

(Carter and Rosa, 1995: pp. 3–4)

Research of this sort is complicated further by issues of definition. The problem is one of distinguishing between true 'gender-based' differences between men- and women-owned businesses and 'sex-based' differences. A gender-based difference is 'one which is attributable to the action of socially determined forces that differentiate the sexes' (Rosa *et al.*, unpublished, p. 5). Meanwhile, sex-based differences reflect underlying non-social factors, for example differences in sector. For instance, women are found to use less finance to start their businesses than men (Brush, 1992). However, most women-owned businesses are in the service sector (Johnson and Storey, 1993) and therefore tend to require less finance at start-up. While many researchers might interpret this finding as a 'gender' difference, what it really shows is evidence of a 'sex' difference (although underlying societal 'gender' differences may explain why women-owned businesses are concentrated in the service sector). Johnson and Storey (1993) have argued that 'this mismatch between the sectoral distributions of male and female-owned businesses complicates any analysis of other differences between them, making it more difficult to disentangle the sectoral effect from any possible gender-related influences' (pp. 73–4).

Following a similar line of argument, Fay and Williams (1993) have argued that there is also a need to make a clear distinction between 'discrimination as a legitimate judgement when assessing risk level and suitability of an applicant in a loan situation, and discrimination as a result of gender prejudice' (p. 365). For example, if a proposal for loan finance is turned down by the bank because of a lack of financial assets, this can only be viewed in terms of the business owner being 'disadvantaged'. It may be that women are more disadvantaged relative to men in certain key areas such as experience, financial track record or financial assets, but this cannot be used as evidence of sex-discrimination by the banks. The problem is that many existing studies have overlooked these inherent complexities and as a result, many 'premature conclusions have been drawn that exceeded the capacity of the data' (Carter and Rosa, 1995: p. 4).

The eighth and one of the most serious methodological shortcomings in existing research has been the frequent lack of a male control group – 'a corresponding group of male business owners with whom to compare experiences' (Riding and Swift, 1990: p. 327). As has already been mentioned, it can be very misleading to rely solely on the perceptions of a small sample of female entrepreneurs as evidence of discrimination but it is particularly misleading in the absence of data from a control group of male entrepreneurs (Fay and Williams, 1993: p. 364), the main reason being that 'the latent hypotheses that women are relatively disadvantaged cannot...be tested empirically when men are not included as respondents' (Fischer *et al.*, 1993: p. 155). However, most of those studies which have included a group of male business owners against which to compare the experiences of a group of female business owners, have frequently failed to compare like with like (i.e. businesses of the same sector, size, age etc.). It has therefore been very difficult to examine the extent to which sex of ownership is the explanatory variable in observed differences or whether there might be other significant factors, apart from sex of ownership, such as business size, sector, age and security or assets (Goffee and Scase, 1983; Clutterbuck and Devine, 1987; Buttner and Rosen, 1989; Department of Alberta, 1990; Carter and Cannon, 1992).

It is widely acknowledged that the financial community evaluates lending risk on a variety of 'structural' factors such as business age, size and sector (Fertuck, 1982; Wynant and Hatch, 1990; Deakins and Hussain, 1992). However, in chapter 2, it was demonstrated that male- and female-owned businesses differ in terms of these structural characteristics. Fabowale *et al.* (1993) use a diagrammatic representation to conceptualise these issues (Figure 3.1).

It identifies the main lending criteria used by banks in the credit-granting decision but also demonstrates how gender may affect business attributes. The model also represents potential gender discrimination in the form of a 'decisional prism'. According to Fabowale *et al.* (1993)

> (i)f gender bias is absent, only structural differences in business attributes would account for gender-related differences in credit terms. However, just as white light is fragmented into different colours when it passes through a prism, so may credit terms differ between female and male small business owners if systematic gender discrimination exists.
>
> Fabowale *et al.* (1993: p. 7)

Therefore, in order to determine the extent to which women are discriminated against in the financing of their businesses, researchers face the challenge of disentangling the effects of gender bias from these other systematic structural differences between male and female-owned businesses (Fabowale *et al.*, 1993: p. 4). According to Fabowale *et al.* (1993), studies which do not take into account the potentially confounding effects of other variables, which may or may not be related to

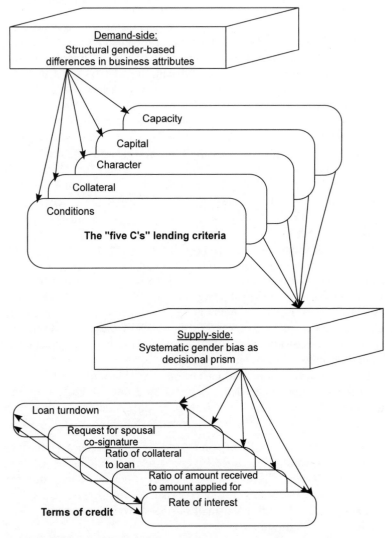

Figure 3.1 Model of factors influencing the credit terms extended to small business owners
Source: Adapted from Fabowale *et al.*, 1993 (p. 26)

gender, are 'susceptible to a "missing variables" error' which will lead to 'biased estimates and inappropriate conclusions' (p. 4).

In the light of these methodological considerations, the following section proposes a research method for the study of the financing of women-owned businesses in the UK.

3.3 THE FINANCING OF WOMEN-OWNED BUSINESSES IN THE UK: RESEARCH METHOD

3.3.1 The matched pairs approach

The challenge for any researcher studying the financing of women-owned businesses is therefore to allow for the fact that '(g)ender is one of a number of factors that affect financing' (Carter and Rosa, 1995: p. 14) and that 'gender-related disparities in business attributes, quite independently of systematic gender discrimination, may lead to discrepancies in credit terms' (Fabowale *et al.*, 1993: p. 2). As argued by Fay and Williams (1993), 'the existence of discriminatory behaviour as a consequence of prejudice and stereotyping can be demonstrated only when all relevant factors up to the point of loan application have been equalised' (Fay and Williams, 1993: p. 365).

A technique which overcomes these problems is the 'matched pairs' approach. A matched pairs design allows two samples of businesses to be compared on a certain issue/factor; in this case, to see whether gender affects the financing of male- and female-owned businesses. The researcher identifies matching criteria, or factors which are likely to distort the comparison. A comparison between men and women in the financing of their businesses is likely to be distorted by systematic differences in the structural characteristics of male- and female-owned businesses (e.g. women-owned businesses tend to be concentrated in the service sector). Once the matching criteria have been chosen, pairs of businesses are selected across the two samples, matched on those key criteria. By holding the match criteria constant in this way, and assuming they have been correctly identified and all relevant criteria have been selected, the effect of gender can be isolated and statistically significant differences between the two samples can be attributed to the owner-manager being a male or a female.

Matched pairs is a technique which has been used widely in fields such as medicine and psychology and, more recently, has been brought into use in the social sciences. In geography, its widest use has been in studies making spatial comparisons of industrial performance. Peck (1985), for instance, pioneered the use of matched pairs in industrial geography with a comparative study of the subcontract linkages in rural and urban manufacturing plants. He employed the technique to find out whether manufacturing firms located in urban areas subcontracted a higher proportion of their processing needs than rural based firms. Realising the importance of influential factors other than location, plants from both rural and urban areas were matched on the criteria of industry type, plant size and ownership type in order to evaluate the location effect.

In more recent years, matched pairs has been adopted as a method of studying small firms (e.g. O'Farrell and Hitchins, 1988a; 1988b; Keeble *et al.*, 1992; Storey *et al.*, 1992; O'Farrell *et al.*, 1993; Westhead, 1995a; 1995b). The work carried out by O'Farrell and Hitchins (1988a; 1988b), for example, used matched pairs to make inter-regional comparisons of small firm performance. O'Farrell and Hitchins (1988b) took samples of small businesses from two regions – Scotland and Mid-West Ireland. By matching the two sets of firms on product, age group and employment size category, they found that the success of small enterprises depends more on the skills of the management team and employees than on location. Both Keeble *et al.* (1992) and Westhead (1995b) have also used this approach to compare the performance of small firms in urban and rural areas and to identify whether and how opportunities, constraints and competitive responses differ by region. Firms were matched on the key characteristics of ownership, product type and size allowing for the identification of critical factors of success. Similarly, Storey *et al.* (1992) compared fast growing firms with normal growth firms of similar age, trade and ownership structure in the North-East in order to identify the key characteristics of fast growing businesses. More recently, Westhead (1995a) has adopted a matched pairs approach to compare the characteristics and performance of non-exporting and exporting businesses.

In the female entrepreneurship literature, the only researchers to have adopted a matched pairs approach are Riding and Swift (1990) who undertook a comparative study of the terms of credit offered to male and female business owners. Their sample was drawn from a national survey of business owners collected by the Canadian Federation of Independent Business via a postal questionnaire survey. Taken on face value, the data appeared to be indicating that financing conditions for women were 'less favourable than those for male business owners' (Riding and Swift, 1990: p. 332). However, in an attempt to control for factors which may confound the analysis of differences in the credit experience of male and female owner-managers, each of the 153 female business owners who replied to the survey was matched with a male business owner of similar business age, size, sector, growth rate and organisational form. In doing so, they found no statistically significant differences between men and women on five of the six terms of credit being measured.

A matched pairs approach has a number of advantages in the study of gender and small firm financing. First, as already discussed, it allows the researcher to compare two samples while controlling for factors which are likely to distort the comparison. For example, in the financing of small businesses, gender may be acting in combination with a number of other factors such as business age, sector, size and premises in the finance application process, all of which can be incorporated into a matched pairs design and their effects examined independently or jointly.

Second, a matched pairs design fits well into the fine-grained/coarse-grained methodological research continuum outlined by O'Farrell and Hitchins (1988a), enabling the researcher to combine the advantages of generalisation which are part of a 'coarse-grained' approach with those of being able to go into detail which are part of a 'fine-grained' approach (Figure 3.2). It therefore has many advantages over traditional techniques such as random probability sampling and has proved to be very appropriate when trying to understand 'the detailed mechanisms of change occurring in small firms' (O'Farrell and Hitchins, 1988a, p. 401), particularly where the mere description

	Fine-grained Methodologies	<->	Coarse-grained Methodologies
Advantages	* Capture subtleties, historical and other details of context * Permits better understanding of detailed processes of change and testing of concepts	<->	* Essential for analysis of patterns Efficient means of estimating population parameters * Simplifies detailed processes and interactions
Disadvantages	* Cannot estimate population parameters	<->	* May ignore important historical and qualitative factors; inferior explanatory capacity

Figure 3.2 A continuum of survey methodologies
Source Adapted from O'Farrell and Hitchins, 1988a (p. 63)

provided by a random or representative sample is insufficient. It is also a technique which has the capacity to incorporate and investigate the causal mechanisms underlying apparent relationships within the data which is an important consideration when studying a relationship as complex as that between gender and small firm financing. Despite these advantages, a matched pairs approach can be problematical if the limitations and sampling needs of the design are ignored. First, in order to select the criteria on which pairs of data will be matched, the researcher already needs a comprehensive understanding of the basic underlying processes involved.

Second, a decision must be made as to the number of matching criteria to be used. Too many criteria will reduce the chances of finding sufficient pairs, while limiting the matching criteria means the researcher risks omitting an influential factor. In the end it is impossible to match on every possible criterion but as Peck (1985) points out, matched pairs is not meant to be 'identical pairs'. Ultimately, a limited number of key variables must be chosen and, as Peck (1985) suggests, other variables which appear to be important can always be included and investigated within the questionnaire if thought to be influential.

Third, in the light of the previous point – that it is impossible to match exactly – a problem arises in deciding how close the matches should be and what deviation from the matching standard can be allowed without distorting the comparison. For example, Carter and Rosa (1995) roughly stratified their sample of male- and female-owned businesses by sector because they recognised that management variables can differ radically across sectors. But, as the authors have acknowledged,[1] there may be large differences between the characteristics of women- and men-owned businesses within the same sector. For instance, it is likely that within one of their sectors, 'textiles and clothing', the same processes that cause women to be segregated into certain types of work within the labour market also cause women business owners to be concentrated in smaller-scale businesses or 'making-up' work on a self-employed basis. Meanwhile, the men tend to run the larger factories (Kaur and Hayden, 1993). Crude matching of this type is bound to distort subsequent comparisons. As O'Farrell and Hitchins (1988a) point out, the criteria employed need to be 'sufficiently unambiguous to avoid errors in matching and yet not too narrow to make matching impossible' (p. 65).

Fourth, the chosen criteria should be measurable prior to interview in order to avoid wasting time and effort. Matching subsequent to interview is generally inefficient as many non-matches will have to be

discarded (although such interviews may be used for contextual information). However, measuring criteria prior to interview is not an easy
task, particularly as a widely recognised problem for any small firms
research is the lack of published data, particularly on women-owned
businesses. In the present study, this problem was avoided by carrying
out a short telephone questionnaire with potential respondents, prior
to inclusion in the survey, to check that they met the matching criteria.

Fifth, while the importance of including a control group of male
entrepreneurs has been demonstrated, Rosa *et al.* (1994) point out
that care must be taken to see that the male respondents included are
not there merely to act as a comparison group. The fact is that they
are also an interesting group in their own right. Similarly, any study of
'gender' and small firm financing must recognise that 'gender' is not
synonymous with 'women' but is about men and women.

Ultimately, a matched pairs design is 'only as good as the researcher's ability to determine how to match the pairs' (O'Farrell and
Hitchins, 1988a: p. 63). What any researcher employing a matched
pairs approach needs to do is give a clear indication of exactly how the
data have been matched, why certain criteria have been chosen over
others and what their significance is within the wider 'framework' of
study (Gibb, 1992). The research is therefore designed to collect data
from forty[2] matched pairs of male and female business owners, taking
the previous caveats into consideration. The method by which the
relevant data were collected is explored in more detail in the following
section.

3.3.2 Interview structure and sample selection

Method used for collecting data

The closest work to this study is that of Riding and Swift (1990).
However, one of the limitations of their study arises from their reliance on a postal survey, using questions answered as part of a wider
national survey of business owners undertaken by the Canadian Federation of Independent Businesses. Postal questionnaires allow for the
collection of a broad sample at fairly low costs and yield standardised,
quantitative data. They need pre-testing to minimise ambiguity, but
careful preparation ensures that all topics are addressed. They also
allow for anonymity. However, postal surveys are renowned for their
low response rates, the fact that they are not always completed fully or
with care (Owens, 1986), and 'respondent bias'. In addition, postal
questionnaires do not allow for in-depth exploration of particular

issues and according to Carter and Cannon (1992), 'researchers have...demonstrated that it is exceptionally difficult to extract experiences of gender discrimination via the use of quantitative techniques' (p. 7). Similarly, Schoenberger (1991) has argued that in-depth investigation is not merely complementary to large-scale quantitative techniques but essential to reveal the underlying causal mechanisms and structures that lie behind observed behaviour. Riding and Swift (1990) were therefore unable to explore in any great depth the more complex interrelationships that exist in the financing of women-owned businesses or the interpersonal dimensions of the banking relationship, particularly as the scope of their survey was much broader than just finance.

In the light of these factors and given that one of the main research aims of the book was to gain a more accurate representation of the underlying processes involved in the financing of women-owned businesses, data were therefore collected by way of in-depth, face-to-face interviews with the owner-managers of the chosen small businesses. Face-to-face interviews have a number of advantages over postal questionnaires. First, it has been argued that, for female business owners in particular, 'in-depth interviews allow them to open up and tell the real story' (Cachon, 1989). Similarly, Oakley (1981) noted that, if the interviewer is able to establish a rapport or a level of trust with the respondent in a face-to-face interview, they are more likely to uncover issues which would have remained hidden in a postal survey.

Second, face-to-face interviews give the interviewer an opportunity to read important non-verbal clues from the respondent in the form of body language and silences, to follow up issues more fully, to query discrepancies, and to probe for verification of certain answers (Healey and Rawlinson, 1993). In addition, it gives both parties the chance to clarify ambiguities of meaning. Face-to-face interviews also allow the researcher to collect visual information, for example, on the state of the business premises or the machinery.

Third, this type of interview can be very beneficial to the respondent (Oakley, 1981). For instance, it offers them an opportunity to share their achievements with an interested listener. In the case of small business owners, particularly those running a business from home, or who have no employees, they are often isolated from the outside world and may not want to burden a domestic partner with their problems. They therefore welcome an opportunity to discuss their business problems with an interested and non-threatening outsider.

An in-depth, semi-structured[3] questionnaire was adopted for two main reasons. First, the structured elements of the questionnaire allowed for an element of comparability and consistency across interviews for the purpose of analysis. In addition they allowed for the collection of quantitative data which was important for studying the mechanics of small business finance (e.g. how much and where from?). Second, the open-ended questions allowed for an insight into the lives of the interviewees and a way of examining the complex, on-going processes that are not always captured by structured questions (Schoenberger, 1991).

A pilot study was undertaken in which five small business owners were interviewed to test the questionnaire for problems of interpretation, wording and length. In addition, meetings were held with other researchers and experts in the field to gain their opinions on the sorts of questions that should be asked. The final questionnaire included around 100 questions informed by the research aims and theoretical framework outlined in chapter 2. Because of the problems associated with sensitising respondents to the issue of gender (outlined in section 3.2), care was taken in the construction of the questionnaire to make the questions gender neutral and to avoid any leading questions or questions relating directly to the issue of gender discrimination. The same questionnaire was therefore used for both the male and female respondents. The research topic was merely introduced to them as the financing of small businesses.

The main survey took place between October 1993 and July 1994 and interviews generally lasted between one and two hours. Interviews were not tape recorded as during the pilot stage respondents had either asked that tape recorders should not be used or had shown signs of discomfort when a tape recorder was present. This was to be expected given the confidential nature of some of the questions. This presented few barriers as in almost all cases verbatim note-taking was possible.

Choosing the matched pairs

In the light of the fact that there is no national database of women-owned businesses and that many women-owned businesses remain 'invisible' because they are small in size and are often run from home, the task of finding a pool of female business owners from which to draw matched pairs was not an easy one. Given that there are fewer women-owned businesses than men-owned businesses and that they are generally more difficult to find, the sample of women-owned businesses was therefore selected prior to the sample of men-owned businesses. The rationale was that it would be easier to find male-owned business matches for the female-owned businesses than vice versa.

Two main sources[4] were identified from which it was possible to identify a sample of women-owned businesses. The sample was supplemented with women-owned businesses drawn from the Yellow Pages (Southampton area), local newspaper articles and by word-of-mouth referrals. It is acknowledged that these sources may have introduced a source of bias into the sample and this, along with other methodological shortcomings are explored in more detail in section 3.4. Having sent out introductory letters to the women-owned businesses in the sample, a follow-up telephone call was made in order to establish whether they were still in business, agreeable to an interview and whether they met the three main criteria for inclusion in the study:

1 Present owner-manager started the business.
2 Business is independent (not part of a larger organisation).
3 Business is small (less than twenty employees).

It was important that the owner-manager to be interviewed had started the business in order to be able to discuss questions relating to raising start-up finance. In situations where there were two or more owner-managers, the interview was undertaken with the one in charge of the finances and who usually deals with the bank. Male–female business partnerships were excluded[5]. Although formal male–female start-up partnerships were excluded, it is acknowledged that even sole traders are not necessarily 'on their own'. Indeed, as pointed out by Rosa and Hamilton (1994), many business owners of both sexes have domestic partners who contribute significantly to the business even though they may not be legal co-owners. Hamilton (1990) argues that an understanding of the issues surrounding the social relations that exist between female business owners and their informal 'partners' and the impact they might have on the business is vital in any study of gender and small business management. Questions were therefore built into the questionnaire which were designed to address these issues.

Having interviewed the female owner-managers, a comparison group of male-owned businesses was selected. The choice of criteria on which pairs of male and female-owned businesses were to be matched was made by referring to existing literature on the financing of women-owned businesses (e.g. Riding and Swift, 1990; Fabowale *et al.*, 1993) and to the criteria used in bank[6] lending to small businesses more generally (e.g. Deakins and Hussain, 1991; Berry *et al.*, 1993). The range of possible match criteria included personal characteristics (e.g. the financial background, managerial background, experience, training, education, qualifications, skills, age, credit track record, personal assets of the owner-manager) and business characteristics (e.g. the sector, legal status, number of owners, annual level of sales, sales growth, number of full-time employees, geographical location, high-technology component of product/process, type of premises, age of the business).

As it would have been impossible to match on all possible criteria and it was essential that the chosen criteria could be measured prior to interview, four of the most important and easily measured of these criteria were chosen on which to match the pairs of female- and male-owned businesses. These were business age, (measured in years from start-up date), size (number of employees), sector (same product/process), and type of premises (home/business premises). As indicated in chapter 2, business age, size, sector and type of business premises are four of the most important factors influencing the amounts and types of finance required by small firms, the problems faced in raising finance, and are also four of the most important structural differences between male- and female-owned businesses. Other factors, for example, turnover or age of owner-manger were not included because their importance in the financing of small firms is less clearly defined or they are too sensitive to be collected prior to interview.[7] The importance of the chosen criteria is explored in greater depth in the remainder of this section.

Business age is one of the most important lending criteria used by the banks and is often used by banks as a surrogate measure for 'risk'. This is because new, start-up companies lack a track record, market share, and have an untried product, high failure rates and the business owner is unlikely to be experienced (Dickson, 1983; Wynant and Hatch, 1990). Young businesses are therefore less attractive to the banks on account of these risk factors. Business age also affects the amount of finance a business generally requires. Younger businesses are found to be able to rely on the internal resources of the owner-manager (Churchill and Lewis, 1983; Hutchinson and Ray, 1986; Brophy, 1989). In addition, business age is an important structural difference between male and female entrepreneurs and research indicates that women-owned businesses are generally younger than men-owned businesses and there are fewer women-owned businesses in the older cohorts of small firms (Riding and Swift, 1990; Clark and James, 1992; Smith, Smits and Hoy, 1992). This is primarily because female entrepreneurship is a relatively recent phenomenon on any scale.

Lenders also prefer to finance certain sectors, particularly those which are able to offer 'hard' assets (e.g. manufacturing) (Loscocco and Robinson, 1991) and therefore service sector businesses are often found to receive less favourable terms of credit (Therrien *et al.*, 1986; Riding and Swift, 1990). In addition, service sector businesses have higher failure or displacement rates than others (Fothergill and Gudgin, 1982; Smallbone, 1990) and are therefore regarded as more risky by the banks. In addition, financing requirements also vary by sector. For example, service sector firms tend to require a lower input of finance than manufacturing firms. However, business sector is an important structural difference between male- and female-owned businesses with women tending to start more businesses in low-capital sectors such as services than men (Brush, 1990).

Again, business size is important as a larger business may be perceived by a lender as being a more secure lending risk. Larger business clients also offer the banks benefits from economies of scale (Binks *et al.*, 1988; Orser *et al.*, 1993). As in the case of newer businesses, smaller businesses also generally require less finance. These findings are of great importance given the fact that female-owned businesses tend to be smaller than male-owned businesses and have few, if any, employees (Goffee and Scase, 1983; Kaplan, 1988; Clark and James, 1992; Scottish Enterprise, 1993b).

Finally, type of premises is important because a business run from external business premises suggests a more 'serious' business to many lenders (Berry *et al.*, 1993). In addition, home-based businesses tend to be less attractive lending prospects because they have obvious constraints on their size and growth potential (e.g. the number of people they can employ). However, research by Curran and Roberts (1989) suggests that businesses run from the owner's home generally require less finance than those run from commercial premises because they have lower overheads. These factors are important because it is found that more women set up and run their businesses from home than men (Carter and Cannon, 1992; Clark and James, 1992; Roberts-Reid and Curran, 1992).

Having located possible male matches from the business directories or Yellow Pages, a short telephone interview was undertaken with them to check that they fulfilled the same initial criteria for inclusion in the study as for the female respondents and that all matching criteria were fulfilled and that they were within the matching ranges allowed.[8] Interviews were then conducted with the male sample of business owners using the same questionnaire as had been used for the female sample. Nevertheless, despite the time spent preparing for the study and the advantages of the matched pairs approach as a method of comparing male- and female-owned businesses, the study was not without problems of both a practical and conceptual nature.

3.4 DATA COLLECTION: PRACTICAL AND CONCEPTUAL DIFFICULTIES

3.4.1 Choosing a representative sample

No claim is made in this study that the sample of businesses was random or representative of the small business population as a whole. However, as Gibb (1992) argues, the search for a representative sample is rarely possible in any small firms research as the small firms sector is so diverse. Nevertheless, there is an awareness in the study that the way in which the matching process was undertaken may have influenced the types of businesses included. In particular, because the female sample was selected first, it is likely that the structure of the sample is influenced by the characteristics of the female-owned business population. Therefore, it is unlikely that the male 'matches' were representative of the general population of male-owned businesses.

It is also acknowledged that the sources by which both the male- and female-owned businesses were selected may have biased the sample. Inevitably, by relying upon businesses included in the South East Hampshire Enterprise Agencies Small Business Directory, the sample will have been biased towards smaller, start-up companies because the small business clients of the enterprise agencies tend to be those requiring help and advice, particularly during the start-up phase. It is anticipated that this may have also had a distorting effect on some aspects of the data collected, for example, attitudes towards training. The sample of businesses drawn from the Yellow Pages is also likely to have been biased towards the types of businesses that can afford a listing. The businesses drawn from the Market Location Directory tended to be the larger, more established and 'visible' business enterprises. Nevertheless, by using a mixture of these sources, in addition to informal referrals and local networking, no one type of small business dominated the sample and possible sample biases may have cancelled each other out.

Given the problems of finding women-owned businesses, the study relied upon a variety of different sources to fill the necessary quota of forty businesses. Because there was a quota that was gradually filled, it is also recognised the sample was not strictly random. As Carter and Rosa (1995) point out, given the relatively small total population of women-owned businesses, a random stratified sample of small businesses would probably not have yielded enough women.

3.4.2   Problems associated with 'matching'

Despite the advantages of a matched pairs approach to compare the financing of male- and female-owned businesses, it is acknowledged that there were problems associated with the method. First, the pairs of female and male business owners were only matched on four of the many criteria possible. As was outlined in section 3.3.2, the four most important criteria to emerge from the existing literature were adopted; however, it is acknowledged that matching on different criteria may have yielded different results.

Second, the matches were not perfect. In other words, the pairs of male- and female-owned businesses were not found to be identical in terms of the match criteria. Nevertheless, in the present study every effort was made to keep matches as close as possible within the matching ranges.

Third, measuring the match criteria was problematical. For example, in the case of the 'size' criteria (measured in number of em-ployees), there were numerous 'types' of employee (full-time, part-time, casual). While it is recognised that a business with four full-time employees might be very different to one with four part-time employees, it would have been almost impossible to match on exact numbers of each type of employee. Therefore, total number of employees (of any kind) was the measure employed. Similarly, pairs of male- and female-owned businesses were matched on 'sector', referring to the product and/or processes used by those businesses. It would have been almost impossible to have matched on exactly the same market as well. The possible effects of these matching issues on subsequent comparisons are duly noted.

3.4.3   Gaining access to the businesses

A more practical problem faced in the study involved gaining access to interview the owner-mangers of the small businesses selected for study. Given that the study involved contacting potential respondents 'cold', the original intention was to make initial contact through a standard letter outlining the research and its aims and requesting an interview. The letter was then to be followed up by a telephone call. However, this approach was found to be very time-consuming because, following the telephone call, many businesses were found not to fit the sample criteria. In addition, the letters invariably ended up at the bottom of the respondents' in-trays, if not in their bins.[9] In any research involving small business owners, it is important to bear in mind that many work incredibly long hours and so the issue of asking them to give up an hour of their valuable time is a very delicate one and requires a great deal of careful negotiation which, it was found, is more difficult to do by letter.

This experience led to a change of strategy with the initial contact being made by means of a telephone call in which an introduction and explanation of the research was given, matching criteria checked and an interview arranged, if appropriate. An 'official' letter of confirmation was sent afterwards. The only problem with this method was overcoming suspicion on the part of some small business owners. In some cases, the business owners needed to be persuaded that they were not being asked to buy anything and that the research was to be undertaken independently. Another of the main problems in negotiating time to interview a busy small business owner is the fact that the researcher generally has nothing to offer in return (McDowell, 1992). In order to tackle this problem, all respondents received a free copy of the executive summary report.

3.4.4 Gaining access to reliable data

Once an interview had been arranged, there were a number of barriers to be negotiated in order to obtain reliable data. First, given the fact that the majority of questions were dealing with issues of business finance, respondents were often reluctant to discuss such issues with a 'stranger', particularly questions of turnover. Some of the respondents were also concerned that their views on the banks should remain anonymous. To counteract these problems, confidentiality was stressed throughout and the questionnaire was designed so as to leave the more sensitive questions until later on in the questionnaire, after a trust and rapport had been established (as suggested by Healey and Rawlinson, 1993). It was often the case that, after the questionnaire had been put away, the respondent was prepared to reveal their views more openly during the informal chats that frequently followed the formal interview. In such cases, notes had to be made from memory after leaving the respondent.

A second barrier to data collection was the tendency for many respondents to discuss issues which interested them but which were not of direct relevance to the study. The world of small business ownership is often very isolated and many small businesses are set up in unhappy circumstances (e.g. bereavement, redundancy, disablement). Small business owners may therefore find the presence of a researcher offers them the opportunity to talk about issues such as personal problems, for example. While this sort of material gives a useful insight into the 'context' of business ownership and is important in order for the interviewer to establish a good rapport with the respondent, it is also important that the interview does not stray off track to any great extent, given the limited time available. Re-directing the conversation back to the line of questioning requires both tact and patience.

Third, a similar problem often arises in the form of distractions. If the business is run from home, these might include pets or children, and whether run from home or external premises, interviews will often be undertaken while the respondent continues to work and with frequent interruptions from telephone calls. While distractions during the interview are far from ideal, the interviewer has to be sympathetic to the respondent's work-load.

Fourth, while the questionnaire was designed and piloted to avoid leading questions and ambiguities, interpretation of certain questions inevitably varied to some extent. For example, one respondent was unsure as to the meaning of the term 'turnover'. The problem is that different people understand and interpret meanings differently. It was therefore necessary to gauge the individual's level of understanding and to offer as much extra clarification for certain questions as was necessary, using an appropriate frame of reference for that respondent. As Schoenberger (1991) points out, '(t)he accuracy and validity of both open-ended interviews and standardised surveys depends on knowing how the respondents use language and what they mean by the way they use it' (Schoenberger, 1991: p. 183).

However, ambiguities and misunderstandings also provide very revealing insights into the ways in which entrepreneurs see things (Schoenberger, 1991).

Fifth, all questionnaire surveys which require respondents to comment on incidents or problems which occurred in the past suffer from problems associated with retrospective recall and this study was no exception. The problems usually stem from the fact that respondents often forget past events or remember them differently to the way that they actually were. The advantage of the face-to-face questionnaire survey is that it allows any contradictions or inconsistencies to be challenged.

Sixth, there was also a need to be aware of the potential effect of the respondent's 'ego' on the answers given to certain types of question.

The effect of 'ego' manifests itself in the attribution of the causes of problems to external factors rather than internal factors. As explained by Gibb (1992),

> (t)hose who work closely with the small business owners will know that, in response to questionnaires about the kinds of 'problems' that he/she faces, most entrepreneurs will place emphasis on the environment or events which are seen to be directly outside their personal control. The filter of ego in answering questions about the business...is of major importance.
>
> (Gibb, 1992: p. 138)

Similarly, there is also a tendency to filter out accreditation to outside influences when reflecting on business successes. Therefore, 'objective statements of the state of the business may be difficult to come by through the owner-manager' (Gibb, 1992: p. 138). These are particular problems in small business research because small business management is generally the sole responsibility of one person and their possible influence on the findings of this study is acknowledged.

A seventh problem in any face-to-face survey is that the respondents may be telling you what they think you want to hear. In this study, for example, a small number of respondents explained that they had a good relationship with their bank manager but then apologised, saying 'oh, but that's not what you want to hear'. In all situations, it was therefore important that the interviewer stressed their impartiality. A pragmatic approach to all qualitative statements was taken by which empirical evidence to support statements was sought. In addition, as advised by Schoenberger (1991), the researcher was alert to the possibility of inconsistencies in given statements and was prepared to challenge them and to look for clarification in the case of ambiguous statements. At the end of each section, a summary was made to the respondent of what he/she had said in order to check that the interviewer's interpretation was correct. It was, however, impossible to interview other parties such as domestic partners, customers, suppliers or employees for further verification of statements, given the additional resources necessary for such an approach.

3.4.5 The influence of the interviewer on data collection

Traditional 'handbooks' on research techniques have tended to advocate a 'hygienic' approach to interviewing, that is, one in which social interaction 'contaminates' the data as little as possible. However, in recent years it has become more widely accepted that, not only is it inevitable that social interaction will impinge on the data collected, but that failure to recognise this fact is misleading (Oakley, 1981). Similarly, Herod (1993) has argued that recognising the effects of factors such as gender, age or race is 'not to abandon scientific concerns for validity' but offers an opportunity to collect richer insights into how such factors shape our understanding of the world (p. 314). It is therefore important as a researcher to state one's 'positionality' (McDowell, 1992) and to take a self-critical stance towards one's research (Schoenberger, 1992). The 'interviewer effect' may take several different forms.

First, in terms of interpreting what the respondent says, it is important to recognise that 'academic researchers are undoubtedly influenced in their approaches by personal ideological beliefs or the "stance" taken within their own discipline' (Gibb, 1992: p. 137). As pointed out by Schoenberger (1992),

> we are people doing research and ... questions of gender, class, race, nationality, politics, history, and experience shape our research and our interpretations of the world, however much we are supposed to deny it. The task, then, is not to do away with these things, but to know them and to learn from them.
>
> (Schoenberger, 1992: p. 218)

Furthermore, because the interviewer is often in a relatively powerful position compared to the interviewee, especially when interviewing small business owners, it up to them not to abuse this power, for example, by asking leading questions (Schoenberger, 1991).

Second, a researcher must also be aware that the 'setting' of an interview might have an important effect on the data collected. Hamilton *et al.* (undated) argue that the 'social roles men and women play and the attitudes they hold are not consistent but vary according to situation and context' (p. 4). In other words, there may be a problem with carrying out interviews in just one setting, for example, the office, because the questions will be answered from that particular social context. If questioned at home or in front of employees or a domestic partner, it is suggested that respondents might give different answers. Nevertheless, these sorts of problems are 'endemic of all cross-sectional social scientific surveys' (Hamilton *et al.*, unpublished: p. 4). In this study, interviews were undertaken from wherever the business was run, usually in the home or in an office. Although the effects are impossible to quantify, an interview undertaken in the owner's home was generally more relaxed than one undertaken in the office. A more holistic approach involving multiple interviews with the same owner-manager in a variety of different settings would have overcome some of these difficulties, but such an approach requires more resources than were available.

Third, the social characteristics of the interviewer, for example their age, race and sex, are important factors because they 'evoke different cultural norms and stereotypes that influence the opinions and feelings expressed by respondents' (Turner and Martin, 1984: p. 271). On no occasion was it felt that race had made a major impact on the data collected, given that no ethnic minorities were interviewed. It is acknowledged that the situation might have been different had there been differences in terms of race. The characteristics of sex and age, however, have raised some important issues with regard to the data collected in this study and the remainder of this section deals with some of these issues.

Much has been written about the 'gender effect' on the interview process (Easterday *et al.*, 1977; Gurney, 1990; Herod, 1993; Kane and Macaulay, 1993; McDowell, 1992). As Herod (1993) points out, '(i)nterviewing as a research practice cannot be conceived as taking place in a gender vacuum' (p. 306). While it is unfruitful to waste time speculating on how things would have been different as a male interviewer, it is important to be self-conscious about the possible effects being a young female researcher has had on the fieldwork (Gurney, 1990: p. 60). According to Easterday *et al.* (1977), 'being young and being female represent two ascribed criteria influencing social interaction in any setting' and 'defines our opportunities and limitations as researchers' (pp. 334–5). Data interpretation, in particular, will be influenced by gender because we are all part of a society in which the terms masculinity and femininity are imbued with certain socially expected characteristics and because interpretation is down to language and men and women are found to use language in different ways (Herod, 1993). In addition, '(g)ender relations are an important dynamic shaping the interview process which can significantly influence the sorts of data obtained' (Herod, 1993: p. 305), particularly when conducting face-to-face interviews. For example, Eagly and Carli (1981) found that interviewees gave significantly different answers to male and female researchers and it was also found that male and female researchers understood interviewees' answers differently.

One of the main disadvantages of being a female researcher, particularly a young female researcher, is that of not being taken seriously, particularly with older, male respondents (Easterday *et al.*, 1977; Gurney, 1990; Herod, 1993). In order to combat such problems, a professional dress code was adopted and the interviewer was well-prepared in order to counteract any potential problems associated with not being taken seriously. On no occasion was it felt that a respondent was overtly patronising or that the researcher had not been treated seriously. However, it was the experience in this study that many of the older respondents of both sexes, particularly those with children of their own, adopted a paternalistic/maternalistic manner, which is not an uncommon experience of young female researchers (see Easterday *et al.*, 1977).

It was also found that the female respondents were more forthcoming in discussions about their children than the men. It is also speculated that the 'ego filter' (Gibb, 1992) was stronger for the male respondents. The men were less likely to highlight their faults and more likely to play up their achievements, and the women vice versa. A final problem which may occur in more in-depth interviews, is that of sexual harassment or 'hustling' (Easterday *et al.*, 1977). Thankfully, in this study there were relatively few examples of this problem but it was recognised that, in an attempt to impress, some men may have exaggerated their achievements.

There are also advantages to being a young female researcher. For instance, not being taken seriously can result in the respondents confiding more readily in the researcher as they are perceived to be powerless and non-threatening. In this study, it was found that during a relatively short time period, respondents could be remarkably frank and open about all aspects of their business and home life. It is also argued that a 'hustler' may be more open in his answers to a female researcher in an attempt to show his co-operation (Easterday *et al.*, 1977). Another advantage is that of access. With many small businesses being run from home, business owners, particularly female business owners, are understandably reluctant to invite in strangers. However, a female researcher is often perceived to be less of a threat to their safety than a male researcher (Gurney, 1990).

3.5   SAMPLE OVERVIEW

3.5.1   Business characteristics

Having outlined the methodological approach adopted in this survey and some of the pitfalls inherent in this kind of research, the remainder of the chapter offers an overview of the sample of businesses included in the survey. To begin this section, the four characteristics on which the pairs of male- and female-owned businesses were matched are explored. Therefore, as the pairs were chosen because they had almost identical characteristics, there is no need to break down the data by sex.

The businesses included in the study were relatively young, 72.5 per cent being under ten years old. The majority of businesses were between the ages of two to four years (Table 3.1). While the age of businesses in this study were younger than those in other studies of small businesses (e.g. Turok and Richardson, 1989), the age distributions of small firms in such studies tend to reflect the way in which samples are selected. In this study, by using an enterprise agency small business directory, the sample may have been biased towards the younger firms, as enterprise agencies tend to have more contact with small business start-ups. In addition, the female sample was selected first and because it is generally the case that the average age of women-owned businesses is lower than that of male-owned businesses (Riding and Swift, 1990; Clark and James, 1992; Smith, Smits and Hoy, 1992), the sample may have reflected the age distribution of women-owned businesses, rather than that of small businesses in general.

Table 3.1 Business characteristics (% of total matched sample, n = 80)

Characteristics	n	%
Business age		
Up to 1 year	12	15.0
2 to 4 years	32	40.0
5 to 9 years	14	17.5
10 years or more	22	27.5
Business sector		
Business services	28	35.0
Consumer services	18	22.5
Other services	16	20.0
Retail	10	12.5
Wholesale	4	5.0
Manufacturing	2	2.5
Transport and distribution	2	2.5
Number of employees (full- and part-time)		
0	30	37.5
1	16	20.0
2 to 3	18	22.5
4 to 9	16	20.0
Business premises		
Owners own home	30	37.5
Commercial premises	50	62.5

There was a predominance of business service sector businesses and a minority of wholesale, transport and distribution and manufacturing businesses. Indeed, 90 per cent of the sample were in retail or services. Again, this was to be expected given that the female sample was selected first and it is widely recognised that women-owned businesses are concentrated in the retail and service sectors (Curran *et al.*, 1987; Brush, 1992). Using the General Household Survey data, Curran *et al.* (1987) found that around 90 per cent of women-owned businesses are in retail or services. This survey therefore makes no claims to be statistically representative of the small business population as a whole, but is more representative of the population of women-owned businesses.

All the businesses in the sample were either very small, 'micro' businesses – under 10 employees, as defined in the Small Business Research Centre study (SBRC, 1992) and the Department of Trade and Industry (DTI, 1995). Just over one-third of the sample were 'one person businesses', defined as 'the small enterprise which employs no other person directly on a full-time basis' (Roberts-Reid and Curran, 1992: p. 249). Nevertheless, many of these businesses did make use of subcontract or casual workers when necessary. None of the businesses were what Roberts-Reid and Curran (1992) have described as 'quasi-self-employed, that is, people formally registered as self-employed but who are, in fact, employees to all intents and purposes' (p. 250).

The small size of businesses in the sample may reflect the fact that over half were selected from the South East Hampshire Enterprise Agencies Directory. As has already been pointed out, because the businesses which use enterprise agencies tend to be new start-ups, it follows that they are likely to be smaller than the general population of small businesses. It may also reflect the fact that female-owned businesses were selected first and female-owned businesses tend to be very small (Goffee and Scase, 1983; Kaplan, 1988; Carter and Canon, 1992; Clark and James, 1992). In addition, the sample was dominated by business service firms and almost 40 per cent of business service firms in the UK are found to be micro businesses (DTI, 1995). However, the findings of the present survey are broadly in line with those of national surveys. For example, research by the DTI (1995) has found that micro businesses make up almost 94 per cent of the total population.

Just under two-thirds of the businesses were run from commercial premises, either leasehold or freehold, with the remaining 37.5 per cent being run from the owner's own home. Many small businesses are started from home because of the need to keep overheads to a minimum in the first few years when undercapitalisation is a particularly severe problem. In addition, very small businesses, particularly service-sector businesses, are frequently run from home because they do not require larger commercial premises. These factors are important, given the fact that most of the businesses in this survey were young, small and in the service sector. It is also the case that around 50 per cent of women set up and run their businesses from home (Carter and Cannon, 1992; Clark and James, 1992; Roberts-Reid and Curran, 1992). Therefore, having picked the female sample first, the total sample may have been biased towards home-based businesses.

The majority of both the male- and female-owned businesses were sole traders (69 per cent) (Table 3.2). The second and third most common business forms were the partnership (15 per cent) and the Limited Company (16 per cent). The high number of sole traders reflects the fact that most of the businesses were very small and very young. In terms of male–female comparisons, it was found that a higher number of female-owned businesses were limited companies than male-owned businesses and there were more male-owned partnerships. However, neither of these differences were found to be statistically significant ($X^2 = 2.044, df = 2$). Similarly, Rosa *et al.* (1994) could find no overall differences between the male- and female-owned businesses in their study in terms of legal status.

The majority of all businesses had an annual turnover of less than £50,000. However, this was more common for the women-owned businesses, with almost 60 per cent of them falling into this category

Table 3.2 Business characteristics by sex of respondent

Characteristics	Total		Female		Male	
	n	%	n	%	n	%
Business form						
Sole trader	55	68.75	28	70.0	27	67.5
Limited company	13	16.25	8	20.0	5	12.5
Partnership	12	15.00	4	10.0	8	20.0
Annual turnover						
Less than £50,000	36	45.00	23	57.5	13	32.5
£50,000 to £99,999	13	16.25	6	15.0	7	17.5
£100,000 to £499,999	18	22.50	6	15.0	12	30.0
£500,000 or over	4	5.00	—	—	4	10.0
Wouldn't say/Don't know/Not applicable	9	11.25	5	12.5	4	10.0
Total	80	100.00	40	100.0	40	100.0

compared to just 30 per cent of men-owned businesses. At the other extreme, just 10 per cent of the businesses had turnovers in excess of £500,000 and in each case these were run by a man. These differences were statistically significant at the 0.01 level using the Wilcoxon Test ($T = 11, N = 16$, two-tailed test). Previous studies have also found the profits, sales and business receipts of women-owned businesses to be lower than those of male-owned businesses. For example, Johnson and Storey (1993) found that 64 per cent of female entrepreneurs had an annual turnover of less than £50,000 compared with only 40 per cent of male entrepreneurs. Similarly, in Canada, Riding and Swift (1990) found 70 per cent of their sample of female-owned firms had gross annual sales of less than $500,000 compared to only 35 per cent of the male-owned firms.

One possible reason why the female sample of businesses was found to have significantly lower turnovers than the male sample of businesses is that many female business owners cannot or choose not to follow a high growth strategy. Some may have domestic commitments which restrict their ability to grow, while others may choose to pursue goals other than growth and performance and place less emphasis on making money than men (Cromie, 1987a; Gregg, 1985; Carter and Cannon, 1992). Another possible reason is that, because many female business owners lack self-confidence, they are often found to under-charge for their products/services (Carter and Cannon, 1992), thus reducing their overall turnover.

3.5.2 Business owner characteristics

The majority of both men and women in the survey were in the 41–55 years age group. However, there were more women (n = 16) in the '40 or under' category than men (n = 9) (Table 3.3). As the male and female samples had been matched on year of start-up, the difference in age group therefore implied that the women were generally younger than the men when they started their businesses. Using the Wilcoxon Test, the difference was found to be significant at the 0.05 level (T = 71.5; n = 23; two-tailed test). These findings are in line with those of other comparative studies of male and female business owners which have also found that female entrepreneurs tend to be slightly younger than their male counterparts (e.g. Watkins and Watkins, 1984; Birley *et al.*, 1986).

The majority of both groups were married or living as married. Nevertheless, only 10 per cent of the men were single, widowed, divorced or separated compared with almost 30 per cent of the

Table 3.3 Business owner characteristics by sex of respondent

Characteristics	Total		Female		Male	
	n	%	n	%	n	%
Age of respondents						
Under 25	1	1.25	1	2.5	—	—
26 to 40	24	30.00	15	37.5	9	22.5
41 to 55	42	52.50	20	50.0	22	55.0
Over 55	13	16.25	4	10.0	9	22.5
Marital status						
Married/Living as married	65	81.25	29	72.5	36	90.0
Widowed/Divorced	8	10.00	7	17.5	1	2.5
Single	7	8.75	4	10.0	3	7.5
Hours worked per week						
Under 40	19	23.75	10	25.0	9	22.5
40–60	26	32.50	15	37.5	11	27.5
Over 60	35	43.75	15	37.5	20	50.0
Education						
Professional/Vocational qualification	31	38.75	18	45.0	13	32.5
Higher education qualification	15	18.75	8	20.0	7	17.5
On-the-job training	15	18.75	6	15.0	9	22.5
None	19	23.75	8	20.0	11	27.5
Total	80	100.00	40	100.0	40	100.0

women. The difference was found to be significant, but at the 0.1 level of significance only ($X^2 = 2.954$, df $= 1$). Similarly, Watkins and Watkins (1984) and Goffee and Scase (1985) also found higher proportions of female small business owners to be single. Nevertheless, the existing evidence as to whether female entrepreneurs are less likely to be married is highly controversial and contradictory (Roberts-Reid and Curran, 1992).

The hours worked by both women and men were high with 75 per cent of the women and 77.5 per cent of the men working more than 40 hours per week. For most, the working week is substantially longer than that of the working population as a whole. Labour Force Survey data reveals that nationally, the average hours worked by the full-time self-employed are 47.3 per week compared with 38.1 for all full-time employees (Curran and Blackburn, 1994). Although numerically more men worked over 60 hours per week than women (50 per cent compared to 37.5 per cent of the women), there was no statistically significant difference ($X^2 = 1.382$, df $= 2$). However, the majority of women in the present survey were found to be working considerably more hours than those in the General Household Survey (Curran *et*

al., 1987) and were far from running 'hobby' or 'pin money' businesses, as suggested by Roberts-Reid and Curran (1992). Both the
male and female business owners in the present survey who were
working under 40 hours per week classed themselves as part-time,
despite the fact that the normal definition of part-time is usually
lower (around 30 hours per week). For the men, reasons for working
part-time included the fact that they were in retirement or that they
had a second job. The women, on the other hand, noted child-care
responsibilities which restricted them from running their businesses on
a full-time basis.

The sample of respondents as a whole was well educated. Almost 40
per cent of respondents had a professional or vocational qualification
and almost 20 per cent had a higher education qualification (e.g.
diploma, degree). Some research has suggested that female small
business owners are better educated than their male counterparts
(Schwartz, 1976; Smith, McCain and Warren, 1982; Watkins and
Watkins, 1984; Welsch and Young, 1984; Curran and Burrows,
1988). Indeed, in this study it was found that more of the female
respondents had professional/vocational and higher education qualifications than their male counterparts. However, the difference was
not found to be statistically significant ($X^2 = 1.947$, df $= 3$). Similarly,
Birley *et al.* (1986) found no significant difference in the levels of
education achieved by male and female business owners.

3.6   SUMMARY AND CONCLUSION

The first aim of the chapter was to explain the inconsistencies and
contradictions that are found to exist in the literature surrounding the
financing of women-owned businesses, as indicated in chapter 2. In
doing so, it identified a number of serious methodological shortcomings in the literature. One of the most serious of these shortcomings
has been the absence, in most studies, of a 'control' group of male
entrepreneurs against which to compare the experiences of female
entrepreneurs in the financing of their businesses. In addition, where
a male control group has been included, it has not compared like with
like because of differences in the structural characteristics of male-
and female-owned businesses.

The second aim of the chapter was to find a research method for the
present study which would respond to the criticisms made of existing
studies. A matched pairs approach was adopted for the study because
it is a method which allows a sample of male- and female-owned
businesses to be compared but in such a way as to cancel out factors

which might distort the comparison – in this case, systematic structural differences which are found to exist between the general populations of male- and female-owned businesses. Bearing in mind the methodological caveats to the approach which are outlined in the chapter, a matched sample of male- and female-owned businesses was interviewed in order to answer the research questions presented at the end of chapter 2. The practical and conceptual difficulties encountered in actually undertaking the survey centred around gaining access to interview the owner-manager, gaining access to reliable data and acknowledging the potential effects of the interviewer on the data collected. However, as indicated, every possible opportunity was taken to counteract these difficulties.

The characteristics of the sample of respondents, although not representative of the small business population as a whole, do tend to reflect the findings of similar small business studies. On the whole, there are few statistically significant differences between the male and female sample of respondents in terms of their business and personal characteristics. Nevertheless, the female respondents were found to have significantly lower levels of annual business turnover, were significantly younger, and were significantly more likely to be single than their male counterparts.

The overall aim of this study is to explore the financing of women-owned businesses in the UK by adopting a methodological rigour and a theoretical framework absent in many previous studies. The remainder of the book therefore seeks to analyse the findings of the matched pairs study outlined in this chapter. The analysis begins in chapter 4 with a comparison of the male and female business owners in their use of and attitudes towards sources of business finance.

4 Raising finance

The use of and attitudes towards sources of small business finance

4.1 INTRODUCTION

Previous research into the financing of women-owned businesses has suggested that female entrepreneurs finance their businesses differently to male entrepreneurs. In almost all cases, women are found to rely solely on personal savings, particularly at start-up (Schwartz, 1976; Stevenson, 1983; Hisrich, 1985; Clutterbuck and Devine, 1987; Hisrich and Brush, 1987; Olm *et al.*, 1988; Department of Industry, Technology and Commerce, 1991). In comparison, male entrepreneurs are found to make greater use of external sources of finance such as bank loans, personal loans and venture capital investors (Hisrich, 1985; Storey and Strange, 1992; Carter and Rosa, 1995; Landström and Winborg, 1995). There is also evidence to suggest that male entrepreneurs use more sources of finance than female entrepreneurs (Carter and Rosa, 1995). Furthermore, businesswomen are found to start their businesses with smaller amounts of finance than their male counterparts (Hisrich and Brush, 1987; Carter and Rosa, 1995).

In addition, as outlined in chapter 2, previous research also argues that female entrepreneurs face more problems than male entrepreneurs in raising finance (Loscocco *et al.*, 1991). It is suggested that women face patronising and discriminatory attitudes by finance providers (Goffee and Scase, 1983; Hisrich and Brush, 1987; Carter and Cannon, 1992). Furthermore, the banks are found to require female business owners to provide more collateral and security on bank finance (Riding and Swift, 1990; Carter and Cannon, 1992; Koper, 1993) and spousal co-signatures more often than male business owners (Collerette and Aubry, 1990).

However, the extent to which differences between male and female entrepreneurs in the financing of their businesses are 'gender-related' is unclear from the existing literature (as explained in chapter 3). It is therefore the aim of this chapter to discover whether 'matched pairs' of male and female business owners exhibit the same differences in the financing of their businesses as are suggested in the existing literature. By studying matched pairs of male and female business owners the study seeks to explore the role of gender in the financing of small businesses.

4.2 THE CHARACTERISTICS OF SMALL BUSINESS FINANCE

4.2.1 Amount used at start-up

All respondents in the survey, regardless of sex, started their businesses with very modest amounts of capital. The frequency distribution of start-up costs indicates that just over one-half of businesses had been started with less than £5,000[1] and that the amount most frequently used was between £1,000 and £4,999 (Figure 4.1). Only 5 per cent of the total number of respondents had used £50,000 or more, while 17.5 per cent were found to have used negligible amounts of capital.

When questioned as to how they had managed to start a business with little, if any, money, the majority of business owners explained that they had used various approaches which go under the heading of 'bootstrapping' (Bhide, 1992). For example, they used equipment that they already owned, that they had borrowed or that they had received as gifts from family or friends. One of the retailers had managed to acquire stock on a sale or return basis. In many cases, businesses were started with little more than the Enterprise Allowance Scheme. The findings of this study are not unusual, given that the majority of small

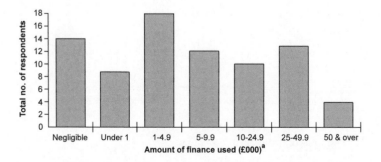

Figure 4.1 Frequency distribution of start-up costs
Note: [a]Amounts are real adjusted figures based on 1992 Retail Price Index

businesses in other studies are found to be launched with very little money (Turok and Richardson, 1989; Carter and Cannon, 1992; Taub and Gaglio, 1995). In addition, bootstrapping techniques are not confined to no- or low-growth enterprises. Indeed, Bhide (1992) found that over 80 per cent of businesses in a sample from the 1989 Inc. '500' (the fastest growing, private companies in the US) were started using bootstrapping techniques (e.g. personal savings, credit cards, second mortgages).

In the light of previous research findings, it was expected that the women-owned businesses in the study would have been started with less finance than the men-owned businesses. For example, a study by Hisrich and Brush (1987) found that, in the US, female business owners started their businesses with under $11,000, roughly half that of male business owners (SBA, 1988). In the UK, Carter and Rosa (1995) found that male business owners used three times more start-up capital than female business owners. However, as can be seen from Table 4.1, there were more similarities than differences between the male and female respondents in the amounts of finance used at start-up and the Wilcoxon Test (N = 32,[2] T = 228; two-tailed hypothesis) revealed no significant differences. There was no evidence that the female respondents had used smaller amounts of capital than their male counterparts.

Table 4.1 Amount of finance used to start the business

Amount[a]	Female n	Female %	Male n	Male %	Total n	Total %
£negligible	7	17.5	7	17.5	14	17.50
Under £1,000	6	15.0	3	7.5	9	11.25
£1,000–£4,999	8	20.0	10	25.0	18	22.50
£5,000–£9,999	6	15.0	6	15.0	12	15.00
£10,000–£24,999	4	10.0	6	15.0	10	12.50
£25,000–£49,999	7	17.5	6	15.0	13	16.25
£50,000 and over	2	5.0	2	5.0	4	5.00
Total	40	100.0	40	100.0	80	100.00

Note: [a] Real adjusted figures based on the 1992 Retail Price Index

4.2.2   The undercapitalisation problem

Undercapitalisation is a problem experienced by many young enterprises (Cromie, 1991; McMahon *et al.*, 1993). Small businesses tend to experience an irregular demand for their product or service at start-up because they are often breaking into a new market in which they are unknown to the customer. While their income may be inconsistent, overheads have to be paid on a regular basis which often leads to cash-flow problems. Similarly, expanding small firms often face difficulties financing growth. The problem for small firms is that growth in sales often exceeds access to new sources of finance to sustain that growth (McMahon *et al.*, 1993). For example, a small manufacturing firm might win a large contract to supply another firm with their product. However, before they are paid for their work, the small business must finance the necessary raw materials, machinery and labour. Small business growth can therefore make severe demands on cash-flow (Drucker, 1985). The problem faced by the small firm is finding enough finance to cushion themselves against such fluctuations in cash-flow (McMahon *et al.*, 1993).

In the present survey, just over half the total sample (forty-two businesses) had faced problems relating to undercapitalisation. As shown in Table 4.2, the majority had experienced cash-flow problems because of late payment and bad debts. This finding is not unexpected. Indeed, a report in the *Guardian* (1994) described late payment of debt as the 'plague of small firms' (p.13). Fifteen respondents explained that undercapitalisation problems had restricted their company's expansion. Gregg (1985) argues that insufficient capital often limits the potential of small firms to expand and grow. Similarly, Carter and Cannon (1992) suggest that '(l)ack of start-up capital is the single, largest constraint on early growth' (p.66). Respondents did not have enough money to purchase essential equipment or to pay for

Table 4.2 Types of problems associated with undercapitalisation (% of respondents who suffered undercapitalisation problems)

	Total[a]	Female	Male	Sig X^2
Late payment/Bad debts	19 (45.2)	8 (40.0)	11 (50.0)	No
Lack of capital for expansion	15 (35.7)	9 (30.0)	6 (22.7)	No
Overheads	7 (16.7)	2 (10.0)	5 (22.7)	—[c]
Working capital	4 (9.5)	1 (5.0)	3 (13.6)	—[c]
Total mentions	45	20	25	—
Total respondents[b]	42 (100.0)	20 (100.0)	22 (100.0)	No

Notes: [a] Total mentions (respondents could mention more than one problem); [b] total number of respondents facing undercapitalisation problems; [c] it was not possible to test the statistical significance of these differences, because in order to perform a *chi*-square analysis, the *expected* number for each cell must not be less than 5 (Clegg, 1994) employees, advertising or marketing. As Carter and Cannon (1992) observe, a lack of capital 'prevents investment in new machinery, it restricts marketing investments and it makes recruitment of new staff impossible' (p.66). A number of respondents noted the dilemma of having to choose between 'getting new business and running the business' as one male respondent put it. For many small business owners, particularly those providing a service, they were unable to afford to take on the employees they desperately needed, particularly to help with the administrative side of the business, and as a result were forced to spend less time selling and providing their service which in turn meant a reduction in business earnings. A further four businesses could not finance their working capital requirements and seven were struggling to meet their overheads.

The literature suggests that women are more likely to suffer from being undercapitalised than men (Allen and Truman, 1991; Carter and Cannon, 1992; *Guardian*, 1992a). According to a report by the National Foundation for Women Business Owners in the USA (1992) 'many women who wish to grow their businesses are hampered by lack of capital' (cited in Atlantic Canada Opportunities Agency, 1992: p.108). In addition, it is suggested that gender 'aggravates' certain business problems such as 'late payment of bills' (Carter and Cannon, 1992). The implication is that, because female entrepreneurs are found to lack management experience and confidence, they will be less proficient at chasing up bad debts.

However, in total fewer women (n = 20) had experienced financial problems than men (n = 22). Using a *chi*-squared analysis,[3] none of the categories in Table 4.2 revealed any statistically significant differences between the male and the female respondents. This finding therefore supports that of Cromie (1991) who similarly found no significant differences between the male and female entrepreneurs on issues such as lack of funds, cash-flow and getting paid.

4.2.3   Sources of finance used at start-up and post-start-up

Number of sources

Respondents were generally found to have used very few sources of finance of any kind. At start-up, 84 per cent of all respondents had used less than three sources (Figure 4.2) and the average number used was just 1.6 per business. Similarly, in a study of small businesses by Cressy (1992), it was found that most businesses only used one or two sources of finance at start-up and no business used more than four sources.

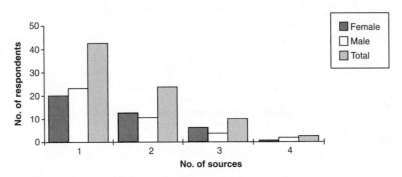

Figure 4.2 Total number of sources used at start-up (per respondent)

Post-start-up, there was a greater diversity of sources used, with 45 per cent of respondents having used three or more sources (Figure 4.3) and the average was 2.7 per business. This is to be expected as the need for and access to more diverse sources of finance tends to increase during the later phases of growth (Churchill and Lewis, 1983; Hutchinson and Ray, 1986; Brophy, 1989).

Internal sources

Consistent with previous small business research findings (e.g. Turok and Richardson, 1989; Holmes and Kent, 1991; Storey and Strange, 1992; McMahon *et al.*, 1993), the majority of businesses in the study had been financed using 'internal' sources of finance. At start-up, almost 60 per cent of all sources mentioned were internally generated Table 4.3. The most common 'internal' sources were personal and/or

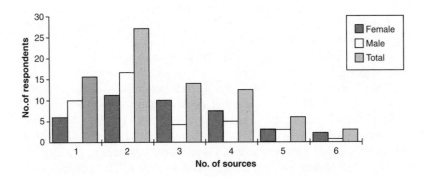

Figure 4.3 Total number of sources used post-start-up (per respondent)

Table 4.3 Sources of finance used by respondents at start-up (% of total number of respondents)

Source	Total n^a	%	Female n^a	%	Male n^a	%	Sig. X^2
Internal							
Personal/Family savings	56	70.00	27	67.5	29	72.5	No
Loans/Gifts (family/friends)	9	11.25	6	15.0	3	7.5	—[b]
Re-mortgage	8	10.00	3	7.5	5	12.5	—[b]
Other 'internal' sources	6	7.50	2	5.0	4	10.0	—[b]
External							
Bank overdraft	16	20.00	9	22.5	7	17.5	No
Bank loan	13	16.25	7	17.5	6	15.0	No
Loan Guarantee Scheme	1	1.25	0	0	1	2.5	—[b]
Supplier credit	5	6.25	2	5.0	3	7.5	—[b]
Leasing/Hire-purchase	4	5.00	4	10.0	0	0	—[b]
Enterprise Allowance Scheme	14	17.50	5	12.5	9	22.5	No
Public sector grant	1	1.25	1	2.5	0	0	—[b]
Informal venture capital	1	1.25	1	2.5	0	0	—[b]
Business Expansion Scheme	1	1.25	1	2.5	0	0	—[b]
Total respondents	80	100.0	40	100.0	40	100.0	—
Total sources used	135	—	68	—	67	—	No

Notes: [a] Number of respondents using each source (many firms used more than one source); [b] it was not possible to test the statistical significance of these differences, because in order to perform a *chi*-square analysis, the *expected* number for each cell must not be less than 5 (Clegg, 1994)

family savings, used by 70 per cent of all business owners. The importance of this source of start-up finance is further reflected in the fact that, for around 45 per cent of respondents, personal or family savings were the *only* sources of finance used at start-up.

Similarly, after start-up, the most commonly used sources of finance were internally generated and accounted for 62 per cent of all sources mentioned (Table 4.4). However, the most important source of post-start-up finance was retained profits which was mentioned by the entire sample. Walker (1989) suggests that retained earnings are a critical source of equity for small firms. Indeed, for 20 per cent of respondents in this study, it was their *only* source of follow-on finance.

Naturally, personal funds may be quite limited, particularly when there is only one business owner. Previous studies have found that the owner's funds are often supplemented with gifts or loans from family or friends (Turok and Richardson, 1989; McMahon *et al.*, 1993). In the present survey, gifts and loans from family and friends were the

Table 4.4 Sources of finance used by respondents post-start-up (% of total no. of respondents)

Source	Total n^a	%	Female n^a	%	Male n^a	%	Sig. X^2
Internal							
Personal/Family savings	20	25.00	12	30.0	8	20.0	No
Loans/Gifts (family/friends)	7	8.75	3	7.5	4	10.0	—[b]
Re-mortgage	2	2.50	1	2.5	1	2.5	—[b]
Retained profits	80	100.0	40	100.0	40	100.0	No
Other 'internal' sources	10	12.50	3	7.5	7	17.5	No
External							
Bank overdraft	24	30.00	13	32.5	11	27.5	No
Bank loan	25	31.25	15	37.5	10	25.0	No
Loan Guarantee Scheme	1	1.25	0	0	1	2.5	—[b]
Supplier credit	9	11.25	7	17.5	2	5.0	—[b]
Leasing/Hire-purchase	9	11.25	5	12.5	4	10.0	—[b]
Other 'external sources'	4	5.00	4	10.0	0	0	—[b]
Informal venture capital	1	1.25	0	0	1	2.5	—[b]
Other 'equity sources'	1	1.25	1	2.5	0	0	—[b]
Total respondents	80	100.0	40	100.0	40	100.0	—
Total sources used	193	—	104	—	89	—	No

Notes: [a] Number of respondents using each source (many firms used more than one source); [b] it was not possible to test the statistical significance of these differences, because in order to perform a *chi*-square analysis, the *expected* number for each cell must not be less than 5 (Clegg, 1994)

next most important sources of finance after personal/family savings and were used by 11 per cent of respondents at start-up and 9 per cent of respondents post-start-up. Other 'internal' sources included loans raised on personal assets (namely second mortgages) and 'other' sources such as credit cards, life insurance policies, inheritances and redundancy payments/early retirement settlements. In addition, it was taken for granted by most business owners interviewed that they themselves were providing a certain amount of 'internal equity' in the form of unpaid or low-paid activity (Ang, 1991).

External sources

In finding with previous studies (Turok and Richardson, 1991; Storey and Strange, 1992; McMahon *et al.*, 1993; Cosh and Hughes, 1994), the most important source of external finance at both start-up and post-start-up was from the high-street banks (Table 4.3 and 4.4). At start-up, banks provided finance for 20 per cent of respondents in the form of overdrafts and 16 per cent in the form of term loans. Post-start-up, these figures had increased to 30 per cent and 31 per cent respectively. Similarly, Cosh and Hughes (1994) found that newer firms raise a lower proportion of their additional finance from banks than older firms. In total, almost 70 per cent of the respondents had ever used the bank for finance, in the form of overdrafts, term loans or both (Table 4.5). These findings are not unusual given that, in the UK as a whole, most small businesses are reliant on short-term debt finance provided by the banks in the form of overdrafts and term loans (Binks, 1993; McMahon *et al.*, 1993). Indeed, the Cambridge University National Small and Medium Sized Firms Survey in 1991 (SBRC, 1992) found that 84 per cent of firms had raised bank finance in the previous three years.

The banks are an important source of finance for the small business owner for a number of reasons. First, as successive reports have shown, small businesses lack access to alternative sources, in particular equity and risk capital (Macmillan Committee 1931, Bolton Report 1971, Wilson Committee 1979; Burns and Dewhurst, 1983; ACOST, 1990). Second, in recent years, the major clearing banks have developed a wide range of new products and services to attract small business customers (Binks, 1991a). Third, virtually all small business owners have a personal bank account and so banks are a convenient source of finance. Fourth, the banks are best able to overcome the acute information asymmetries associated with small firm financing because they have a large customer base, well developed branch networks and can therefore design relatively standardised lending contracts which can be monitored and enforced at low cost (Keasey and Watson, 1993b). Fifth and most importantly, the banks are virtually the only sources which provide small business owners with the type of

Table 4.5 Total use[a] of bank finance and type at start-up and post-start-up (% in brackets)

Type	Total	Female	Male
Overdraft and loan/s	26 (47)	15 (47)	11 (48)
Overdraft only	20 (36)	11 (34)	9 (39)
Loan/s only	9 (16)	6 (19)	3 (13)
Total[b]	55 (100)	32 (100)	23 (100)

Notes: [a] Includes overdrafts facilities that had been arranged but not necessarily used; [b]percentage totals may not = 100 due to rounding finance they most commonly require (short-term debt finance in the form of overdrafts and term loans) (Keasey and Watson, 1993b).

The most common type of bank finance used by respondents in the survey was found to be the overdraft facility, used by over half (58 per cent) of the total sample. Similarly, the CBI Cleveland study (1994) found that 57.4 per cent of small businesses had borrowed by overdraft or overdraft extension. Cressy (1992) suggests that the bank overdraft is the most important source of institutional finance for small firms nationally. Indeed, a study by the Bank of England (1994) revealed that 56 per cent of small businesses in the UK rely on overdrafts as their main source of finance. According to the Pecking Order Hypothesis (POH) (Myers, 1984), as outlined in chapter 2, finance is sought by small business owners in an order which minimises external interference and ownership dilution (Cosh and Hughes, 1994). Therefore, overdraft finance is a particularly attractive external source of small business finance because it tends to be exempt from the regular monitoring that accompanies fixed and long-term loans, thus enabling the owner-manager to maintain a level of independence and freedom of control (Cressy, 1992; Cosh and Hughes, 1994). Overdraft finance is also attractive because interest is only charged on the amount actually borrowed on a day-to-day basis, unlike term loans where interest is charged on the whole loan even if it is not all being used. In addition, the overdraft allows the small business owner to overcome fluctuations in cash-flow and working capital which tend to be more acute for the smaller firm (Cressy, 1992). Indeed, 17 per cent of those respondents who said they had an overdraft had not actually used it, but were keeping it for such 'emergencies' as one respondent put it.

Apart from bank finance, respondents in this survey were found to use very few external sources finance, either at start-up or post-start-up (Tables 4.3 and 4.4). None of the businesses had sought formal venture capital. In addition, only three respondents in the survey had raised informal equity finance and in all three cases, equity stakes were taken either by friends or relatives. The low overall usage of equity finance in this study is not surprising given that small business owners generally avoid equity finance because they do not want the interference or dilution of ownership perceived to accompany it (Myers, 1984; Holmes and Kent, 1991). Less significant is the fact that, on the supply side, venture capital organisations are known to have shifted away from start-ups and early stage ventures and towards less risky investments in corporate restructuring projects (e.g. Management Buy-Outs and Buy-Ins) (Murray, 1990; 1993; BVCA, 1993; Mason and Harrison, 1994).

A minority (6 per cent) of respondents had succeeded in arranging supplier credit at start-up. Post-start-up, there was a slight increase in the use of supplier credit to just over 10 per cent of respondents. However, these respondents tended to have already established relationships with suppliers, either previously as employees of other companies or as owners of other businesses. Despite the spectacular growth in the use of hire-purchase and leasing among many firms in recent years (Berry *et al.*, 1990), only 5 per cent of business owners in the present survey had used leasing or hire-purchase for financing equipment at start-up which increased to just over 10 per cent post-start-up. This figure is much lower than that of the Cambridge study (SBRC, 1992) which found that hire-purchase and leasing had been used by 33 per cent of 'micro' businesses (under 10 employees). This may reflect the fact that the present survey included a much narrower sectoral mix of firms dominated by service sector firms which tend to have low equipment needs and therefore have a lower need for hire-purchase or leasing arrangements.

In terms of public sector finance, 17.5 per cent of respondents had taken advantage of the Enterprise Allowance Scheme (EAS), or Business Start-up Scheme as it is now known. This figure may be higher than that of the general population of small business owners because over half of the respondents in this survey were drawn from the South East Hampshire Enterprise Agencies small business directory. Only two respondents (2.5 per cent) had ever raised finance through the Loan Guarantee Scheme (LGS). Similarly, only one business owner in the present survey had raised finance through the Business Expansion Scheme (BES). The latter two findings are not surprising given the low take-up rate for the schemes nationally (Storey, 1994). Only one business owner had ever received a public sector grant (from the Training and Enterprise Council) to assist with employing staff.

Male–Female Comparison

Although all small businesses in this study used relatively few sources of finance, either at start-up or post-start-up, it was expected that the male business owners would have used more sources of finance than the female business owners, given the findings of existing research into the financing of women-owned businesses. For example, Smith *et al.* (1982) found only 8 per cent of their sample of female entrepreneurs used more than two sources of finance in their businesses, whereas 47 per cent of the male entrepreneurs used multiple sources. In this study, however, there was virtually no difference between the number of sources of finance used by the male and female respondents. Indeed, 17.5 per cent of the female business owners had used more than two sources of finance at start-up compared to 15 per cent of the male business owners. Post-start-up, 57.5 per cent of the female respondents had used more than two sources of finance compared to 32.5 per cent of the male respondents. These findings were not found to be statistically significant using the Wilcoxon Test (Start-Up – N = 22, T = 118; Post-Start-Up – N = 23, T = 95.5).

Previous studies into the financing of women-owned businesses have also found that, in almost all cases, women rely solely on personal savings, particularly at start-up (Schwartz, 1976; Stevenson, 1983; Hisrich, 1985; Clutterbuck and Devine, 1987; Hisrich and Brush, 1987; Olm *et al.*, 1988; Department of Industry, Technology and Commerce, 1991) and also for on-going finance (Carter and Rosa, 1995). In comparison, male entrepreneurs make greater use of external sources of finance such as bank loans, personal loans and venture capital investors (Hisrich, 1985; Carter and Rosa, 1995). Studies have also found that female business owners borrow less frequently from banks and in much smaller amounts than their male counterparts (Hisrich, 1985; Brown and Segal, 1989). The pervasive belief is that this is because female entrepreneurs suffer from gender discrimination by external finance providers and as a result lack access to external finance or avoid it altogether. It was therefore expected that female respondents in the present study would be found to have used more internal sources of finance and less external finance, particularly bank finance, than the male respondents.

However, in the present study, there were no significant differences between the male and female business owners in terms of the individual sources of finance they used to start or grow their businesses. In particular, there was no evidence to suggest that the female business owners were more reliant on their own internal sources of finance and less likely to use bank finance (Tables 4.3 and 4.4). Indeed, the male business owners generally used internal finance more often than the female business owners and more of the female respondents were found to have used bank overdrafts and loans than the male respondents. When the total number of respondents using bank finance (overdrafts and loans) was analysed (Table 4.5), it was found that significantly more of the female respondents (n = 32) had used bank finance than their male counterparts (n = 23) ($X^2 = 4.713$; df = 1, 0.05 level of significance, two-tailed test).

One possible suggestion as to why significantly more female business owners had used bank finance than their male counterparts is the fact that fewer women (n = 7) started their businesses as a direct result of unemployment following redundancy or forced early retirement than men (n = 11). Storey and Strange (1992) found that business owners who were unemployed prior to start-up use bank finance less than those who were employed prior to start-up. The suggestion is that the banks are more wary of lending to unemployed business owners, although Storey and Strange (1992) could find no evidence to suggest that firms founded by the unemployed are significantly less profitable than others. It is more likely, in the case of the present survey, that the male business owners did not need to raise bank finance because they had access to redundancy money, unlike the female business owners. Indeed, 64 per cent of those men starting a business due to unemployment were found to have invested their redundancy settlements but none of the women. The fact that a smaller proportion of the unemployed female founders had used redundancy settlements to finance their businesses than the male founders probably reflects the fact that the female business owners in the survey were significantly younger than their male counterparts (see chapter 3) and therefore less likely to qualify for large redundancy payments or early retirement settlements. It is also likely to be a reflection of women's position in the labour market more generally. As pointed out in chapter 1, women are less likely to have a long, uninterrupted career history with a single employer and are therefore only eligible for a smaller redundancy payment. They are also more likely to work part-time and therefore would not qualify for a redundancy payment at all. In addition, it is likely that, because the male respondents were found to be older, they were more likely to have accumulated personal savings and therefore did not need bank finance. The fact that women tend to be concentrated in low-paid jobs in the labour market (chapter 1) may also mean that the female entrepreneurs in the survey were less likely to have large personal savings.

Other noteworthy, although not statistically significant, differences between the male and female business owners are as follows. First, twice as many of the female respondents had raised finance in the form of loans or gifts from family or friends at start-up than the male respondents (15 per cent of women compared to 7.5 per cent of men), although the significance of this finding could not be tested given the small numbers concerned.[4] Similarly, Storey and Strange (1992) found that 33 per cent of female founders compared with just 6 per cent of male founders had used loans or gifts from friends or relations at start-up. Storey and Strange (1992) found that the younger the new firm founder, the more likely they were to use loans or gifts from friends or relations. Although Storey and Strange (1992) did not suggest a reason as to why this might be the case, it is likely that the parents of younger business owners will still be alive and have disposable cash and therefore be in a position to give such gifts. In addition, the younger the business owner, the more socially acceptable it is for them to be 'supported' financially by their family. The reason why more female respondents in the survey had raised finance in the form of family gifts or loans may therefore reflect the fact that the sample of female business owners was significantly younger than the sample of male business owners (see chapter 3).

Second, the female respondents were also found to have used more leasing/hire-purchase at start-up and more supplier credit post-start-up than the male respondents. Again, however, the significance of all these findings could not be tested given the small numbers concerned. Nevertheless, these findings are surprising given that previous studies of the problems faced by female entrepreneurs (as outlined in chapter 1) show that women are not taken seriously in business compared to men and lack business credibility, particularly in the eyes of suppliers (Hisrich and O'Brien, 1981; Hisrich and Brush, 1983; Goffee and Scase, 1985; Hisrich, 1986; Clutterbuck and Devine, 1987; Carter and Cannon, 1992). Although it is difficult to make generalisations, given the small numbers involved, it may be that the findings of this study reflect an increase in the credibility of female entrepreneurs among suppliers or that being a woman is a positive asset when dealing with suppliers (e.g. the 'novelty' of doing business with a woman – *Cosmopolitan Magazine*, July 1995). However, it may also be a reflection of the fact that women have less access to their own personal sources of finance and therefore have to search more widely for alternative sources of finance (e.g. leasing, hire-purchase or supplier credit).

Third, almost twice as many male respondents as female had used the Enterprise Allowance Scheme (22.5 per cent of men compared to 12.5 per cent of women). This may be a reflection of the fact that more of the men had been unemployed prior to start-up and were therefore eligible for the scheme or, conversely, that many women are ineligible for the Enterprises Allowance Scheme. Indeed, 'there has been a widely voiced concern that the scheme discriminates against women' (Kaur and Hayden, 1993: p.103). Many women are at home, bringing up a family before they start a business. They are therefore not in receipt of unemployment benefit and therefore do not meet the main criterion of the scheme. According to one of the accountants interviewed in the study, these rules are gradually being relaxed to account for such problems, but on an unofficial basis only.

4.3   EXPLAINING THE RELIANCE ON INTERNAL SOURCES OF FINANCE

4.3.1   Problems raising external sources of finance

Despite the apparent abundance of finance options available to the small business, it is often argued that the financial needs of small businesses are not well served by existing financial institutions and that small firms face a 'finance gap' (Macmillan Committee 1931, Bolton Report 1971, Wilson Committee 1979; Burns and Dewhurst, 1983; ACOST, 1990). These problems have become particularly acute during the recession of the early 1990s. Not only has this been a period in which the banks have become more cautious in their lending decisions towards small businesses and tightened their lending criteria (Bank of England, 1994), but in addition, almost all venture capitalists have moved away from start-ups and early-stage companies (Mason and Harrison, 1990). Small firms are therefore faced with a 'debt gap' as well as an 'equity gap'. As a result, many small firms have been forced to rely increasingly on their own internal sources of finance.

While a number of authors have questioned the evidence to support the existence of a 'finance gap' and of market failure in the supply of funds (Keasey and Watson, 1993a; Storey, 1994), it cannot be denied that many small businesses experience difficulties in raising particular amounts and types of finance (Binks *et al.*, 1988; Storey *et al.*, 1992). In the present study, it was therefore expected that the heavy reliance on internal sources of finance was the result, at least in part, of the fact that many small businesses had been unable to raise external sources of finance. However, the data revealed that only 12.5 per cent (n = 10) of the respondents had ever been refused finance. A further 7.5 per cent (6 respondents) had been offered the finance they requested, but on terms and conditions which prevented them from accepting the offer (e.g. they were asked to put up their homes as security).

In total, eight of the ten refusals were for bank finance, the majority of applications being for term loans (75 per cent). One respondent had been refused finance from a leasing company, the other from a building society. Three-quarters of refusals occurred during the post-start-up period and the amounts of finance which were being sought ranged from £200 to £60,000 (median amount = £7,000). In all but three cases, the finance had been sought to fund capital assets such as premises, cars and equipment. The other three applications were for cash-flow and working capital.

Almost one-third of all business owners who had been refused finance were not given a reason by their finance provider. However, of the two-thirds that had been given a reason, it was generally due to a lack of collateral/security or insufficient turnover (Table 4.6). This is not surprising given that the banks are well-known for seeking collateral/security to protect themselves from the agency-related risks associated with lending to the small business sector (chapter 2) and that in a study by the CBI (1994), 40 per cent of firms were turned down for bank finance because of insufficient assets. Other reasons given in the present study included poor cash-flow, and one businessman was even told that he was too young for a bank loan.

The business owners themselves often had their own ideas as to why they had been refused finance. This often involved them externalising the blame, a characteristic of small business owners which is frequently noted in the entrepreneurship literature (Gibb, 1992). For example, one businessman had been refused a bank loan on the grounds of insufficient turnover. However, his personal view was that the bank was unprepared to finance the equipment he needed because it was high-technology in nature. Another was refused a bank loan on the basis of mediocre trading figures. He blamed a poor banking relationship. One businesswoman was given no reason for having her bank loan request denied but blamed it on the arrival of a new bank manager who did not understand her business.

In only three of the ten cases did respondents not manage to find the finance required in a different way. In almost all cases this involved finding the money from a different source, or by changing banks. One of the female respondents was so annoyed with her bank manager's refusal to grant her a term loan and his unhelpful attitude that she

Table 4.6 Reasons given by finance providers for refusing to finance businesses (% in brackets)

Reason for refusal	Total	Female	Male
None	3 (30)	2 (40)	1 (20)
Lack of collateral	3 (30)	1 (20)	2 (40)
Insufficient turnover	2 (20)	1 (20)	1 (20)
Poor cash-flow	1 (10)	1 (20)	0
Age of business owner	1 (10)	0	1 (20)
Total refusals[a]	10 (100)	5 (100)	5 (100)

Notes: [a] Percentage totals may not = 100 due to rounding

removed all her accounts, including personal accounts, to another bank and raised the finance by re-mortgaging her house. Another of the businesswomen who was refused a bank loan was subsequently able to raise half the capital from a finance company and the other half from her parents who re-mortgaged their house for her. For approximately half of those who had faced problems raising finance, there were no serious, long-lasting effects on the business. For the other half however, they were faced with problems which included the stagnation of business growth, the extra costs associated with raising more 'expensive' finance, the inconvenience and for two of the businesswomen, the added personal stress of being reliant on their parents for money.

The study, however, offers no evidence to suggest that female business owners faced more problems raising external finance than their male counterparts. Exactly the same number of male and female respondents had been refused finance and the same number had been offered finance but on terms and conditions which meant they could not accept. However, it does appear that the women were refused on smaller amounts than the men. The median amount refused to a woman was £7,000 compared to £10,000 for the men. This may simply reflect the fact that the women in this survey were generally seeking less external finance than the men anyway. For instance, it is noted later in this chapter that the female business owners in the survey were also found to have smaller bank overdraft facilities and loans than the men. In particular, there was no evidence to suggest that the female respondents were more likely to be refused bank finance because they lacked collateral (Kaur and Hayden, 1993; Carter and Rosa, 1995). Neither was there any evidence to suggest that discrimination was the explanatory factor in bank finance refusals for female-owned businesses, although one female respondent felt the bank had become much less lenient towards her business since she and her husband (the other director) had divorced.

4.3.2   Attitudes towards external finance

Existing studies of the financing of small firms have argued that the way in which small businesses are financed is not related purely to gaps in the supply of small finance but also to gaps in demand (DTI, 1991; Holmes and Kent, 1991; Cosh and Hughes, 1994; Landström and Winborg, 1995). In order to explore reasons for the reliance on informal sources of finance among small business owners in the present survey, the following section seeks to examine the demand side of the financing relationship by exploring the reasons why small business owners had decided not to use one of the most important sources of external finance – the banks.

As indicated in Table 4.5, 31 per cent (n = 25) of the sample fell into the 'non-users of bank finance' category. This is not an unusual finding. For example, 38 per cent of small businesses interviewed for the Scottish Birth Rate Study (Scottish Enterprise, 1993a) had never sought an overdraft or loan. When asked why they had not used the bank as a source of finance, Table 4.7 indicates that most respondents were not anti-banks but 'anti-borrowing' (e.g. 'I don't like borrowing' or 'I don't believe in borrowing'). For example, one respondent explained how he was

> taught as a child never to borrow. It may take longer to get what you want by saving for it but it's nice to wake up in the morning and know that you don't owe anyone any money.
>
> (survey respondent)

Other reasons for their 'anti-borrowing' behaviour included the belief that bank borrowing is too risky. Although the reasoning behind this cautious behaviour was not explored directly, the implicit message being sent by the respondents was that the recession had forced them to become more cautious. Similarly, in a study by the CBI (1994), it was suggested that a resistance to borrowing was, in part, due to economic uncertainty. One respondent in the present survey had lost his home when his previous business had collapsed due to the recession. He explained, 'I am determined never to make the same mistakes again. I was determined not to borrow any money or even to invest any of my own money in the new business' (survey respondent).

Table 4.7 Reasons for non-use of bank finance (% in brackets)

Reason	Total	Female	Male	Sig. X^2
Anti-borrowing	37 (47)	13 (39)	24 (52)	No
Do not need	23 (29)	8 (24)	15 (33)	No
Too expensive	11 (14)	6 (18)	5 (11)	—[b]
Don't know/no reason	8 (10)	6 (18)	2 (4)	—[b]
Total reasons[a]	79 (100)	33 (100)	46 (100)	—
Total non-users	25	8	17	Yes

Notes: [a] Adds together reasons for not using bank overdrafts and loans, therefore exceeds total number of non-users. Percentage totals may not = 100 due to rounding; [b]it was not possible to test the statistical significance of these differences, because in order to perform a *chi*-square analysis, the *expected* number for each cell must not be less than 5 (Clegg, 1994)

Another six respondents had friends whose businesses had recently collapsed. A further four were not prepared to provide the banks with the necessary collateral (i.e. their homes) for fear of failure and therefore the loss of their home. Two respondents, having started their businesses due to redundancy, said they were cautious about 'making a big commitment to borrowing' until they were sure the venture would be viable. This is not surprising given that the interviews took place in the period immediately following the peak of small business failures (1991–1993) (George, 1994). Media attention at the time also portrayed the banks as being 'out of touch, insensitive and greedy' (The *Observer*, 1994a: p.3) which will have deterred many business owners from seeking bank borrowing. In addition, three respondents were against bank borrowing because, as predicted by the Pecking Order Hypothesis (Myers, 1984), they felt it would deny them their independence and control over the business and would create an unwelcome source of interference. As one businesswoman put it, 'once you have involved the bank, it's no longer your own business. You are, in effect, working for the bank once you borrow' (survey respondent).

Of course, others openly enjoyed the challenge of starting a business with little financial input. One male respondent said that he 'got a kick out of starting businesses with no money'. The second most important reason for not using bank finance was that the respondents felt that they could meet all of their financing needs from internal sources. Most felt that they had more than enough finance from internally generated sources and the remainder felt that the scale of their business did not warrant more finance than was available internally. While this may have been true for the smaller, home-based businesses in sectors with low capital requirements, it cannot be ignored that just over 50 per cent of all businesses in the survey were suffering from undercapitalisation problems (section 4.2.2). This suggests that many respondents may have underestimated their financial needs. Holmes and Kent (1991) argue that small firms are often found to be suffering from undercapitalisation because of the 'knowledge gap', rather than the 'finance gap' discussed in section 4.3.1; in other words, because owner-managers frequently lack the skills to assess adequately their company's financial needs. However, respondents in the present survey may have also been ignoring the financial needs of their businesses because of recession-related caution.

As expected, the third most important reason for not using bank finance was related to cost which is not surprising given that one of the most frequent causes of conflict in the small business–banking relationship is found to be bank charges (Binks *et al.*, 1988; Keasey and Watson, 1993a). In particular, the banks were perceived by respondents to impose excessively high charges and interest rates on small firm borrowing.

Given that the male business owners were found to use bank finance significantly less than the female business owners, it is not surprising that the male respondents gave more reasons for not using bank finance than the female respondents. In general however, the female respondents were found to give very similar reasons for not using bank finance to the male respondents and there were no statistical differences between the male and female business owners in the reasons they gave (Table 4.7). These findings therefore make no suggestion that female entrepreneurs exhibit a stronger version of the Pecking Order Hypothesis, as suggested in chapter 2. Indeed, it was the male entrepreneurs who indicated that they were more 'anti-borrowing' than the female entrepreneurs, despite existing research which suggests that female business owners are generally more cautious about borrowing than men (Brown and Segal, 1989). Nevertheless, two of the female business owners had avoided bank borrowing because of perceived gender-related problems. One female respondent had avoided the bank because, in her words, 'I was a full-time mother for ten years and had no track record. In addition, my husband was unemployed at the time. What bank would have wanted to know?' (survey respondent). Another had avoided the banks because she 'knew how notorious banks are at rejecting women and how they ask questions that wouldn't be asked of a man' (survey respondent). However, it must be noted that these were perceptions only. In addition, two women said there was no need for external finance as they had their husbands to 'fall back on'. In comparison, none of the men said that they did not need external finance because they could rely on their wife's salary. This finding is to be expected because, given the traditional position of women in the workforce (in lower paid jobs) or in society (home-makers) (see chapter 1), male business owners are less likely to be in the position where they can rely on the salary of their domestic partner to support them.

4.4 RAISING BANK FINANCE: AN IN-DEPTH ANALYSIS

The findings of the study, so far, indicate that bank finance is the main source of external debt finance for small firms, regardless of whether the owner is male or female (SBRC, 1992; Bank of England,

1995). In the remainder of this chapter, the study therefore investigates the use of bank finance in more depth, comparing the amounts and terms and conditions of the bank finance used by male and female small business owners.

4.4.1   Amount of bank finance used

The majority of the overdraft facilities held by the respondents were fairly small in size (size as measured at time of interview). They ranged in size from £200 to £55,400. However, as illustrated in Figure 4.4, there was a skew towards the smaller sized overdrafts and 40 per cent of respondents had an overdraft facility of less than £5,000. Indeed, the average (median) overdraft was £5,350 (mean £10,225). The bank loans were generally of a higher value than the overdrafts (Figure 4.5). They ranged in size from £520 to £277,500 and 70 per cent of were between £5,000 and £20,000. The average (median) loan was £9,900 (mean £14,658).[5]

Previous studies into the financing of women-owned businesses have found that female business owners generally borrow from the banks in much smaller amounts than their male counterparts (Hisrich, 1985). In the present survey, the women were found to have smaller overdraft facilities and bank loans. This was most evident in the case of the overdraft facilities where the median limit for the female respondents was £2,143 but £8,785 for the male respondents. Using the Wilcoxon test (N = 10, T = 8), these findings were found to be statistically significant at the 0.05 level (two-tailed hypothesis). In the case of the bank loans, there was less of a difference – the median loan

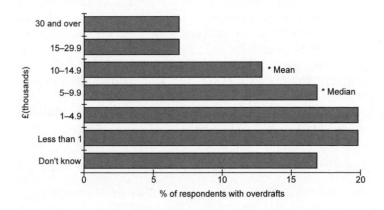

Figure 4.4 Size of overdraft limit

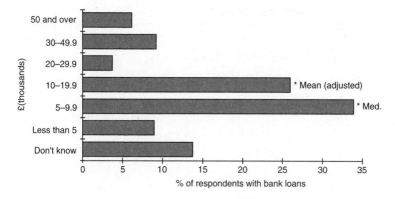

Figure 4.5 Size of bank loans

size for the women was £8,550 and £10,590 for the men. Using the Wilcoxon test (N = 5, T = 7; two-tailed hypothesis), there was no statistically significant difference.

Although the female respondents were found to use smaller amounts of bank finance, there was, however, no evidence to suggest that they had been restricted in their access to larger loans/overdrafts. It is possible that the female business owners in the study did not require larger amounts of bank finance or they did not want to have a large debt burden. The latter suggestion is consistent with the finding that female business owners are generally less inclined to take risks in their businesses than men (Therrien *et al.*, 1986; Sexton and Bowman-Upton, 1988; O'Hare and Larson, 1991), particularly risks which might impinge on personal or family well-being. In this way, female business owners may decide to rely upon smaller amounts of bank finance so that they do not have to risk personal assets (for security/ collateral), a risk that might be detrimental to the family (Brush, 1992; Koper, 1993). Indeed, Brown and Segal (1989) have argued that the desire not to jeopardise the family home may explain why women tend to be more cautious in their bank borrowing (Carter and Cannon, 1992).

4.4.2 Terms and conditions

Just over 40 per cent of respondents were required to provide the bank with some form of security or guarantee on their overdraft facilities. In addition, almost 60 per cent of respondents were required to provide security on their bank loans (Table 4.8). As outlined in chapter 2,

Table 4.8 Security/guarantees required on bank finance
(overdrafts and loans)

	Total	Overdrafts Female	Male
Security	20 (43)[a]	11 (42)	9 (45)
No security	26 (57)	15 (58)	11 (55)
Total	46 (100)	26 (100)	20 (100)
	Total	Loans Female	Male
Security	26 (59)	17 (68)	9 (47)
No security	18 (41)	8 (32)	10 (53)
Total	44 (100)	25 (100)	19 (100)

Note:[a] Percentages in brackets = % of total number of
respondents with overdrafts/loans

agency theory explains that banks are more likely to demand security/
collateral from small business borrowers in order to protect themselves from the increased risks of adverse selection and moral hazard
associated with small business lending (Deakins and Hussain, 1992;
Keasey and Watson, 1993a; McMahon *et al.*, 1993). Security/collat-
eral is also used by the banks as a signal of the owner-manager's
commitment to the business (McMahon *et al.*, 1993).

Security was more commonly required on those loans and overdrafts acquired at start-up. Indeed, two-thirds of both loans and
overdrafts were guaranteed at start-up, compared to 57 per cent of
loans and 24 per cent of overdrafts post-start-up. This was to be
expected given the fact that lending to new businesses is most risky
for the banks. Information asymmetries, in particular, tend to be
greater for new businesses, because they lack track record (Pettit
and Singer, 1985; Storey, 1994). Many lenders are also reluctant to
finance new start-up companies because the founders are often inexperienced and lack a track record (Dickson, 1983).

Although the pattern was not consistent, security also tended to be
required more often on the larger overdrafts and loans. The median
secured overdraft limit was £26,000 and £12,000 for secured loans.
Again, this reflects the increased risk burden being taken on by the
bank with larger loan and overdraft facilities. It is also the case that
banks will not consider securing smaller levels of loan and overdraft
finance because it is not worth the effort or cost in taking security.
However, it was not possible to analyse the ratio of collateral/security

to size of loan/overdraft in the present survey because the majority of respondents did not know the value of their collateral/security or were not prepared to give this information.

Previous studies into the financing of women-owned businesses have suggested that female entrepreneurs are required to provide the bank with security or guarantees more often than male entrepreneurs (Clutterbuck and Devine, 1987; Carter and Cannon, 1992; Koper, 1993). However, in the present study, fewer of the female respondents were required to provide security on their overdrafts than their male counterparts. Nevertheless, more women were required to provide security on their loans. However, these differences were not significant (Overdraft – $X^2 = 0.032$, df $= 1$; Loan – $X^2 = 1.854$, df $= 1$). Similarly, there was very little difference between the men and women in the size of overdrafts or loans on which they were required to provide security. The median overdraft limit on which security was required was £6,625 for women and £9,250 for men and the median term loan £13,800 and £12,000 respectively.

In the light of previous research, it was also expected that the female business owners would have been requested to provide spousal co-signatures on their bank borrowing more often than the male business owners (Collerette and Aubry, 1990; Carter and Cannon, 1992; Fabowale *et al.*, 1993). However, once the co-signatures of spouses/domestic partners, who were also business partners, were omitted, the opposite was found to be true. In fact, six of the women and ten of the men were required to provide spousal co-signatures on loans and overdrafts. Even as a percentage of the total number of married respondents, more of the men (27.8 per cent) were required to provide spousal co-signatures than the women (20.7 per cent).

4.5 CONCLUSION

The majority of the findings presented in this chapter are therefore found to challenge existing theoretical and empirically based expectations surrounding the role of gender in the financing of small businesses. First, the female business owners did not use less money to start their businesses than the male business owners. Second, the female respondents were not found to suffer more from the problem of undercapitalisation. Third, they had not used fewer sources of finance than their male counterparts. Fourth, not only did the women use less internal and more external sources of finance than their male counterparts, but significantly more of the female business owners had used bank finance than the male business owners. Fifth, there is no evidence to suggest that the female respondents had been refused finance more than the male respondents. Sixth, they were not required to provide more collateral/security or spousal guarantees on bank finance. Seventh, although the female respondents were found to borrow smaller amounts of bank finance than their male counterpart, as suggested in the literature, there was no evidence to suggest that they had faced barriers in their access to larger amounts of finance.

The overall picture is one of female business owners choosing to use a wider range of financial sources than men. As the female respondents were found to use similar amounts of finance in their businesses as men, this suggests that female business owners choose to use lots of small 'packages' of finance from lots of different sources. By way of an explanation, female entrepreneurs are generally found to be less inclined to take risks in their businesses than men (Therrien *et al.*, 1986; Sexton and Bowman-Upton, 1988) and may therefore decide to spread the financial risk burden across a number of different sources. Female entrepreneurs are also found to plan their businesses more thoroughly than male entrepreneurs (Thomas, 1991). They are therefore more likely to be aware of the wide range of sources of finance available to them.

Another possible reason for the finding that female business owners finance their businesses with a much wider range of sources than their male counterparts is that, if they perceive the banks to discriminate against women in business, they are likely to search for alternative external financing sources (Bowman-Upton *et al.*, 1987), adapting to the prevailing conditions, whether real or perceived (Godfrey, 1992). Although, in the present study, there was no evidence of direct discrimination by the banks or any other finance providers against women in business, a very small number of female respondents were found to hold perceptions that the banks do have discriminatory practices.

Nevertheless, it must be remembered that this study is only based on the experiences of those women who have successfully started businesses and are still trading. By only covering the experiences of the 'successes', it fails to explore the attitudes and experiences of two groups of female entrepreneurs –

1 those women who take active steps to initiate a new business but who never actually get the business established ('nascent entrepreneurs' – Reynolds and White, 1992);
2 those women who start a business and later fail.

The importance of the nascent female entrepreneur has been recognised by Scottish Enterprise (1993a) in their strategy to improve the business birth rate in Scotland. Indeed, in a survey conducted by MORI for the Scottish Enterprise Business Birth Rate Inquiry in 1992, it emerged that there were around 280,000 potential female entrepreneurs in Scotland (those women who were interested in becoming an entrepreneur) but only a 31 per cent conversion rate (the proportion of people interested in becoming an entrepreneur who actually established a business). However, to date, there has been no research comparing male and female nascent entrepreneurs and the role of finance. However, Carter and Cannon (1992) did include a sample of ten female entrepreneurs who had started businesses but had later failed as part of their general survey of female entrepreneurship. Nevertheless, they found that problems raising finance were seldom given as reasons for business failure. For future research, it would be very valuable to explore, in greater depth, the financing of 'failed' women-owned businesses and nascent female entrepreneurs, using the matched pairs methodology.

The fact that male and female business owners closely matched on four key structural factors exhibited more similarities than differences in the financing of their businesses also further confirms suggestions made in chapter 3, that previous studies may have been drawing out structural differences between male- and female-owned businesses, rather than true gender-based differences. Similarly, Riding and Swift (1990) and Fabowale *et al.* (1993) find that, by controlling for structural characteristics, male and female business owners generally exhibit more similarities than differences in the financing of their businesses.

However, the findings of this study also highlight the complexity of the subject of small business financing and the need to control for more than just four structural factors. Indeed, what has come through most strongly is the importance of the behavioural element in the financing of small businesses and the fact that the financing of small businesses is closely entwined with the small business owner's life situation (Sargent and Young, 1991; Brush, 1992), as argued in chapter 2. For instance, the way in which a small business is financed is very much related to availability of finance within the family unit and to the circumstances by which the owner came to start the business (e.g. redundancy). Financial decision-making is therefore a product of the firm's characteristics plus the manager's background, values, ambitions, motivations, aspirations and risk willingness (Levin and Trevis, 1987; Barton and Matthews, 1989; Ang, 1991; 1992). Future research might therefore consider comparing the financing of male- and female-owned businesses matched on these characteristics.

5 The characteristics of the banking relationship

5.1 INTRODUCTION

Another area in which previous studies have found differences between male and female business owners is in the 'banking relationship'. According to Bannock (1994), the 'banking relationship' can be seen as the bank's 'relationship with the customer that is not confined to contact when a credit limit is exceeded, or a new application made for a loan, but which is renewed on a regular basis so that the banker builds up a real understanding of the firm's progress and financial needs' (p. 34). The small business–banking relationship therefore incorporates elements such as the provision of business support and advice, trust, two-way communication, and other interpersonal/social interaction factors (Berry *et al.*, 1993; Koper, 1993).

A good banking relationship is vital to both the small business owner and the banks. From the point of view of small business owners, the relationship that they have with their banks is particularly important for a number of reasons. First, they generally only use one bank. They are therefore totally reliant on the support, advice and understanding of that particular bank (Binks *et al.*, 1992; Howcroft and Beckett, 1993). Second, Howcroft and Beckett (1993) have found that many customers believe they will receive a better service if they are customers in an established banking relationship. Third, small business owners will tend to have more trust and confidence in a bank with whom they have a long-standing relationship. Fourth, many small business owner-managers find the financial services offered by banks to be very complex and therefore substitute a good banking relationship for knowledge, trusting in their bank to recommend the right products for their situation (Howcroft and Beckett, 1993).

From the bank's point of view, a long-standing relationship with a small business customer is likely to reduce information asymmetries as the bank will have had time to build up a good understanding of the business. A sound understanding of their small business customers will also help to reduce the bank's exposure to bad debts (Bannock, 1994). In an environment of growing competition, the ability of a bank to retain loyal small business customers is also a competitive advantage (Binks *et al.*, 1992), and the trust built up within such a banking relationship will help the bank to sell more of its financial services to the small business owner.

In addition, good small business–banking relations also have important implications for the economy as a whole. According to a study by the Forum of Private Business (1994), in order for small firms to fulfil their potential as the wealth and job creators of the UK economy, they need 'an efficient working relationship with their banks that is based on good communication and mutual trust' (p. 2).

However, as indicated in chapter 2, the literature suggests that female entrepreneurs are less likely to have a satisfactory banking relationship than male entrepreneurs. In order to explore this suggestion further, the chapter aims to seek answers to seven main questions:

1 Do female business owners choose their banks for different reasons to male business owners, given that women generally have different perspectives and expectations of small business ownership than men (Reilly, 1989; Brush, 1992; Koper, 1993)?
2 Are female business owners in contact with their bank managers less frequently than male business owners? Given that many female business owners perceive that they are not taken seriously by their bank managers (Goffee and Scase, 1983; Carter and Cannon, 1992), do they avoid contact with their banks?
3 Do female business owners use 'straw men' in the banking relationship? A number of studies in the past have found that female business owners often use 'straw men' (Hertz, 1987: p. 189) or 'sleeping' partners (Goffee and Scase, 1985: p. 45) to negotiate credit on their behalf because they are not taken seriously by their banks.
4 Again, in light of the fact that women generally have a different perspective on small business ownership than men, do they place the same importance on key elements of the banking relationship?
5 Are female business owners less satisfied with their banking relationship than male business owners, given the weight of existing research and anecdotal evidence to suggest that bank managers discriminate against female entrepreneurs and treat businesswomen with a condescending attitude (Goffee and Scase, 1985; Reilly, 1989; Still and Guerin, 1991; Fabowale *et al.*, 1993)?

6 Do female business owners face more problems in the banking relationship than male business owners, as suggested in previous research (see chapter 2)? In particular, do they suffer from problems of gender-related discrimination?

7 In response to problems in the banking relationship, do female entrepreneurs adopt different coping strategies to male entrepreneurs?

Before exploring the answers to these questions in more detail, however, it is necessary to set the context of the small business–banking relationship more generally.

5.2   THE SMALL BUSINESS–BANKING RELATIONSHIP: AN OVERVIEW

5.2.1   Introduction

As outlined in chapter 4, bank finance is the most important source of external funding for the small business (Binks, 1993; McMahon *et al.*, 1993). The latest figures indicate that around £37 billion in bank finance was outstanding to small firms on 30 June, 1994, in the form of overdrafts and term loans (Bank of England, 1995). However, the small business–banking relationship is frequently characterised by negative feelings from the small business sector towards the banks. As Chrystal (1992) points out, the banks 'have been subjected to a flood of criticism by the media, and by groups claiming to represent consumer and small business interests' (p. 44). The banks have been accused of

> insensitivity over the handling of small firm accounts, over-charging in terms of interest payments, of applying bank charges without informing the customer, being overly eager in calling in their loans and demanding too high a level of security.
>
> (Keasey and Watson, 1993a: p. 35)

Indeed, 'the banks are widely regarded as out of touch, insensitive and greedy – and that's what their friends say' (*Observer*, 1994a: p. 3). Many small business owners feel that the banks have fuelled the recession by withholding vital credit from small businesses which would otherwise have allowed them to 'turn the corner' to recovery, and by imposing higher margins and additional collateral requirements just when the 'going gets rough'. Indeed, 'if most of the media are to be believed, the bank manager is to most owner-managers of small businesses what Dracula was to the inhabitants of Transylvania – at best a pain in the neck; at worst someone who will bleed you dry' (*Network*, 1994: p. 4).

In their defence, the banks have emphasised that, they themselves, suffered as a result of the recession and that they do not actually benefit from the difficulties of their small business customers and are not 'simply waiting for an opportunity to pounce' (George, 1994: p. 1), neither are they public services. They are faced with the challenge of meeting the needs of the recession survivors, many of whom have over-borrowed and have an eroded capital base with little to offer in terms of collateral (Binks, 1991a), in addition to meeting the needs of new business start-ups. Meanwhile, they also have a duty to protect their shareholders from bad debts.

The causes of conflicts in the small business–banking relationship are complex and can be viewed both in terms of the internal conflicts which result from the very nature of the contractual relationship itself and also in terms of the external environment in which the relationship is based. In the remainder of this section, both internal and external sources of conflict are explored in more detail.

5.2.2 The contractual relationship

The small business–banking relationship, as seen through the agency theory lens (see chapter 2), is one which is inherently problematical. A significant cause of conflict in the small business–banking relationship is the fact that the distribution of information between the parties is asymmetric (Barnea *et al.*, 1981); in other words, the small firm owner is generally more informed about the financial circumstances and prospects of their business than the bank (McMahon *et al.*, 1993; Storey, 1994). The existence of information asymmetries means that banks tend to be more wary of lending to small firms because there is greater risk and uncertainty involved. Banks are also subject to moral hazard, or the risk that the small business will not perform in a manner consistent with the contract (Keasey and Watson, 1993a). In order to protect their investments, the banks are required to monitor their small business customers which is very expensive. In order to cover their costs, the banks are therefore forced to pass them on to the small business customer in the form of charges. These charges are not popular with the small business population, especially those small business owners who never borrow from the bank. In return for the risks associated with the debt contract, banks also look for 'signals' from borrowers, usually in the form of personal security or collateral, to indicate the commitment of the owner to the business and to ensure that the bank could cover its losses in the event of the business failing (McMahon *et al.*, 1993).

The bank charges and security/collateral inherent in such a contractual relationship are therefore the most frequent causes of conflict in the small business–banking relationship. The impression from a survey of small business owners by Binks *et al.* (1988) is that bank charges are too high and that the collateral required to cover loans is excessive. According to a number of authors (e.g. Wynant and Hatch, 1990; Keasey and Watson, 1993a), many of these problems are exacerbated by the fact that the majority of small business owners do not fully understand the bank's situation. For instance, they do not appreciate that the banks do not share in the 'up-side' of the debt contract and bear all the 'down-side' risks and costs. It is also the case that many small business owners do not understand the way in which banks evaluate loan applications and what they expect from their small business customers in return for the provision of finance. This tends to be the result of confusing terminology used by the banks, a general lack of financial skills, over-optimism among many small business owners, and poor communication between the two parties (Wynant and Hatch, 1990). Indeed, Bradford (1993) suggests that clear, two-way communication is the 'backbone of an enduring relationship between bank and customer' (p. 15). Failure to communicate often causes misunderstandings which frequently lead to resentment on the part of the small business owner and strained relations.

A further cause of conflict is the powerful position that the banks are perceived to exert in the relationship. The bank is in the position of 'holding the money' and the bank manager is perceived as having a relatively stable ('cosy') job in comparison to the perceived instability of the small firm owner's position (Storey, 1994). This also causes resentment among many small business owners.

5.2.3　The external environment

The inherent problems associated with the small business–banking relationship which have been outlined above are frequently exacerbated by the external environment in which the relationship is operating. Over the last two decades, the relationship between small businesses and their banks has evolved dramatically as a result of changes in the legislative environment of the UK banking sector (Binks, 1991).

Until 1971, UK clearing banks operated in a highly regulated environment, characterised by low levels of competition because there were quantitative ceilings on the amounts they were allowed to lend (Chrystal, 1992). However, reforms under the 1971 Competition and Credit Control Act removed these ceilings and therefore encouraged competition. In the early 1970s, following the 1973 oil crisis and the collapse of property and equity prices, quantitative constraints known as the 'corset' were reintroduced. The 'corset' was later abolished in June 1980 and since then there has been a gradual deregulation of the financial markets to encourage increased competition (Binks, 1991). In particular, the UK banks have come under increasing pressure from the building societies which were allowed to compete more directly with the banks following the Building Society Act of 1986 (Binks, 1991). In addition, the banks have come under increasing supervision from the Bank of England which was given statutory responsibility to license and monitor all UK banks under the 1979 and 1987 Banking Acts.

In the light of these developments, the 1980s saw the banks being forced to re-evaluate their approach to small business lending. As competition for the business of larger corporations increased (Bannock, 1994) and the potential profit margins in this and the personal sector decreased, so the small business sector was viewed more and more as a new and profitable market to be exploited. The banks began to develop a 'more market-oriented approach' (Binks, 1991: p. 54), acknowledging that particular groups of consumers have particular needs to be met by tailor-made products. The 1980s therefore witnessed a 'revolution' in the bank financing of small firms (Figure 5.1). While the 1970s had been characterised by a basic product range (loan and overdraft), the 1980s saw an increase in the provision of a whole range of products and services specifically designed for the business start-up to the more established small firm (e.g. special start-up loans, free first year banking, and specialist small business advisors) (Thornhill, 1989; Binks, 1991; Chaston, 1994).

During the boom years of the 1980s, the major clearing banks were therefore only too keen to lend to the small business and relations were generally good. However, the 1990s have heralded a period in which the banks have had to make some fundamental changes to their small business lending policies. As a result of the recession, small business failures were at their peak between 1991 and 1993 and it has been suggested that clearing banks had to provide over £3 billion against losses on a total small business loan book of some £45 billion during this period (George, 1994). Indeed, Barclays Bank was having

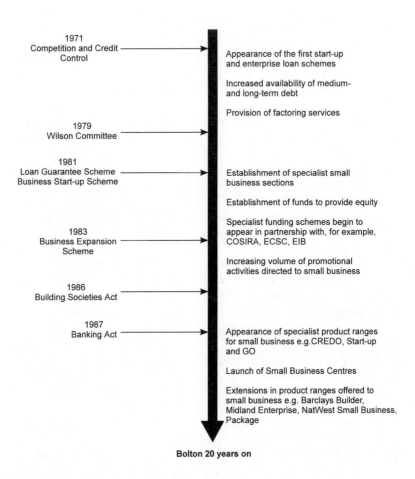

The Bolton Committee

1971
Competition and Credit Control

Appearance of the first start-up and enterprise loan schemes

Increased availability of medium- and long-term debt

Provision of factoring services

1979
Wilson Committee

1981
Loan Guarantee Scheme
Business Start-up Scheme

Establishment of specialist small business sections

Establishment of funds to provide equity

Specialist funding schemes begin to appear in partnership with, for example, COSIRA, ECSC, EIB

1983
Business Expansion Scheme

Increasing volume of promotional activities directed to small business

1986
Building Societies Act

1987
Banking Act

Appearance of specialist product ranges for small business e.g.CREDO, Start-up and GO

Launch of Small Business Centres

Extensions in product ranges offered to small business e.g. Barclays Builder, Midland Enterprise, NatWest Small Business, Package

Bolton 20 years on

Figure 5.1 The development of banking services for small businesses
Source: Binks, 1991 (p. 156)

to write off bad loans to small businesses at a rate of £1 million per day during the second half of 1991 and all of 1992 (Gapper, 1993). Similarly, the National Westminster Bank was forced to put aside almost 47 per cent of its £1.3 billion bad debt provision to cover loans of less than £50,000 in 1992 alone. At the same time, the banks were attempting to rebuild their capital base in the light of the 1980s legacy of vast Third World debt losses and international property debts (Gapper, 1993; Bannock, 1994). Therefore, the balance sheets of most major clearing banks were similar to that of the National Westminster Bank which showed pre-tax profits of £405 million in 1992 but bad debts of £1.9 billion (Kane and Whitebloom, 1993).

These developments have had a great impact on the small firm–banking relationship. During the early 1990s in particular, the banks were generally seen, not only as fallible, but 'downright incompetent' (Kane and Whitebloom, 1993: p. 40). In response to criticisms of over-lending in the 1980s and increased risk associated with small business lending in the recession, the 1990s have witnessed the banks becoming 'more cautious in their lending decisions. They admit that their lend-ing criteria have tightened' (Bank of England, 1994: p. 7). They have also limited small firm access to overdraft finance because it is fre-quently used as a substitute for equity by undercapitalised businesses rather then as working capital (Gapper, 1993). In addition, the banks have recognised the high agency costs and risks associated with the financing of small firms and so have raised their charges on many of their small business loans (Gapper, 1993) and tend to require more security and equity from their small business customers (Deakins and Hussain, 1991), placing much more importance on the level of gear-ing. However, small businesses have been faced with problems provid-ing collateral for security on loans because of the decline in the value of their property and other assets. In order to cut their costs further, the banks have been 'pruning' the branch networks (Howcroft and Beckett, 1993) and creating business centres serving small businesses from a wide area. Although this was expected to improve the banking relationship, many small businesses have lost the local branch which they chose for its proximity and convenience and many 'micro' busi-nesses are not big enough to be included in the business centre portfolios. None of these developments have endeared the banks to the small business population (Bannock, 1994).

However, media attention has also had a major part to play in the anti-bank feeling amongst the small business community. Reports of conflicts, particularly in the early 1990s, were rarely out of the news (*Guardian*, 1991a; 1991b; 1991c; 1991d). As pointed out in *The Times* (1994a), 'bank-bashing is an ever popular pastime' (p. 27). Although, with hindsight, it is possible to see that many of these reports were the horror stories of 'an unrepresentative minority' (Keasey and Watson, 1993a: p. 35), they did prompt inquiries from the Treasury, Bank of England and the Director General of Fair Trading. These inquiries could find no evidence that the banks had been operating as an organised cartel in their dealings with small firms, but the relationship between small businesses and their banks still remains problematical and these inquiries eroded the trust and confidence in banks that many small business owners used to hold (Chaston, 1993). A survey carried out by the Forum of Private Business in 1992 revealed that small business respondents perceived the quality of bank services to have declined since 1990 (Bannock, 1993). More recently, the case of a couple who successfully sued Lloyds Bank for poor business advice, which received widespread media coverage, is likely to have eroded the small business–banking relationship further (*The Times*, 1995).

One of the main problems that banks face is that, in an economic crisis, the bank is often the 'only visible object to kick' (*Guardian*, 1992b: p. 16). As Chrystal (1992) explains,

> money lenders have had a bad press in recessions ever since Biblical times. In this regard, banks do not cause the problem – rather it is the inevitable outcome of a business downturn. The bank simply conveys the news that negative cash-flow cannot go on for ever.
>
> (Chrystal, 1992: p. 44)

Another factor which has contributed to the growing tensions seen in the general small business–banking relationship, is that the 1990s have witnessed an increase in the demands for an improved level of service quality and greater 'accountability' from the banks from an increasingly discriminating consumer.

In the light of developments in the overall small business–banking relationship, as outlined above, the remainder of this chapter seeks to compare the experiences of male and female business owners in the banking relationship.

5.3 THE USE OF BANKS

5.3.1 Choice of bank

In the present study, the four major UK clearing banks were found to hold the greatest market share (Figure 5.2). The National Westminster Bank was used by 34 per cent of respondents; Lloyds Bank by 28 per cent; Barclays Bank by 21 per cent; and Midland Bank by 10 per cent of respondents. In addition, two business owners (3 per cent) banked with the Royal Bank of Scotland, one (1 per cent) with the Trustee Savings Bank (TSB) and another (1 per cent) with the Co-operative Bank. In the latter case, the owner had chosen the Co-operative Bank because of the bad press surrounding the major high street banks. The remaining small business owners (n = 2) were found to use building

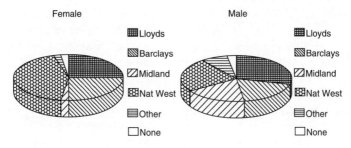

Figure 5.2 Distribution of firms by bank

society accounts, one because he had faced personal banking problems in the past and therefore wanted to avoid banks, the other because she did not want to have to pay business charges.

A breakdown of bank used by sex of owner shows that more of the female business owners had chosen to bank with the National Westminster and more of the male business owners had chosen the Midland Bank (Figure 5.2). However, these differences were not found to be statistically significant.

In terms of the reasons behind their choice of bank, the majority of business owners in this study chose their bank because they already had their personal account with that bank (Table 5.1). Similarly, in a study by Binks *et al.* (1988), two-thirds of small business owners chose to do their business banking at the same branch as their personal

Table 5.1 Reasons given by respondents for choosing their bank (n = total number of mentions)

Reason given	Female		Male		Total		X^2
	n	%	n	%	n	%	
Personal account already there	24	61.5	17	43.6	41	52.6	1.79
Offered best services/terms	5	12.8	8	20.5	13	16.7	0.90
Personal recommendation	5	12.8	4	10.3	9	11.5	—[b]
No previous association with	4	10.3	7	17.9	11	14.1	1.05
First year free banking	4	10.3	4	10.3	8	10.3	—[b]
Proximity to business premises	4	10.3	3	7.7	7	9.0	—[b]
Know someone at bank	3	7.7	4	10.3	7	9.0	—[b]
Other	2	5.1	3	7.7	5	6.4	—[b]
Total[a]	51	100.0	40	100.0	101	100.0	—

Notes: [a] Total number of respondents answering question = 78 (1 man and 1 woman did not have a bank account); [b] It was not possible to test the statistical significance of these differences. In order to perform a *chi*-square analysis, the *expected* number for each cell must not be less than 5 (Clegg, 1994).

banking, usually for the sake of convenience. Other less important factors included the type of services and terms being offered by the bank, personal recommendations, a year's free banking, geographical proximity of the branch to the business premises, knowing someone at the bank, and for many, not having had any previous dealings with that particular bank before. A number had already tried other banks and left on bad terms. Others did not want their personal account at the same bank as their business account: as one businesswoman put it, 'I don't want to put all my eggs in one basket'. In terms of male/ female differences, it was found that there were more similarities than differences between the male and female respondents in their reasons for choosing a bank and none of the differences were statistically significant (Table 5.1).

5.3.2   The bank as a source of advice

Neither the female, nor the male business owners used their banks as a source of advice on a frequent basis. Indeed, only 24 per cent of respondents had ever used the bank for advice. This is not surprising, given the fact that small business owners generally do not use external sources of advice very frequently (Storey, 1994). In the present survey, almost 25 per cent of all the respondents had *never* used any external advice sources (see chapter 6). The low level of usage may also reflect the fact that the majority of businesses in the study are in the service sector and have small capital bases and are therefore not in such a great need for 'constant upgrading of capital equipment and product development, which will inevitably require more financial advice than other businesses', especially those experiencing higher rates of technological and market change (Curran and Blackburn, 1994: p. 96).

However, the study does indicate that a higher number of female respondents had used their bank for business advice than male respondents (37.5 per cent compared with only 10 per cent of men), a difference which is statistically significant at the 0.01 level ($X2 = 6.9025$, df $= 1$). For the female respondents, the most common type of advice sought was general business advice, followed by financial advice (e.g. insurance, loans, bank charges), and start-up advice. The male respondents simply used the bank for general business advice. These differences were not found to be significant, however, given the small number of respondents involved (Table 5.2).

When asked to rate[1] their satisfaction with the standard of advice received by the bank, it was found that a similar proportion of female business owners (73 per cent; (n = 11) and male business owners (75 per

Table 5.2 Type of assistance provided by banks (% in brackets)

Type of assistance	Total[a]	Female	Male	Sig. X^2
General business advice	13 (68.4)	9 (60.0)	4 (100)	—[c]
Financial advice	9 (47.4)	9 (60.0)	0	—[c]
Business start-up	2 (10.5)	2 (13.3)	0	—[c]
Total no. using banks[b]	19 (100)	15 (100)	4 (100)	Yes

Notes: [a] Total number of mentions; [b] percentage of total number of respondents that had used the bank for advice (% totals do not add up to 100 as respondents could mention more than one type of assistance); [c] it was not possible to test the statistical significance of these differences, because in order to perform a *chi*-square analysis, the *expected* number for each cell must not be less than 5 (Clegg, 1994)

cent; n = 3) were either 'quite' or 'very' satisfied. When assessing the standard of advice provided by the banks, respondents were, not only looking for the quality and usefulness of the advice, but also the way in which it was delivered. For example, the bank's ability to give 'straight' answers to their questions was greatly valued by respondents as was the helpful manner of the banking staff. Nevertheless, there were a number of sources of dissatisfaction, the most common being that the bank staff did not always appear to be very helpful or sympathetic to the respondents' problems. In addition, a number of respondents felt that the bank often failed to give straight answers to their questions, or as one male business owner put it, 'they skirt round the issue and won't commit themselves to helping you in any way'. Finally, there was a high level of concern about the lack of impartiality of bank advice, particularly in the light of the bank's increased interest in selling other financial products such as insurance (Chrystal, 1992).

Almost all of the respondents (92 per cent of women; 94 per cent of men) who had never approached the bank for advice added that they had no intention of doing so in the future. As indicated in Table 5.3, the majority of respondents felt that the banks do not understand the needs of or problems faced by small businesses and therefore are not a good source of advice. As one respondent put it, 'they don't know anything about running a small business. They [bank managers] have never run a business before so what advice could they offer?' (survey respondent).

Similarly, Curran and Blackburn (1994) found the main theme to emerge from business owners' comments on the bank as a source of advice was 'the poor knowledge they felt bank managers had about their business sectors' (p. 97). A further 10.5 per cent of business owners perceived bank advice to be problematical, primarily for

Table 5.3 Reasons for non-use of bank advice (% in brackets)

Reason	Total	Female	Male	Sig.X^2
Banks unsuitable for small business advice	30 (52.6)	10 (43.5)	20 (58.8)	No
Other sources of advice preferred	13 (22.8)	8 (34.8)	5 (14.7)	Yes
Advice not needed	8 (14.0)	2 (8.7)	6 (17.6)	—[b]
Bank advice perceived to be problematical	6 (10.5)	3 (13.0)	3 (8.8)	—[b]
Total[a]	57 (100.0)	23 (100.0)	34 (100.0)	—

Notes: [a] Percentage totals may not = 100 due to rounding; [b] it was not possible to test the statistical significance of these differences, because in order to perform a *chi*-square analysis, the *expected* number for each cell must not be less than 5 (Clegg, 1994)

reasons of impartiality. These findings have important implications for bank marketing, given that they are the perceptions of business owners who have never used the bank for advice before. A number of business owners (n = 13; 23 per cent) said that they would prefer to contact their accountant or another independent organisation if the need for external advice were to arise. Naturally, there were some business owners who felt that they did not need advice from any source.

There is a question mark over whether banks should provide small business advice at all (Bannock, 1994). Bannock (1994) likens the provision of small business advice by the banks to an airline trying to teach its customers how to be passengers. The suggestion is that it should not be attempted at all. It is true that the banks are not always best placed to provide the advice that small businesses need (e.g. marketing or training). However, because many small business owners cannot afford to buy in training or consultancy services, they often make do with the banks but complain when the bank fails to deliver an adequate service (Wynant and Hatch, 1990). In the light of the fact that a couple have recently been successful in suing their bank for poor business advice, it seems increasingly likely that banks will offer less specific advice in the future, rather than more (*The Times*, 1995).

In terms of male/female differences, Table 5.3 shows that similar numbers of male and female business owners avoid using their banks for advice because they feel that banks are unsuitable providers of small business advice. However, significantly more of the female business owners would have preferred to use other sources of advice ($X^2 = 3.25$, df = 1; 0.1 level of significance), and numerically more of the male business owners felt that they did not need advice. These findings suggest that female business owners are generally more willing than their male counterparts to use a variety of external sources of advice. These suggestions are explored in greater depth in chapter 6.

5.3.3 Frequency of contact

Respondents in the survey generally did not meet with their account manager[2] very frequently. As indicated in Table 5.4, only 21 per cent were in contact with their account manager more than twice a year while 33 per cent had never met their account manager. Reasons for this lack of contact included the fact that the owners did not borrow from the bank and therefore did not see the need for contact. Some respondents blamed the banks, saying that it was their fault that the frequency of contact was so low. They believed it was the bank's place to make the effort to contact the business owner. The majority felt that their banks failed to make contact because they were not large enough borrowers. A number of the male respondents noted that, since the centralisation of many banking services, there is no longer a contact at their local branch with whom to discuss business matters.

However, it appears that female business owners see their bank managers more frequently than their male counterparts – 21 (52.5 per cent) of the female business owners but only 15 (37.5 per cent) of the male business owners saw their bank manager every 6 months or more frequently. Meanwhile, 42.5 per cent of the male business owners and 22.5 per cent of the female business owners had never met with their bank manager or had not done so for over a year. Although these differences in contact were not found to be statistically significant using the Wilcoxon Test, they are important because they contradict what is expected given the existing literature. In the introduction to this chapter, it was hypothesised that businesswomen would be less inclined to meet their account manager on a frequent

Table 5.4 Frequency of contact with account manager

Frequency	Total	Female	Male
More than every 6 months	17 (21.25)	7 (17.5)	10 (25.0)
Every 6 months	19 (23.75)	14 (35.0)	5 (12.5)
Once a year or less	18 (22.5)	10 (25.0)	8 (20.0)
Never/NA	26 (32.5)	9 (22.5)	17 (42.5)
Total	80 (100)	40 (100)	40 (100)

Note: Wilcoxon Test - T = 220.5; N = 33 (omitting pairs where difference = 0)

basis because many perceive there to be problems of discrimination associated with bank finance (Goffee and Scase, 1985; Reilly, 1989; Still and Guerin, 1991; Fabowale *et al.*, 1993). However, there is no evidence to suggest that this is the case for any of the female respondents in this survey.

Although the majority of respondents had retained a fairly constant level of contact with their bank since start-up, 15 per cent (n = 6) of the women and 18 per cent (n = 7) of the men reported a decrease in contact over time. This was largely attributed (38 per cent) to the high turnover of banking staff which had destroyed the relationship between owner and bank manager (Table 5.5) (see discussion in section 5.4.3). A further 31 per cent of those entrepreneurs who had experienced a decrease in contact with their bank, had deliberately reduced contact as a result of problems they had experienced in the banking relationship. The few entrepreneurs (n = 11) who reported an increase in contact tended to be those facing financial problems which required them to be reviewed by the bank more frequently. However, a very small number (n = 3) noted an increased effort on the part of their bank manager to establish greater contact, which would suggest that the recommendations made for a better small business–banking relationship are being followed to some extent (Bannock, 1994).

In terms of male–female differences, it was impossible to compare reasons for the decrease in contact with the bank because of the small numbers involved. However, it does appear that more of the male respondents (n = 5) had experienced a reduction in contact with their bank because of problems relating to staff turnover than the female respondents (n = 0). This is to be expected given that more of the male respondents were found to have experienced a high turnover in account managers than their female counterparts (see section 5.4.3). Nevertheless, there was no indication that female business owners had

Table 5.5 Reasons for decrease in frequency of contact with bank (% in brackets)

Reason	Total	Female	Male
Staff turnover	5 (38)	0	5 (71)
Problems in the banking relationship	4 (31)	3 (50)	1 (14)
Stopped borrowing	3 (23)	2 (33)	1 (14)
Other	1 (8)	1 (17)	0
Total[a]	13 (100)	6 (100)	7 (100)

Note: [a] Percentage totals may not = 100 due to rounding

reduced contact with their banks because of discrimination or unfair treatment, as might have been expected, given previous research findings (chapter 2).

5.3.4 The involvement of external parties in raising bank finance

It is widely acknowledged that business owners of both sexes frequently have domestic partners, family or friends who contribute significantly to their business, even though they may not be legal co-owners or partners (Rosa and Hamilton, 1994). Indeed, it was revealed that 12.5 per cent (n = 10) of respondents frequently involved people, other than business partners, in the banking relationship. In the light of previous research findings, it was anticipated that more of the female respondents than the male respondents would be found to involve external parties, particularly other men, in the banking relationship. As pointed out in the introduction, because of problems associated with not being taken seriously by banks and discriminatory practices, businesswomen are often found to use 'straw men' or 'sleeping partners' (Goffee and Scase, 1985; Hertz, 1987) to negotiate credit on their behalf. However, contrary to expectations, more men (15 per cent) than women (10 per cent) had involved external parties.

Of the four female respondents who had involved other people in the banking relationship, two had handed over responsibility for dealing with the bank manager almost entirely to other people, one to her father, an accountant, and the other to her boyfriend, a businessman and also the major source of finance in her business. The main reason for doing so, as explained by one of the women was that 'he can speak the language of the banks more fluently than I ever could'. Another of the female respondents had involved her supplier after he had offered to act as an unofficial guarantor in her application for a loan, using his established position in the business world as backing. Of the six male business owners, one usually let his father visit the bank manager instead of him because the bank manager and his father had a long-established business relationship. Another of the male business owners was always accompanied by his business consultant who, in his words, 'can speak their [the bank's] language and knows the magic words to get what the business needs'. A third male business owner was accompanied by an accountant on the bank's advice.

There is also anecdotal evidence in the literature to suggest that the banks prefer female business owners to bring their husbands with them when they visit the bank manager because they lack credibility on their own (Goffee and Scase, 1985). However, in this survey there was no evidence to suggest that this was the case. It was true that the husband of one woman, a businessman himself, always accompanied her to bank interviews, but for 'moral support' rather than for added credibility. As she explained, her business 'affects his life just as much as mine'. Another woman, not only dealt with all her own banking but also that of her husband who runs his own business as well. They both felt that she could deal with the bank better than he could and in her words, 'I can get round them [the bank] more easily and get what I want'. Three of the male respondents were found to include their wives in the banking relationship but only to sign documents which required joint signatures, their accounts being in joint names.

5.4   THE BANKING RELATIONSHIP

5.4.1   Important elements in the banking relationship

Using a 3-point scale similar to that employed by Binks *et al.* (1988) and Fabowale *et al.* (1993), respondents were asked to rate the importance of ten factors in relation to a good banking relationship. The results presented in Table 5.6 show that there was a very strong agreement among the respondents with regard to the importance of the interpersonal elements of the banking relationship. Over 50 per cent of respondents rated the factors 'bank manager is easy to talk to', 'bank manager makes me feel comfortable' and 'bank manager

Table 5.6 Importance of key factors in the banking relationship (total n = 80)

	Importance		
Factor	*Very*	*Imp.*	*Not*
1 Business	n	n	n
Banker knows me and my business	*45*[a]	21	14
Bank provides helpful business advice	16	31	33
Bank offers best rates/lowest fees	36	26	18
Bank offers a wide range of services	7	*45*	28
Bank handles credit requests quickly	19	*41*	20
Banker is easily accessible	21	*44*	15
Bank has specialised small business bankers	15	34	31
2 Interpersonal			
Bank manager is easy to talk to	*50*	19	11
Bank manager makes me feel comfortable	*48*	17	15
Bank manager treats me with respect	*49*	17	14

Note: [a]Figures in italic denote agreement among 50% or more of total no. of respondents treats me with respect' as being 'very important' for a good banking relationship. These findings are broadly in line with those of a survey by the Forum of Private Business (Binks *et al.*, 1988) and also support previous studies which have found small business owners to place the most importance on the 'interpersonal', or 'human' element of the banking relationship (Fabowale *et al.*, 1993; Koper, 1993; Carty, 1994).

Similarly, in the open-ended section of the questionnaire, respondents were asked to talk more generally about what they felt to be the key to a successful banking relationship and the majority felt that a 'personal relationship' was most important. They explained that by this they meant a situation in which the bank manager understands their business and makes an effort to get to know them personally. The second most important factor was felt to be 'communication' where both the bank manager and business owner were in frequent contact and could participate in a two-way working relationship. Business owners of both sexes felt that, in the best banking relationship, the business owner would be able to warn the bank of impending problems and negotiate with them, thus avoiding a situation, for example, where the bank cuts their overdraft facility 'overnight' or puts their business into liquidation unnecessarily. As one businessman in the present survey put it, 'the heart of any business, but particularly small business, is understanding people and establishing personal relationships'. In his view, the banks are failing because 'they don't take the time to get to know their customers or to understand their businesses'.

In terms of the 'business' elements of the relationship, Table 5.6 indicates that the most important factor was 'banker knows me and my business'. Indeed, it was rated as being 'very important' to the small business–banking relationship by more than 50 per cent of respondents. The majority of business owners (n = 36; 45 per cent) also felt that the offer of 'best rates or lowest fees' was also 'very important'. The remaining business-related factors were rated 'important' by the majority of respondents ('bank offers a wide range of services', 'bank handles credit requests quickly', 'banker is easily accessible', and 'bank has specialised small business bankers'). However, 41 per cent (n = 33) of respondents felt that the provision of business advice was 'not important'. These findings are in line with the attitudes expressed earlier in the chapter in relation to bank advice – that the majority of small business owners feel that it is not the bank's place to provide small business advice and that, more importantly, the banks are not qualified to do so.

Table 5.7 Male–female comparison of the four most important banking relationship factors

| | Female | | | Male | | |
Very important	Rank	n	%	Rank	n	%
Bank manager is easy to talk to	1	28	70	= 2	22	55.0
Bank manager treats me with respect	= 2	26	65	1	23	57.5
Bank manager makes me feel comfortable	= 2	26	65	= 2	22	55.0
Bank manager knows me and my business	= 2	26	65	3	19	47.5

Female and male respondents were found to ascribe similar degrees of importance to many of the key factors associated with the banking relationship. In particular, there was strong agreement between the sexes about the importance of the 'interpersonal' element of the banking relationship (Table 5.7). However, for all of the factors rated, more women than men rated them as very important (Figure 5.3).

By using the Wilcoxon test to compare the ratings for each factor across the sexes, significant differences were only found on three of the factors. There were significant differences in the importance ascribed

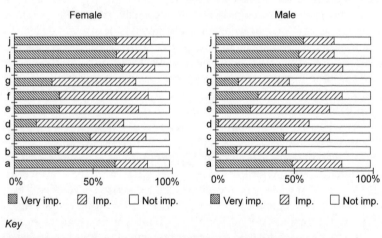

Figure 5.3 Importance of key factors in the banking relationship: breakdown by sex of respondent

to the bank 'offering a wide range of services' (T = 54; N = 19)[3] and 'providing specialised small business bankers' (T = 99.5; N = 26), at the 0.10 significance level (two-tailed test). In both cases, the female respondents gave the factors a higher rating than the male respondents. The fact that the female respondents rated the provision of specialised small business bankers and a wide range of services significantly higher than the male respondents suggests that they are less averse to the changes which have been occurring in small business banking in recent years, namely the move towards providing a variety of financial services (Chrystal, 1992) and the provision of specially trained small business officers (Chaston, 1994). It also reflects their orientation towards seeking and valuing external advice. Indeed, the female respondents rated the importance of the bank providing advice consistently higher than the men (T = 77, N = 27; 0.01 level, two-tailed test). This finding, coupled with the fact that more women in the survey had used their bank for advice than men, suggests that the banks are seen as a more important source of advice by female business owners than their male counterparts. A number of tentative suggestions can be made as to why this may be the case.

First, female business owners are found to have less management experience than male business owners (Watkins and Watkins, 1984; Welsch and Young, 1984; Hisrich and Brush, 1987; Simpson, 1991; Barclays Bank, 1992; Fabowale *et al.*, 1993; Scottish Enterprise, 1993b; Barrett, 1995) and have less training and fewer skills in areas relevant to running a business, in particular financial skills (Hisrich and Brush, 1983; Watkins and Watkins, 1984; Belcourt *et al.*, 1991; Sexton and Bowman-Upton, 1991a). In addition, in the present study, it was found that the female respondents were significantly younger than their male counterparts. It is therefore likely that they had fewer years' experience than the male respondents. As a result, many more of the female sample may have felt it necessary to seek external advice in the running of their businesses to fill the 'gaps' in their own skills and experience.

Second, female business owners are found to lack confidence in their own business abilities and have a lower self-assessment than male business owners (Hisrich and Brush, 1983; 1986; Honig-Haftel and Martin, 1986; Batchelor, 1987; Still and Guerin, 1991). As a result, female business owners may be more keen to seek external advice in order to fill the knowledge gaps they perceive themselves to have.

Third, female business owners may seek advice from the banks more than their male counterparts because they lack access to alternative sources of advice. It has been argued that female business owners find it very difficult to gain access to the more traditional, male-dominated business networks (Therrien *et al.*, 1986; Smeltzer and Fann, 1989). Aldrich (1989) has also suggested that many women lack the necessary experience and skills with which to undertake networking activity. These issues are explored in greater depth in chapter 6.

5.4.2   Satisfaction with the banking relationship

When asked to rate their satisfaction with the overall banking relationship, the survey revealed that the majority of respondents (70 per cent) found it to be 'very good' or 'fairly good'. Only 5 per cent felt that their banking relationship was 'poor' or 'very poor'. Similarly, 61 per cent of respondents thought the overall quality of service provided by the banks was 'very' or 'fairly good' and only 8 per cent thought that it was 'poor' or 'very poor'.

These findings are paradoxical given the weight of evidence, both in the research literature (e.g. Binks *et al.*, 1988; Binks, 1991) and in the media (e.g. *Financial Times*, 1994: p. 12), to suggest that most small business owners have a problematical banking relationship. They are also paradoxical given the fact that in 1994, when the study was undertaken, the banking relationship was at an all time low due to the fact that the major clearing banks were having to be more cautious in their lending decisions to small businesses in the face of substantial losses on their small business portfolio (Bank of England, 1994: p.7).

This study is not alone, however, in finding unexpectedly high ratings given to the overall banking relationship. Similarly, studies by Woods *et al.* (1993) and the *Observer* (1994c) found the majority of small businesses to have either a satisfactory or good to very good relationship with their bank. The *Observer* interpreted the favourable response as an indication that recent action by the banks to improve their relationship with small firms is having some effect. However, in the present study, further in-depth analysis reveals that almost 20 per cent of those respondents who rated their relationship as satisfactory or very good qualified their reply with the point that they have little contact with the bank and most implied that their relationship might be less satisfactory if they did. In addition, section 5.4.3 indicates that the banking relationship was far from unproblematic for the respondents. The satisfaction ratings given in this survey may have been influenced by the generally low expectations of the entrepreneurs concerning what the bank can offer in terms of a relationship.

In addition to this general overview, the respondents were also required to rate their bank's performance on the same ten factors

Table 5.8 Performance of banks on key factors in the banking relationship
(total n = 80)

Factor	GD[a]	AC[b]	UN[c]	NA[d]
1 Business	n	n	n	n
Banker knows me and my business	33	20	11	16
Bank provides helpful business advice	19	9	10	*42*[e]
Bank offers best rates/lowest fees	7	32	22	19
Bank offers a wide range of services	22	26	1	21
Bank handles credit requests quickly	29	17	0	34
Bank manager is easily accessible	*41*	13	3	23
Bank has specialised small business bankers	27	14	8	31
2 Interpersonal				
Bank manager is easy to talk to	*43*	14	4	19
Bank manager makes me feel comfortable	*40*	15	5	20
Bank manager treats me with respect	*41*	13	5	21

Notes: [a] GD – Good/Very good; [b] AC – Acceptable; [c] UN – Unsatisfactory; [d] NA – Not
applicable/Don't know; [e] figures in italic denote agreement among 50% or more of total
no. of respondents

used in the previous section. On this occasion, ratings were again
made using a 3-point scale (Table 5.8). What is most evident from
the table is the fact that many respondents answered in the 'not
applicable/don't know' category. Indeed, 31 per cent of all responses
were in this category. A large number of both male and female
respondents felt they could not answer all the questions relating to
perceptions of bank facilities because they had never used these facilities and therefore did not feel qualified to comment on them. This
was particularly evident in questions relating to the perceived quality
of 'business-related' factors (e.g. provision of bank advice, speed with
which credit requests are handled, and the provision of specialised
small business bankers). In addition, there was one male and one
female respondent who were unable to comment on *any* of the questions because they did not have a business bank account, opting
instead for a building society account.

If the respondent's satisfaction with the banking relationship is
analysed in terms of the 'scores' awarded to each factor by each
respondent (Table 5.9), the banks are found to perform least well on
'best rates and lowest fees'. This is to be expected given the fact that
bank charges are one of the most frequently cited causes of conflict
in the small business–banking relationship (Binks *et al.*, 1988; Keasey
and Watson, 1993b). Meanwhile, the banks were found to perform

Table 5.9 Performance scores of banks on key factors in the banking relationship

Factor	Bank performance scores	
	Total	Average[a]
1 Business		
Banker knows me and my business	22	0.34
Bank provides helpful business advice	9	0.24
Bank offers best rates/lowest fees	−15	−0.25
Bank offers a wide range of services	21	0.36
Bank handles credit requests quickly	29	0.3
Bank manager is easily accessible	38	0.67
Bank has specialised small business bankers	19	0.39
2 Interpersonal		
Bank manager is easy to talk to	39	0.64
Bank manager makes me feel comfortable	35	0.58
Bank manager treats me with respect	36	0.61

Scores: Good/Very good = 1; Acceptable = 0; Unsatisfactory = −1; N/A are omitted
Note: [a] Omits respondents who answered NA

consistently highly on the 'interpersonal' elements of the banking relationship – 'bank manager is easy to talk to' (0.64), 'bank manager treats me with respect' (0.61) and 'bank manager makes me feel comfortable' (0.58). In addition, 'bank manager is easily accessible' also scored highly (0.67).

In order to quantify these findings more accurately, a satisfaction rating was created which measured each factor in relation to the importance placed on that factor by each respondent and the performance of their bank. Using the method adopted by Fabowale *et al.* (1993), an index value was computed for each respondent by multiplying the level of importance ascribed to each factor (not important = 0; important = −1; very important = 2) by the degree of perceived performance expressed on each factor by each respondent (unsatisfactory = –1; acceptable = 0; good/very good = 1). The scores from each respondent were then summed. For example, overall satisfaction with the factor 'bank knows me and my business' was calculated in the following way:

$$\sum I_i \times P_i$$

i = 'bank knows me and my business'
I = importance rating
P = performance rating

Table 5.10 Satisfaction with the banking relationship

Relationship factors	Total	Female	Male	Sig[a]
1 Business				
Banker knows me and my business	0.48	0.94	−0.07	0.05
Bank provides helpful business advice	0.53	0.80	0	0.10
Bank offers best rates/lowest fees	−0.56	−0.34	−0.79	No
Bank offers a wide range of services	0.53	0.58	0.46	No
Bank handles credit requests quickly	0.87	0	0.65	No
Bank manager is easily accessible	0.94	0.97	0.89	No
Bank has specialised small business bankers	0.43	0.75	−0.18	0.01
2 Interpersonal				
Bank manager is easy to talk to	1.13	1.32	0.89	No
Bank manager makes me feel comfortable	1.00	1.12	0.85	No
Bank manager treats me with respect	1.07	1.15	0.96	No

Note: [a] Significance level, using the Wilcoxon matched-pairs signed ranks test (two-tailed test)

Each element of the banking relationship was calculated in the same way. Table 5.10 presents the average values for each measure of satisfaction. Again, these figures show that respondents were most satisfied with the interpersonal elements of the banking relationship ('bank manager is easy to talk to', 'bank manager makes me feel comfortable', 'bank manager treats me with respect') and least satisfied with the 'bank offers best rates/lowest fees). Given the findings of existing research that women feel discriminated against in their dealings with the bank, it was expected that the female respondents would record a lower level of satisfaction with their banking relationship. In fact, however, 87.5 per cent of the women compared to just 52.5 per cent of the men rated the overall relationship as very or fairly good. These differences were found to be statistically significant at the 0.01 level using the Wilcoxon Test (T = 86.5; N = 28; two-tailed test). Similarly, 77.5 per cent of the female respondents and 45 per cent of the male respondents felt that the overall quality of service was very or fairly good. Again, these differences were significant at the 0.01 level (T = 99; N = 26; two-tailed test).

On the ten separate performance indicators, Figure 5.4 indicates that the female respondents rated their bank's performance higher than the male respondents on every factor. In particular, the female respondents were found to rate their banks significantly higher on four of the 'business' elements of the relationship ('bank manager knows me and my business', 'bank provides helpful business advice', 'bank offers best rates/lowest fees', and 'bank provides specialised

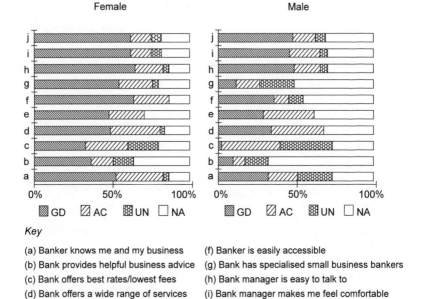

Key

(a) Banker knows me and my business
(b) Bank provides helpful business advice
(c) Bank offers best rates/lowest fees
(d) Bank offers a wide range of services
(e) Bank handles credit requests quickly

(f) Banker is easily accessible
(g) Bank has specialised small business bankers
(h) Bank manager is easy to talk to
(i) Bank manager makes me feel comfortable
(j) Bank manager treats me with respect

Figure 5.4 Performance of banks on key factors in the banking relationship: breakdown by sex of respondent

small business bankers'). Using the Wilcoxon Test, significant differences at the 0.10 level (two-tailed test) were found between the men and women in the performance of their banks on 'bank manager knows me and my business' (T = 41; N = 17), 'bank provides helpful business advice' (T = 7; N = 9), and 'bank offers best rates/lowest fees' (T = 30; N = 15). A significant difference was also found in terms of the 'provision of specialised small business bankers' (T = 13.5; N = 13; 0.05 level; two-tailed test).

Using Fabowale's satisfaction index (Table 5.10), female respondents were found to be significantly more satisfied with three elements of the banking relationship ('banker knows me and my business', 'bank provides helpful business advice' and 'bank has specialised small business bankers'), than their male counterparts. These findings are very important as they contradict expectations based on findings from previous studies. Indeed, there was no evidence to confirm that female business owners have a worse perception of the banking relationship than their male counterparts because they face discrimination and lack of credibility in the banking relationship (e.g. Goffee and Scase, 1985; Carter and Cannon, 1992).

One possible suggestion for this finding is that, because female business owners expect to be treated badly because they are women, when their treatment by the banks is better than expected, their rating of the banking relationship increases. Indeed, in the present survey there was evidence to suggest that a number of the female respondents in the sample expected the banking relationship to be poor – 'I was a full-time mother for ten years and had no track record. In addition, my husband was unemployed at the time. What bank would have wanted to know?' (survey respondent). 'I try and avoid the banks because I know how notorious banks are at rejecting women and how they ask questions that wouldn't be asked of a man' (survey respondent).

Similar issues have been raised by Fletcher (1995), who suggests that small business owners in Scotland may rate their banks higher than their English counterparts because they have lower expectations of the banking relationship.

The fact that female business owners experience a more satisfactory banking relationship may also reflect the way in which they utilise the bank and its services. The study has already indicated that female business owners are more likely to use the bank for advice and place significantly more importance on the banks offering a wide range of services, providing specialist small business advice and advisors. This suggests that female business owners tend to be more 'participative' in the banking relationship. These findings are important because, as Binks (1995) argues, small business owners who are more 'participative' in the banking relationship tend to have a better experience of the banking relationship and are less likely to be considering changing banks.

Nevertheless, it is also possible that the male respondents in the survey had actually experienced a worse banking relationship than the female respondents. Indeed, it was found that the male respondents felt that they had suffered from significantly more problems in the banking relationship than their female counterparts (see next section).

5.4.3 Problems faced in the banking relationship

As suggested in the previous section, despite the generally high rating assigned to the overall banking relationship, when probed in more detail, small business owners were revealed to have faced a number of problems in their banking relationship and levelled a number of criticisms at the bank. The four most commonly cited bank-related

Table 5.11 The six most commonly cited bank-related problems (% of total number of respondents facing problems)

Problem	Total Rank	n	%	Female Rank	n	%	Male Rank	n	%
(a) High charges	1	46	69.7	1	20	64.5	1	26	74.3
(b) Unhelpful attitude	2	31	47.0	2	13	41.9	2	18	51.4
(c) Impersonal relationship	3	21	31.8	4	6	19.4	3	15	42.9
(d) Poor small business knowledge	4	17	25.8	= 5	5	16.1	4	12	34.3
(e) Mistakes/Inaccuracies	5	12	18.2	= 5	5	16.1	5	7	20.0
(f) Discriminatory behaviour	6	8	12.1	3	8	25.8	—	—	—
Total facing problems[a]	—	66	100	—	31	100	—	35	100

Male–female differences ($X^2 - a = 0.05$; b = 1.72^{-3}; c = 1.94; d = 1.85; e = 3.74^{-3}; f = †).

Notes: † It was not possible to test the statistical significance of these differences. In order to perform a *chi*-square analysis, the *expected* number for each cell must not be less than 5 (Clegg, 1994); [a] May be lower than column total as respondents could mention more than one problem

problems were high charges, unhelpful attitude, impersonal relationship and poor small business knowledge (Table 5.11).

The most common cause for concern of respondents in this study, as in other similar studies (e.g. Binks *et al.*, 1988), was that of bank charges being too high, particularly for those business owners who never borrow or rarely use their accounts. Almost 70 per cent of respondents who had faced problems in the banking relationship felt that they were being charged too much. There was a feeling, particularly amongst the male entrepreneurs, that small business owners are being made to pay for the banks' lending mistakes of the late 1980s/ early 1990s. Even when charges are reduced it can be problematical. As Smith (1989) found, reduction of charges may take place but it tends to be a random occurrence and highly negotiable, but not across the board. Such inconsistencies had not inspired the small business owners in this survey with trust in the fairness of the banks' charging structures.

The second most commonly cited problem was the perception that the banks do not have a supportive small business policy and that they are unhelpful, inflexible, and lack the interest or experience to enable them to understand small business needs and problems. Common issues raised included examples of banks refusing to extend overdraft facilities, withdrawing loans and overdraft facilities 'overnight', and of being unwilling to negotiate on charges and interest rates. Many business owners felt that the banks are only interested in protecting their own interests and do not care about the small business or its owner-manager. Similarly, small businesses in a study by Wynant and Hatch (1990) found bank managers to be arrogant and unsympathetic. A further 26 per cent of respondents in the present survey felt that banks do not have a sufficient knowledge or understanding of how small businesses operate and what their needs are. Indeed, this was the primary reason why respondents had not used their bank for advice.

Paradoxically, despite the relatively high scores respondents were found to award to their banks on the 'interpersonal' elements of the banking relationship (section 5.4.2), 32 per cent of respondents found the impersonal nature of the banking relationship to be problematic. The concern for most respondents was that they felt the 'relationship banking' element had been declining in recent years and that they were increasingly being treated as 'numbers' and not real people. Many respondents linked their relationship banking problems to the great upheavals which have been taking place in banking in recent years. Indeed, recent restructuring and centralisation of bank facilities and the associated rapid turnover in bank managers at branch level was found to have destroyed the long-established, close working relationships which used to exist between many of the respondents and their banks. In total, 60 per cent of respondents had experienced a change of bank manager in the previous three years or since start-up (if less than three years) and 31 per cent had dealt with three or more different managers. Fifteen (19 per cent) respondents were not sure how many managers there had been, the turnover being so frequent.

Almost all business owners who had experienced staff turnover felt that it had been detrimental to their banking relationship. According to one male respondent, 'the main effect is that a rapid turnover of managers destroys established working relationships and it becomes increasingly difficult to establish 'personal' relationships with a long string of replacement managers' (survey respondent).

Similarly, it has been argued in the literature that, because of staff turnover, the relationships between bank managers and small business owners are often disturbed with sometimes uncomfortable consequences (Gibb, 1993; Binks, 1991). For example, in September, 1995, Barclays Bank was taken to court by a small business owner who had his loan and overdraft facilities removed 'overnight' and without warning when his bank manager was replaced.

Respondents in the present survey explained how it takes time to build up a good working relationship which hinges on trust and communication. Many of the new replacement managers appear not to be prepared to put in the time or the effort to get to know their business customers. Furthermore, the entrepreneurs appeared to distrust the new managers brought in to replace the 'old school' style of manager. The feeling was that the younger managers are arrogant, do not speak the same language, do not understand small businesses, and are inexperienced and inflexible – 'little Hitlers' as one businesswoman put it. Although these feelings could simply reflect an age barrier or resistance to change, it should be noted that these problems were echoed by entrepreneurs of all ages.

Although the range of problems noted by the male and female respondents were similar,[4] as were the total numbers of male and female business owners who had faced problems in the banking relationship,[5] the male respondents were found to have faced more problems than the women. Indeed, between them, the male respondents mentioned 96 bank-related problems compared to the female respondents who mentioned only 65 problems. This difference was found to be significant at the 0.05 level ($X^2 = 5.590$, df $= 1$), and is important as it contradicts the expectation that women usually face more problems in the banking relationship.

One possible explanation for this finding is the fact that the male respondents were found to have experienced a significantly[6] higher level of staff turnover than the female respondents, a factor which is known for causing problems in the banking relationship (Wynant and Hatch, 1990). Another possible explanation is that, because the male respondents were less 'participative' in the banking relationship, they may have had a more problematic experience of the relationship (Binks, 1995) (as discussed in section 5.4.2).

Nevertheless, a minority of female business owners (20 per cent of the entire female sample) felt that they had experienced different treatment by the banks because they were women (Table 5.11). Indeed, this was the sixth most important problem faced by the sample as a whole and the third most important problem faced by the female respondents, although sex discrimination was not a problem cited by any of the male respondents. The female respondents who cited this problem did so quite independently and without prompting and therefore it might be the case that these figures under-represent the actual number of women who have ever felt discriminated against by the banks.[7] Like the female entrepreneurs in previous studies (Goffee and Scase, 1985; Carter and Cannon,

1992), these women felt they had not been taken seriously as business owners and had been treated in a patronising way by their bank manager. One of the female respondents felt that the male-dominated banking structure was to blame because male bank managers have little experience of dealing with women and therefore do not know how to treat female business owners. She herself had experienced a male bank manager not treating her seriously and had been on the receiving end of a number of sexist jokes which, although not being 'sexism at its worst' were, nevertheless, highly irritating and had an adverse impact on the overall banking relationship. Another woman had found her bank to be extremely supportive overall but that her bank manager was 'no good with women'. She found him to be a male chauvinist, patronising and was particularly irritated by his insistence on calling her 'sweetheart'. She also felt that he treated her as if she was stupid. This discriminatory treatment was even more noticeable when she was accompanied by her male business partner, a fact that he himself had also noted.

One businesswoman in the present study had found her first bank manager to be very narrow-minded. In her words, 'he had never heard of women in business other than hairdressers or those running clothes shops' and could not understand why she (a woman) would want to set up a business at all, particularly a public relations business. Indeed, the existing literature often highlights the fact that many bank managers are less supportive of women entering into 'non-traditional' or male-dominated sectors (Charbonneau, 1981; Hisrich and O'Brien, 1982; Buttner and Rosen, 1988b). Even though this particular manager had left the bank, she found it 'amusing' that the bank still treated her as their 'token woman' and often 'paraded' her as such at bank functions. Another female entrepreneur, whose boyfriend was her main source of business finance and who usually let him deal with the banking side of the business, felt that, on occasions when they saw the bank manager together, she was treated as the 'silent partner' even though it was her business and the boyfriend had nothing to do with its running. Moreover, when she saw the manager alone, she felt she was 'not taken at all seriously'. Another woman complained of the bank manager 'talking to her like she was his daughter', while another had her overdraft limit reduced by the bank when her ex-husband left the business and got the distinct feeling that the bank felt she would not succeed on her own.

It was expected that female business owners who had faced sexist treatment and attitudes by their banks would be less satisfied with the banking relationship than those female business owners who had

Table 5.12 The relationship between sexist treatment by the banks and satisfaction scores

| Relationship factors | Total[a] | Satisfaction scores | | Sig. level[d] |
		Discrim[b]	Non-discrim[c]	
1 Business				
Banker knows me and my business	0.94	0.50	1.07	0.09
Bank provides helpful business advice	0.80	0.83	0.79	No
Bank offers best rates/lowest fees	−0.37	−0.38	−0.36	No
Bank offers a wide range of services	0.58	1.00	0.48	0.05
Bank handles credit requests quickly	0	1.57	0.82	0.02
Bank manager is easily accessible	0.97	0.88	1.00	No
Bank has specialised small business bankers	0.75	0.86	0.72	No
2 Interpersonal				
Bank manager is easy to talk to	1.32	0.86	1.44	0.1
Bank manager makes me feel comfortable	1.12	0.29	1.35	0.03
Bank manager treats me with respect	1.15	0.29	1.39	0.02

Note: [a] Total female sample; [b] 'discriminated' female sample; [c] 'non-discriminated' sample; [d] significance tested using the Mann–Whitney U test

faced no such problems. In order to test this hypothesis, satisfaction scores (explained in section 5.4.2) were calculated for both female respondents who felt they had experienced sexist treatment and for those who had not (Table 5.12).

As expected, the results indicate that female respondents who had faced patronising or sexist attitudes in the banking relationship rated the interpersonal dimensions of the relationship significantly lower than those female respondents that had not faced such attitudes. In particular, they were less satisfied with the bank manager making them feel comfortable and treating them with respect and less satisfied that their bank manager knew them and their business. These findings correspond with the feelings expressed by female entrepreneurs in previous studies. For example, anecdotal evidence suggests that female business owners often feel that they have not been treated with respect:

> he just didn't take me seriously... with bank managers there's two things to be said. One, they're nicer to you because you're a woman. Two, they're worse because they think you're stupid.
> (Goffee and Scase, 1985: p. 45)

However, it was also found (Table 5.12) that the poorly treated sample of female respondents were significantly more satisfied with the range of services provided by the bank and the speed with which their credit requests were handled. A tentative explanation for this finding is that female entrepreneurs who have used the bank's facilities and services are more likely to have come into contact with sexist treatment than those female entrepreneurs who rarely use the bank and its services. However, there was no evidence to suggest a significantly different level of contact between those female entrepreneurs that had been treated badly by their banks and those that had not ($U = 128$, $N_A = 8$, $N_B = 32$; Mann–Whitney U test).

On all the occasions when sexist treatment was alleged to have taken place, the bank manager concerned was a male. None of the male respondents reported feelings of being discriminated against because of their sex. However, the vast majority of both male and female business owners had male account managers. Indeed, only 16 per cent of the women and 9 per cent of the men had female account managers. It was therefore impossible to meaningfully compare the experiences of male and female small business owners with regard to the sex of their bank manager.

5.4.4 Ways in which problems are dealt with

In total, 55 per cent (n = 36) of those respondents who had faced problems in their banking relationship had taken positive action in response to their problems (e.g. complained or changed banks). A further 6 per cent (n = 4) had considered taking action and 39 per cent (n = 26) had decided to do nothing about their problems. All of the latter group felt that they would not achieve anything by complaining.

The majority of respondents (67 per cent) had reacted to problems faced in the banking relationship by writing letters of complaint or by telephoning the bank to complain (Table 5.13). These complaints generally included a threat to change banks. Only one respondent (a male) had taken his complaint to the Banking Ombudsman. In many cases, particularly where the complaint centred around excessively high charges, the bank reduced these charges as a result of complaints. A further 22 per cent described their action in terms of becoming 'more forceful' in their approach to the banking relationship, in other words making their wishes known and demanding changes.

It has been suggested by observers that small business owners should stop whinging about banking problems and 'exploit the free market' that exists in banking today (Pennington in *The Times*, 1994a: p. 27). However, in practice, it is argued that small business customers do not actually have as much of a choice in terms of the bank they use

Table 5.13 Ways in which respondents deal with banking problems (% of total number of respondents who took action)

Method	Total[a]	Female	Male	X^2
1 Complained (letters/telephone calls)	24 (66.7)	8 (53.3)	16 (76.2)	4.40
2 Changed banks	13 (36.1)	6 (40.0)	7 (33.3)	0.07
3 Became 'more forceful'	8 (22.2)	7 (46.7)	1 (4.8)	—[b]
4 Other	8 (22.2)	5 (33.3)	3 (14.3)	—[b]
Total taking action	36 (100.0)	15 (100.0)	21 (100.0)	0.89

Notes: [a] Total number of mentions (respondents could mention more than one method); [b] it was not possible to test the statistical significance of these differences because, in order to perform a *chi*-square analysis, the *expected* number for each cell must not be less than 5 (Clegg, 1994)

as might be expected (Storey, 1994: p. 236). A study for the Forum of Private Business (1994) found that, although many small business owners had considered changing banks (43 per cent), only 5 per cent had actually done so. A major problem for many small business owners is that the wish to move banks often occurs at a time when they have been denied credit facilities. However, this is usually at a time when they are also having difficulties and so are unattractive to alternative banks. Banks generally have a cautious attitude towards customers arriving from other banks. This is illustrated in a comment by Sir John Quinton (chairman of Barclays Bank) to the Treasury Select Committee:

> We find, as a matter of experience, something like half of our bad debts are from customers we have taken on from other banks in the last year or two, so we have issued instructions for a number of years from the centre, and I have no doubt other banks have done the same if they are sensible, saying if you get offered business from another bank look at it hard ... before you take it.
>
> (Sir John Quinton to the House of Commons Treasury and Civil Service Committee, 1991; Storey, 1994: p. 238)

In the present survey, 36 per cent of respondents had actually changed banks in response to the problems faced in the banking relationship. Reasons given by respondents for changing banks included unsatisfactory terms, numerous mistakes, and high charges. The most frequently cited cause, however, centred around problems with individual bank managers. One businesswoman had found her manager's attitude unhelpful and inflexible, which coupled with regular statement mistakes was sufficient to make her change banks.

Another felt that she had been treated rudely in her loan application and was given no reason for the refusal. Similarly, one businessman, when refused an extension to his overdraft facility without explanation, decided to 'cut his losses', as he put it, and move elsewhere.

However, changing banks can cause problems. It may result in the loss of an existing relationship, however inadequate, and means that the small business owner has to start again from scratch. There are also 'adjustment' costs associated with transferring facilities over to a new bank. In addition, most small business owners perceive there to be little difference between the quality of service offered by the different banks (Forum of Private Business, 1994). In the present study there was no evidence to suggest that those respondents who had changed banks had successfully eradicated all the problems experienced in their previous banking relationship.

In terms of male–female differences, it was found that fewer (48 per cent) of the female respondents had taken positive action in response to their banking relationship problems than the male respondents (60 per cent). However, this difference was not found to be significant (Table 5.13). Nevertheless, there were some important differences between the male and female respondents in terms of the ways in which they had dealt with their banking relationship problems. First, significantly more of the male respondents had complained in writing or by telephone ($X^2 = 4.40$; df $= 1$; 0.05 significance level). Meanwhile, although its significance could not be tested, more of the female respondents claimed to have dealt with their banking relationship problems by becoming more forceful in their approach. For many of the women, this was the strategy adopted to cope with the bank's perceived discriminatory behaviour. For instance one female respondent said,

> The banks are generally very narrow-minded about women. I therefore lay down the ground rules. I have had to lay down clear rules. I basically told him [the bank manager] at our first meeting that I would require basic information sometimes but that I did not want to be spoken to as if I was a child.
>
> (survey respondent)

Another businesswoman felt that she was not being treated fairly and therefore confronted her bank manager in the following way,

> my general feeling was that he was not giving me the credibility that I deserved because I am a woman and so I confronted him and

asked if he actually believed in backing women at all...yes, I suppose I became more forceful in my approach.

(survey respondent)

The female respondents often described their action in terms of standing up to the bank manager and demanding improvements. As one woman put it, 'being a woman on your own, you have to learn to fight'. The importance of this finding is not that the female respondents were shown to take very different action compared to their male counterparts, but that they interpreted their own behaviour in a subtly different way to the male respondents. Carter and Cannon (1988) suggest that many female entrepreneurs 'sublimate their gender and personal position to gain confidence and credibility [in the eyes of the lender] for the benefit of the enterprise' (Carter and Cannon, 1988: p. 15). It may be that female business owners in this survey saw being more 'forceful' in their approach to the banking relationship as a way of 'sublimating their gender'.

Of course, as a number of respondents (both male and female) pointed out, banking relationships do change over time. The following statements illustrate this point. 'When I started out, the bank manager frightened me to death. But it soon turns around and now I tell him what to do. It comes with confidence I think' (female respondent).

At first, I used to wear my suit to see the bank manager but now he has to accept me as I am and I usually say to him that if he wants to see me then he will have to come to me as I am far too busy.

(male respondent)

Important factors influencing the relationship are therefore track record, confidence and very often the attitude in which a business owner approaches their bank manager. This can be particularly important for female business owners as the following statement illustrates.

The key to getting what I wanted was I think in the determined way I went about getting it. So often women are in awe of bank managers and are too 'coy' about asking for what they want. Men stride in, put their plans on the table and look the bank manager in the eye.

(survey respondent)

Similarly, Carter and Cannon (1992) found that many of the female entrepreneurs in their study had responded to gender-related problems with their bank by preparing well for interviews and wearing business suits. This is described in terms of a 'depersonalisation' strategy and is commonly associated with achievement oriented women.

5.5 CONCLUSION

The results presented in this chapter suggest that there are considerably more similarities than differences between female and male entrepreneurs in their experiences of the banking relationship than would have been expected given the findings of previous research and theory (chapter 2). The men and women made their choice of bank on similar criteria. Neither the female nor the male business owners used their banks as a source of advice on a frequent basis and neither group was in contact with their bank managers very frequently. Both had faced similar problems when dealing with their banks and there was no evidence to suggest that the female business owners had to use 'straw men' in response to problems with the banking relationship.

Nevertheless, there are some noteworthy differences between the male and female small business owners. First, the most consistent differences throughout the chapter centre around the provision of advice by the banks. Not only were the female respondents found to have used their banks significantly more often for business advice than the male respondents, but they also rated the importance of bank advice significantly higher. In addition, the women rated their banks more highly on the quality of advice provided than the men. Female respondents were also in contact with their bank managers more frequently than their male counterparts. The question is why? As has already been discussed, many businesswomen are found to lack confidence and have a low self-assessment. The fact that more of the female respondents were prepared to take advice may reflect an underlying lack of confidence in their own abilities. It may also be a reflection of the fact that many women feel they have to 'work harder' to be successful in business (Godfrey, 1992). However, it may also reflect the fact that male business owners perceive that they do not need to take advice. Indeed, it is generally accepted that businesswomen have less experience and fewer skills than businessmen, in particular, financial skills. Female business owners might therefore be more aware of their need to take more external advice.

Second, the female respondents were found to rate the importance of all factors associated with the banking relationship more highly than the male respondents. In particular, the female respondents felt that the provision of 'specialised small business bankers' and of 'a wide range of services' was significantly more important than their male counterparts. The former may reflect the fact that the female respondents in the study were more willing to seek and take advice from the bank and therefore required specialised small business bankers to give them the advice they needed. The latter may reflect the fact that the female respondents place more importance on convenience than their male counterparts. If their bank provides all the financial services that they might require, it saves the inconvenience of looking elsewhere. Similarly, although the difference was not significant, more women were found to have chosen their bank because they already had their personal account there, suggesting a desire for convenience.

Third, in terms of their bank's performance, both the overall relationship and quality of service received were given a significantly higher rating by the female respondents than the male respondents. The female respondents also gave a significantly higher rating to their banks on the factors 'bank manager knows me and my business', 'bank offers best rates/lowest fees', 'bank provides helpful business advice' and 'bank provides specialised small business bankers'. Using the satisfaction index developed by Fabowale *et al.* (1993), the female respondents were also found to be significantly more satisfied with their bank's provision of specialised small business bankers, helpful business advice and with the bank knowing their business. In addition, the male respondents were found to have experienced significantly more problems than the women.

A study by the Forum of Private Business (1994) showed that business owners who are more 'participative' in the banking relationship generally find their banks more helpful and have a better relationship than 'non-participative' owner-managers. The research indicates that the female business owners in this sample were in contact with their account managers more frequently than their male counterparts and discussed their business with the bank more readily when seeking advice. One suggestion is therefore that, because the female business owners were more participative in the banking relationship, they had a better experience than their 'non-participative' male counterparts. On the other hand, because there is a common belief that women are discriminated against in the banking relationship, it is possible that the female respondents had lower expectations as to the quality of relationship they could expect. It is therefore possible that, when they did not experience any problems, they rated the relationship more highly than if they had gone in without any expectations. The fact that the male business owners had faced more problems than the female business owners may also reflect the fact that the male respondents had experienced a higher turnover in banking staff than their female counterparts.

Fourth, although there was no evidence in chapter 4 to suggest that the female respondents had been discriminated against in their access to bank finance, one in five of the female sample felt that they had been patronised or not taken seriously by their account managers. Similarly, Fabowale *et al.* (1993) could find no differences in the terms of credit applied to male and female business owners by the banks but a significant number of women had come away from the banking relationship with a sense of having been treated disrespectfully. The findings of this study suggest that this kind of treatment does have an adverse effect on the banking relationship. Indeed, the poorly treated sample were significantly less satisfied with the interpersonal dimensions of the banking relationship and were not satisfied that their bank knew their business well enough. These findings have important implications for the marketing of bank services to female entrepreneurs which are discussed in chapter 7.

In the light of findings from chapters 4 and 5, it is therefore argued that, while there is a small minority of female business owners who feel that they have been treated in a different way by individual bank managers because they are women, there is little evidence to suggest that banking policy directly discriminates against women, and that women have less access to bank finance than men. However, as concluded in chapter 4, it is acknowledged that this study has only concentrated on those male and female business owners who had successfully launched a business enterprise. The study therefore needs to be complemented by research which looks at the banking relationship of 'nascent' female entrepreneurs who were unsuccessful in starting a business (Reynolds and White, 1992) and female entrepreneurs who start businesses but later fail. Carter and Cannon (1992) found that, in their subsample of ten female-owned business failures, the banking relationship was generally poor, with virtually no interaction with the bank manager. Respondents blamed patronising behaviour and attitudes for the failure to establish good working relationships. However, Carter and Cannon (1992) did not use a male control group against whom to compare the experiences of female-owned business failures. There is therefore scope to extend the use of the matched pairs methodology to a study of the banking relationship amongst nascent female entrepreneurs and 'failed' female-owned businesses. Future research might also consider examining the differences between male and female business owners in their treatment by the banks depending on whether they have a male or a female bank manager.

6 The role of networking in the financing of male and female-owned businesses

6.1 INTRODUCTION

6.1.1 Overview

The findings that have been reported in chapters 4 and 5 have been in sharp contrast to expectations based on theory, existing research, and anecdotal evidence (as presented in chapter 2). Indeed, there are many more similarities than differences between male and female business owners in the financing of their businesses. Chapter 4 found that male and female business owners use similar amounts and sources of finance in their businesses, face similar problems in raising finance, and receive finance from the banks on similar terms and conditions. The main difference is that significantly more of the female respondents use bank finance than their male counterparts. In terms of the banking relationship, chapter 5 found that male and female respondents choose their banks for similar reasons, neither are in contact with their bank managers on a frequent basis, and they both face similar problems in the banking relationship. However, significantly more of the female business owners were found to use their bank for advice than the male business owners. In addition, they were found to rank the importance of key banking relationship factors more highly and were significantly more satisfied with the banking relationship than their male counterparts. Only a small minority of female business owners felt that they had not been treated with respect in the banking relationship; and there was no evidence to suggest they had been discriminated against in their access to bank finance.

The question raised is, why should there be such a contrast between the findings of this study and those of previous studies? One possible answer lies in the fact that previous research failed to use the matched pairs methodology. It is therefore quite possible that, in previous studies, the differences found between men and women in the financing of their businesses were simply a reflection of the differences that exist in the structural characteristics of male- and female-owned businesses, rather than an indication of true gender-based differences (see chapter 3 for a discussion). The matching process adopted in the present survey would therefore explain the similarities found between male and female business owners in the financing of their businesses (chapter 4). However, it does not provide an explanation for the differences which have been identified, in particular why female respondents in this study are found to have a much better experience of the banking relationship than the male business owners (chapter 5), a finding that is in total contrast to expectations based on existing research (chapter 2). In chapter 5, it was suggested that the difference might be explained by the finding that female business owners in the study had a more 'participative' approach to the relationship (Binks, 1995). In particular, significantly more of the female respondents were found to use the bank for advice, value the provision of bank advice, and rate the performance of their bank on the provision of advice more highly than their male counterparts. These findings therefore raise the possibility that the differences between male and female business owners in the financing of their businesses and in their banking relationship may be associated with differences in the networking behaviour of female and male business owners.

6.1.2   Networking: a definition

A network is a specific type of relation linking a defined set of persons, objects or events. Small firm networks generally consist of a mixture of 'formal' contacts (e.g. advice agencies, professionals, bank managers) and 'informal' contacts such as friends and business associates (Carswell, 1990). Szarka (1990), using Mitchell's work (1973), identifies three types of linkages which can be used to examine the external assistance networks of small firms:

- *Exchange networks* – linkages with organisations with which the small firm has commercial transactions (e.g. customers, suppliers).
- *Communication networks* – linkages with individuals or organisations with which the small firm has non-trading links (e.g. accountants, banks, public and semi-public business support agencies).
- *Social networks* – formed by family, friends and acquaintances.

6.1.3   Networking and the financing of small businesses

It has been argued that networking is the 'essence' of entrepreneurship (Dubini and Aldrich, 1991; Cromie *et al.*, 1993), and that the personal network of an entrepreneur should be regarded as his or her major asset and 'the strategically most significant resource of the firm' (Johannisson, 1990: p. 41). There is a 'growing recognition that new firms are shaped by the relationships their founders are able to nurture and maintain with a range of external agencies' (Steier and Greenwood, 1995: p. 337; Birley, 1985; Jarillo, 1989; Reuber *et al.*, 1991).

Networking is of utmost importance in the financing of small businesses for three main reasons. First, networks give entrepreneurs access to vital resources, in particular finance (Birley, 1985; Starr and MacMillan, 1990; Dubini and Aldrich, 1991; Reuber *et al.*, 1991; Cromie *et al.*, 1993; Scottish Enterprise, 1993a; Zhao and Aram, 1995) which are fundamental for business survival and growth (Aldrich and Zimmer, 1986; Aldrich, 1989; Jarillo, 1989; Carswell, 1990; Szarka, 1990; Blackburn *et al.*, 1992; Curran and Blackburn, 1994; Zhao and Aram, 1995).

Ostgaard and Birley (1994) have found that

> (o)wner managers whose firms generate capital mainly through outside sources tend to receive both general advice and particular assistance in obtaining this capital through their personal network. They also tend to spend a significant amount of their time developing other new contacts.
>
> (Ostgaard and Birley, 1994: p. 291)

Similarly, Olm *et al.* (1988) found that female entrepreneurs who had greater access to a network of contacts were found to have better access to formal sources of capital. Again using research on female entrepreneurs, Reese (1992) argues that a 1 per cent increase in network size is found to increase an entrepreneur's access to external resources by 2 per cent, finance being one of the most important resources. The importance of the network in gaining access to sources of finance is illustrated in the case of informal venture capital. Mason and Harrison (1994) found that the majority of equity investments in small firms made by 'business angels' (informal investors) are based on information supplied to them by a network of business associates and friends. It therefore follows that, 'the more people you know, the more likely you are to know someone who has what you need', or who can introduce you to someone that has (Reese, 1992: p. 9).

Second, networks are also an important way in which many small business owners compensate for the fact that they lack the necessary financial skills to successfully manage their business finances and to raise finance (Curran and Blackburn, 1994; Donckels and Lambrecht, 1995; Young, 1995). The ability of the owner-manager to manage the finances of his/her business is recognised as being critical in the formation and growth of small businesses. Indeed, a business owner may be an excellent innovator or capable salesperson, but without sound financial management, those skills will 'not bear fruit' (McMahon *et al.*, 1993: p. 20). According to research sponsored by the National Westminster Bank, two-thirds of small firms fail due to a lack of financial skills and information (*Guardian*, 1993a; McMahon *et al.*, 1993). The banks are also well-known for making lending judgements based on the ability of the small business owner to supply financial information and also to be able to understand it (Berry *et al.*, 1993). Therefore, entrepreneurs often turn to outsiders for financial advice and assistance. Certain contacts within the small business network will be called upon to provide advice and assistance on specific financial issues (e.g. tax specialists, accountants) or on preparing business plans and loan applications (e.g. enterprise agencies). Meanwhile, other contacts within the network will act as 'signposts' to the most relevant source of advice for solving a particular financial problem (e.g. national small business organisations, banks, accountants) (Lavarack, 1994).

Third, it has also been argued that networking activity improves the small business–banking relationship. The banks tend to be more positive towards those businesses that have sought advice in the preparation of loan applications (Berry *et al.*, 1993), particularly advice from accountants (Fletcher, 1995). Indeed, in a study of the decision-making of Scottish bank managers, Fletcher (1995) found that 42 per cent of bank managers asked specifically if a chartered accountant had been or would be employed. This is because bank managers see an accountant as 'an important adviser in business planning and for producing financial information' (Fletcher, 1995: p. 47).

Intermediaries such as accountants, enterprise agencies and trade associations also act as 'brokers' in the banking relationship (Aldrich and Zimmer, 1986; Cromie at al, 1993; Bannock, 1994; Fletcher, 1995). Aldrich and Zimmer (1986) define the role of the 'broker' as 'linking persons having complementary interests, transferring information, and otherwise facilitating the interests of persons not directly connected to one another' (Aldrich and Zimmer, 1986: p. 16).

For example, bank managers often have long-established working relationships with local accountants whom they trust to recommend good small business proposals, primarily because taking recommendations reduces their exposure to the risks and costs associated with moral hazard and information asymmetries (chapter 2). The small business that enters the banking relationship via an accountant or another intermediary/broker is therefore less likely to experience difficulty in establishing a level of trust with the bank manager. Indeed, this is implied in a study by Carter and Rosa (1995) who found that small business owners are more likely to be refused bank finance if they are not members of The Rotary Club or similar organisations.

The bank itself is also an important source of well-informed advice and has a wealth of experience to offer the small business (Lavarack, 1994). Binks (1995) have suggested that those small business owners that take a more 'participative' approach in the banking relationship, which includes using the bank for advice, are likely to have a better banking relationship. Indeed, in chapter 5, it was found that the female respondents were more participative in the banking relationship and had also experienced a much more satisfactory banking relationship than the male respondents.

6.1.4   Networking and female entrepreneurs

Existing research suggests that female owner-managers frequently face distinctive problems in accessing support and advice networks (Turner, 1989). In a study of seventy female entrepreneurs, Carter and Cannon (1992) found that a number of women had confronted patronising attitudes when seeking advice from bankers and accountants. Still and Guerin (1991) found that the third major entry barrier to women wishing to start their own business, after 'confidence' and 'access to finance', was finding adequate sources of assistance and advice. In the US, Hisrich and Brush (1984) also revealed that, although the female entrepreneurs in their survey were aware of their need for 'guidance and counsel', they had problems acquiring it. One female entrepreneur explained, 'I approached both the SBA and SCORE for assistance (not money) and felt I was treated in a patronizing way' (Hisrich and Brush, 1984: p. 34). A study by Reuber *et al.* (1991) argues that female business owners are treated differently from male business owners by business consultants. They found that the advice hypothetical female business owners received from a sample of consultants was significantly greater in volume and less complex in content than that received by hypothetical male business owners, which suggests that consultants see women as being 'more helpless' and therefore in need of more advice, and men as being 'more capable' and able to process more complex advice (Reuber *et al.*, 1991: p. 249).

Five main reasons can be put forward to explain why female business owners may face barriers in their access to networks of assistance, advice and support. First, women are disadvantaged in the labour market. Most entrepreneurs work for someone else before they start their own businesses. During these pre-start-up years, entrepreneurs build up a network of formal and informal contacts that they subsequently draw on when starting and running their own businesses (Aldrich, 1989). However, as outlined in chapter 1, research on labour market segmentation indicates that there are sexual divisions in the organisational distribution of the workforce which mean that women tend to remain at the bottom of the occupational hierarchy (Carter and Cannon, 1992). In particular, many women suffer form workplace discrimination and stereotyping which place constraints on their career advancement, particularly to senior management levels (Kanter, 1977). However, it is found that managerial positions afford the best opportunities for developing a wide network of contacts (Aldrich, 1989). Therefore, many female entrepreneurs who leave employment to start their own businesses face a 'network deficit' in comparison to male entrepreneurs who are more likely to have enjoyed direct access to the top managerial positions in organisational hierarchies (Aldrich, 1989: p. 118; Stevenson, 1983; Hisrich and Brush, 1985; Carter and Cannon, 1992). Female managers are also found to be inclined to turn to other females for advice and assistance (Nicholson and West, 1988; Noe, 1988). However, because of the scarcity of other female business owners and senior women in their professions generally, it is not surprising to find that female business owners seek advice outside of informal networks because they rarely have friends in a position to give business advice (Cromie and Birley, 1992).

Second, many women who start businesses do so having been economically inactive for some time, usually because they have been raising a family. However, by staying at home to raise a family, women are often isolated from important networks of colleagues and business contacts (Fogarty, 1972). Work by Fischer and Oliker (1983) found that married women, especially those with children, had significantly fewer persons in their networks. The critical period in which potential entrepreneurs accumulate the resources and contacts that help to sustain a business start-up is found to be between the ages of late twenties and early thirties (Aldrich, 1989), the most common period for women to be taking a career break to raise a family.

Third, domestic responsibilities are also likely to detract from female entrepreneurs' ability to develop an extensive network of colleagues and business contacts (Fogarty, 1972; Aldrich, 1989; Cromie and Birley, 1992). For example, many women may be excluded from important networking activity, which frequently takes place after work hours, because they have domestic responsibilities.

Fourth, Aldrich (1989) argues that many women lack the necessary experience and skills with which to undertake networking activity. Indeed, as indicated in chapter 1, female business owners are found to have, or perceive themselves as having, less experience and fewer skills in areas relevant to running a business (Belcourt *et al.*, 1991; Kalleberg and Leicht, 1991; Simpson, 1991; Barclays Bank, 1992; Carter and Cannon, 1992; Fischer *et al.*, 1993; Scottish Enterprise, 1993b; Barrett, 1995). Without experience, many women may not realise the importance of networking activity. In addition, the finding that many women lack confidence in their business abilities (Hisrich and Brush, 1983; 1986; Honig-Haftel and Martin, 1986; Batchelor, 1987; Still and Guerin, 1991; Carter and Cannon, 1992) may hinder them from seeking to participate in networking activity.

Fifth, on the supply-side, few 'formal' business support organisations actively target female entrepreneurs (Watkins and Watkins, 1984; Truman, 1993). Many female entrepreneurs are alienated because the advisory services on offer are generally oriented to the needs of male entrepreneurs, which are often very different to those of female entrepreneurs. Indeed, female business owners tend to have different attitudes towards business ownership, many lack management experience and skills, female-owned businesses are concentrated in different sectors to male-owned businesses, and many women have particular needs which need to be incorporated into the supply of business advice and assistance (e.g. crèche facilities). Turner (1993) summarises these issues as follows,

> conventional sources of business information and advice tend to be oriented towards the reality, motivations, and background of male entrepreneurs, with the result that many women feel these services do not address their needs and thus they are discouraged from using them.
>
> (Turner, 1993: p. 138)

In Britain, most schemes aimed at meeting the needs of women in business are fairly *ad hoc* and localised. One of the only national initiatives to be set up is the scheme run by the Women's Enterprise

Forum which encourages existing enterprise agencies to become more 'women-friendly'. The result has been the development of Women's Enterprise Centres, set up alongside many enterprise agencies, which offer advice and training specifically tailored to the needs of business-women (e.g. female business counsellors, crèche facilities). However, recent research by Bennett (1995) indicates that, since enterprise agencies have become contractors to the Training and Enterprise Councils (TECs) in England and Wales, the number of women-owned businesses that are counselled by the enterprise agencies has decreased from 27 per cent to 22 per cent of clients (1988–1992). Bennett (1995) argues that the reason for this decrease is, in part, due to the emphasis placed by the TECs on 'performance' which has led many enterprise agencies to 'cream-off' the clients most likely to succeed in business, the implication being that they view women-owned businesses as being less likely to succeed.

According to Simpson (1991) and a survey by Scottish Enterprise (1993b), the biggest problem for female entrepreneurs in their search for advice is that most business advisors are male and therefore less likely to understand the specific needs of women in business. Similarly, most of the traditional, well-established business networks are male-dominated (e.g. The Rotary, The Masons) (Smeltzer and Fann, 1989; Scottish Enterprise, 1993b). As well as experiencing difficulty in gaining access to such male-dominated groups (Reskin and Hart-mann, 1986), Therrien *et al.* (1986) suggest that many women will shun such formal business groups because they are male-dominated and will rely instead on informal sources of advice. However, many female business owners are also sensitive about joining women-only groups, 'as they want to be seen to succeed on the same terms as men' (Scottish Enterprise, 1993b: p. 25).

6.1.5 Justification for further research

The networking literature therefore suggests that female owner-managers will encounter problems in raising finance and in dealing with banks (Moore *et al.*, 1992; Rees, 1992). However, as already noted in chapter 4, there were more similarities than differences between male and female owner-managers in their access to and use of finance, and in chapter 5 there was little evidence to suggest that female business owners encounter more problems in the banking relationship. In fact, the female respondents were found to have a significantly more satisfactory banking relationship than the male respondents.

One possible reason for the paradoxical findings is that previous studies on the networking behaviour of female entrepreneurs suffer from the same problems as previous studies on the financing of women-owned businesses; namely, they do not control for structural differences between male- and female-owned small businesses. In chapters 2 and 3, it was demonstrated that structural factors (e.g. business age, size, sector) are an important influence on the lending decisions made by the financial community, and are also an important influence on the amount and type of finance required by small businesses. However, in chapter 2, it was shown that the general populations of male- and female-owned businesses differ in terms of structural characteristics. It is therefore likely that previous studies finding differences between male and female business owners in their networking behaviour may have simply been highlighting differences in the structural characteristics of male- and female-owned businesses rather than true gender-based differences.

Further examination of the networking behaviour of male and female small business owners using the matched pairs approach is therefore justified. The expectation is that, contrary to previous studies, differences between the male and female business owners in their networking behaviour will be largely eliminated once structural differences are controlled for, as in the financing of their businesses (chapter 4). However, the specific intention in this chapter is to examine whether there are any differences in the networking behaviour of male and female small business owners which might explain the differences found in the financing of their businesses.

6.2   NETWORKING BEHAVIOUR AND THE SIZE OF SMALL BUSINESS NETWORKS

6.2.1   General overview

Respondents were asked to indicate the sources of external assistance[1] that they had ever used in the start-up and running of their businesses. As shown in Table 6.1, just under three-quarters (74 per cent; n = 59) of the total number of respondents had used some form of assistance or advice in their businesses. However, the size of the networks was generally very small. Indeed, the average number of contacts per respondent network was found to be just 2.7. In fact, this figure probably overstates the size of networks normally used by respondents because the question asked for sources *ever* used and therefore

Table 6.1 Sources of assistance used by respondents (% of total mentions in brackets)

Sources of assistance	Total	Female	Male	Sig X^2
1 Informal	*n*	*n*	*n*	
Friends/business colleagues	30 (18.5)	10 (11.4)	20 (27.0)	Yes
Family	17 (10.5)	13 (14.8)	4 (5.4)	Yes
Domestic partner	10 (6.2)	6 (6.8)	4 (5.4)	No
2 Formal				
Accountants	58 (35.8)	27 (30.7)	31 (41.9)	No
Public and semi-public agencies	20 (12.3)	10 (11.4)	10 (13.5)	No
Banks	19 (11.7)	15 (17.0)	4 (5.4)	Yes
Other formal sources	8 (4.9)	7 (8.0)	1 (1.4)	—[a]
Total no. of mentions	162 (100.0)	88 (100.0)	74 (100.0)	—
Total no. using external assistance	59	28	31	No
Average network size	2.7	3.1	2.4	Yes[b]

Notes: [a] It was not possible to test the statistical significance of this difference, because in order to perform a *chi*-square analysis, the *expected* number for each cell must not be less than 5 (Clegg, 1994); [b] Using the Wilcoxon Test

answers may have included sources used on a single occasion, perhaps some time in the past.

The reasons for the reliance of small business owners on a narrow range of contacts are three-fold. First, many business owners have a limited awareness of the range of sources of advice and assistance available to them (Maidment, 1994). For example, Curran and Blackburn (1994) have suggested that many small business owners are unaware of the existence of Training and Enterprise Councils (TECs). The suggestion is that many support organisations, such as the TECs, have not done enough to market themselves to the small business owner (Curran and Blackburn, 1994).

However, the second reason why many small business owner-managers do not seek external assistance is that they are found to be highly independent (Bolton Report, 1971; Kets de Vries, 1977; Goffee and Scase, 1985; Walker, 1989). Indeed, many of the respondents in the present survey explained that they had not sought external assistance because they preferred to 'go it alone' and therefore avoided turning to anyone else for help or advice. According to Curran and Blackburn (1994), 'network participation is often incompatible with such values and attitudes because it necessitates an open reliance on advice from others or other implicit admissions of dependence' (p. 92). A common characteristic shown by respondents was determination and often pride in building up their business without help. There was a dislike displayed for what was seen as 'interference' from outside. The *Guardian* (1993b) similarly found this sort of resistance from small business owners towards any external assistance or schemes 'that hint at telling them how to run their companies' (p. 12). Similarly, Sowman (1994) talks of the small business owner's 'stubborn resistance to seek, let alone accept, advice' (p. 5). This appears entirely consistent with the fact that many business owners set up their own business to be independent and to be 'their own boss' (Hertz, 1987; Carter and Cannon, 1992; Carter, 1993).

Third, according to Curran and Blackburn (1994), another major factor which mitigates against networking activity is the time involved, which many small business owners find difficult to spare. As explained by one of the respondents in the present survey, the reason that he had not sought more formal business advice was because 'it takes too much time and money to establish a relationship with an external business advisor so that advice can *really* be tailored to individual needs' (survey respondent).

6.2.2   Male–female comparison

A comparison of the male and female respondents indicates that a larger proportion of the male sample (78 per cent; n = 31) had used external sources of assistance than the female sample (70 per cent; n = 28) (Table 6.1). Although, this difference was not found to be significant using the *chi*-square test ($\chi^2 = 0.581$, df=1; two-tailed hypothesis), it meets the expectations formed by the existing literature which suggests that women have less access to networks (see section 6.1.4).

However, despite the fact that fewer of the female respondents were found to have used external advice/assistance, it was found that the average size of business network used by the female respondents was larger than that of the male respondents. Indeed, the average female network was found to consist of 3.1 contacts compared to just 2.4 contacts per male network. Using the Wilcoxon Test, this difference was found to be significant at the 0.01 significance level (N = 27; T = 69.5; two-tailed test). These findings are in contrast to expectations formed by studies of female entrepreneurship and networking behaviour which suggest that the problems faced by female business owners are likely to restrict their ability to form extensive networks (section 6.1.4). They are also in contrast to findings from a study of the networking behaviour of male and female owner-managers in Northern Ireland (Cromie and Birley, 1992) which could find no significant differences between the male and female respondents in terms of the average size of their current business network (measured by the number of people with whom they discussed their business). However, the findings do correspond with those of Brown and Segal (1989) who similarly found that female entrepreneurs are more likely to use multiple sources of advice at start-up than male entrepreneurs.

A number of suggestions can be put forward as to why female business owners use significantly more sources of advice than their male counterparts. First, as suggested in chapter 1, female business owners are generally found to have much less experience than equivalent male business owners, in particular less managerial experience (Welsch and Young, 1984; Cromie, 1987a; 1987b; Barclays Bank, 1992). In addition, female business owners are generally found to have fewer skills in areas relevant to running a business, in particular financial skills (Hisrich and Brush, 1983; 1984; Watkins and Watkins, 1984; Chaganti, 1986). They may therefore feel it more necessary to seek external advice and assistance than male business owners. In other words, a large, diverse and closely knit network of associates offers the potential for female entrepreneurs to overcome their skill deficiencies (Welsch and Young, 1984; Brown and Segal, 1989; Cromie and Birley, 1992).

Second, the literature suggests that businesswomen lack confidence and have a lower self-assessment than men (Hisrich and Brush, 1983; 1986; Honig-Haftel and Martin, 1986; Batchelor, 1987). In particular, women are more frequently conditioned by society to regard themselves as weaker in areas such as finance and business operations, regarding these as 'male' attributes (Hisrich and Brush, 1984; Goffee and Scase, 1985; Hisrich and Brush, 1985; Chaganti, 1986). Many female business owners may therefore seek external assistance to counteract the lack of confidence in their own abilities and to confirm the validity of their ideas and strategies. Indeed, Jennings and Cohen (1993) suggest that many female owner-managers tend to understate their own knowledge and abilities and, as a result, feel that they have much to learn from others.

Third, women tend to be risk-averse (Therrien *et al.*, 1986; Sexton and Bowman-Upton, 1988). They may therefore attempt to minimise risks by learning from the experiences of others (Brown and Segal, 1989) and by taking a lot of advice before making important decisions.

Fourth, women are generally found to 'plan and research their enterprises more thoroughly than their male counterparts' (Thomas, 1991: p. 92) and are therefore more likely to be aware of the wide range of sources of advice and assistance available to them. Nelson

(1989) found female entrepreneurs to be 'rather... pragmatic in their solicitation of aid', targeting 'significant others' for the specific contribution they could make to the business (p. 16). These findings also suggest that female entrepreneurs regard the importance of networking more highly than male entrepreneurs.

The finding that female respondents in the present survey had significantly larger networks of contacts, not only contradicts expectations based on previous research, but also suggests that female business owners may have greater access to sources of finance than their male counterparts, given that previous research has identified a positive association between the size of a small business network and access to external resources (Reese, 1992). The finding that the female business owners had more extensive networks than their male counterparts may therefore go some way towards explaining the findings in chapter 4 that female respondents were found to have used a slightly wider range of sources of finance, more of the female respondents had used external sources of finance, and significantly more had used bank finance.

Their more extensive networks may also explain why, in chapter 5, the female business owners were found to have had a more positive experience of the banking relationship than the male business owners. Indeed, in section 6.1.3 it was suggested that banks tend to be more positive towards those businesses that have sought advice, in particular because the process of seeking advice from a wide range of sources acts as a 'signal' to the bank that the owner-manager is committed to the success of the business.

6.3   NETWORK PROFILES

6.3.1   Informal sources

In total, informal sources of advice (provided by friends/business colleagues, family and domestic partners) accounted for 35 per cent of the total number of sources of advice mentioned by respondents (Table 6.1). Similarly, Birley (1985) and Nelson (1987) found entrepreneurs to be heavily reliant on family, friends, and business contacts for advice. This is to be expected, given that informal sources of advice and assistance are relatively cheap and easy to come by (Katz, 1994). In addition, it is likely that the Pecking Order Hypothesis described in relation to the preference for 'internal' sources of finance (chapter 2) also exists in relation to the preference for certain sources of assistance/advice. As described in section 6.2.1, small business owners tend to be highly independent and are therefore likely to choose sources of advice which minimise external interference (i.e. informal sources).

The most frequently used informal source of advice/assistance was that provided by friends and business colleagues. Indeed, 38 per cent of all respondents (n = 30) had ever received advice from friends or business colleagues. A further 21 per cent of all respondents (n = 17) had received advice/assistance from family members. The advice of domestic partners was less frequently used with only 13 per cent of the total sample citing them among their networks of contacts.

There were two significant differences between the male and female business owners in terms of the profile of their informal contact networks (Table 6.1). First, twice as many of the male respondents (n = 20) had used friends/business colleagues as a source of assistance and advice as the female respondents (n = 10). This difference was found to be significant at the 0.05 level ($\chi^2 = 5.333$; df = 1). The finding that significantly fewer of the female business owners used friends/business colleagues probably reflects, to a certain extent, the fact that the female respondents in the sample were significantly younger than their male counterparts (chapter 3). Because they are likely to have worked for less time in the formal labour market than the male respondents, the female respondents are therefore less likely to have had the opportunity to develop an extensive network of business colleagues (Aldrich, 1989).

Second, despite the female respondents' lack of access to, or use of, friends/business colleagues as a source of assistance and advice, it appears that they make up for this by their use of family support, which is significantly higher than that of the male respondents ($\chi^2 = 6.050$; df = 1; 0.05 level of significance). Again it is speculated that the reason why more female respondents in the survey had received advice and assistance from family is because they are significantly younger than the male respondents. As suggested in chapter 4, the parents of younger business owners will also tend to be younger and are more likely to still be in employment. In addition, younger business owners are likely to be 'closer' to their parents (either living at home, and/or financially dependent on them). It is also the case that the younger the business owner, the more socially acceptable it is for them to be 'supported' and assisted by their family. They will therefore be in a better position to receive advice and assistance from their family than older business owners.

The impact of these findings on the financing of the women-owned businesses is not clear-cut, primarily because in chapter 4, finance from 'friends and family' was considered as one category and not individually. However, the finding that significantly more of the female respondents had used family members in their networks may go some way towards explaining why more of the female respondents were found to have used gifts and loans from family/friends than their male counterparts (chapter 4). However, there is no evidence to suggest that, because the female respondents lacked access to networks of friends and business colleagues, they lacked access to either internal or external sources of finance. Indeed, the female respondents were found to use a wider range of sources of finance, more external sources of finance, and significantly more bank finance than their male counterparts.

6.3.2 Formal sources

The formal sources of advice used by respondents included accountants, banks, public/semi-public agencies (TECs and enterprise agencies) and 'other' sources – independent financial advisors, suppliers, customers, solicitors, business consultants, and the Inland Revenue (Table 6.1). The three most important sources were found to be accountants, banks and public/semi-public agencies. In the remainder of this section, the use of each will be explored in turn.

Accountants

The most frequently used 'formal' source of advice was found to be that of accountants. Indeed, almost three-quarters of all respondents were found to have used the services of an accountant in the management of their businesses (Table 6.1). Similarly, Curran and Blackburn (1994) found that accountants were the most likely 'outsiders' to be used as sources of advice by business owners. The importance of the accountant as a provider of small business advice has also been highlighted in a study for the *Observer*, conducted by Barclays Commercial Services (*Observer*, 1994a), which found that for 71 per cent of respondents, the accountant was *the* main source of business advice outside of the company. Similarly, the Office World Quarterly Small Business Survey (undertaken by the Small Business Research Centre at Kingston University) found that, of those small businesses that had sought advice over the previous three months, the majority (45 per cent) had favoured the advice of an accountant (*The Times*, 1994b).

In the present survey, there was no significant difference between the number of female (n = 27) and male respondents (n = 31) who had used accountants for advice and assistance in the running of their businesses ($\chi^2 = 1.003$; df $= 1$). Differences exhibited between the male and female business owners in the financing of their businesses and in the banking relationship cannot therefore be explained by differences in the use of accountants.

The banks

In comparison to accountants, the banks were not found to be a frequently used source of assistance in the networks of respondents in the present survey. Only 24 per cent (n $= 19$) of the total sample of respondents had ever used the bank for advice (see chapter 5). Similarly, only 16 per cent of small businesses in the Barclays Commercial Services survey (discussed above) cited the bank as their main source of external advice (*Observer*, 1994a). However, Curran and Blackburn (1994) found the figure to be somewhat higher with just over a third of all business owners seeking help or advice from their bank manager 'beyond routine cash transactions' (p. 96).

In terms of male–female differences, it was found in chapter 5 that significantly more female business owners had used their banks for advice than their male counterparts. Again, this finding is contrary to expectations based on the literature which suggests that, because of discriminatory attitudes in the banking relationship, female business owners are less likely to approach their bank manager for advice (see chapter 2).

The fact that the women used their bank for a wider range of advice than their male counterparts has already been suggested as a possible reason why the female business owners had a better experience of the banking relationship than the male business owners (chapter 5). As suggested by Binks (1995), small business owners that take a more 'participative' approach to the banking relationship, which includes using the bank for advice, are found to have a more satisfactory banking relationship. The highly rated banking relationship may, in turn, explain why the female business owners used bank finance significantly more than their male counterparts (chapter 4).

The TECs and enterprise agencies

Since the early 1980s, there has been a great increase in the amount of government support for small businesses (Curran and Blackburn, 1994). Indeed, Curran and Blackburn (1994) quote evidence to suggest that between 1979 and 1985, £1 billion of government money was spent on small business assistance. However, in the present study, only

25 per cent (n = 20) of the total sample of respondents were found to have used public/semi-public business support agencies (Table 6.1). In all cases, advice and assistance was sought from either the local enterprise agency or the Training and Enterprise Council (TEC). None of the firms had used national level government assistance or advice (e.g. the Department of Trade and Industry). Similarly, Storey and Strange (1992) found that 26 per cent of small firms in Cleveland had sought advice from public sector agencies. However, although the overall use of public sector advice by the respondents was fairly low, it is probably higher than that of the general small business population as a whole because approximately half of the businesses in the sample were drawn from the South East Hampshire Enterprise Agencies Small Business Directory.[2]

Just over one in five respondents (n = 17) were found to have sought advice and training from their local enterprise agency.[3] Similarly, less than one in five businesses in the study by Curran and Blackburn (1991) had used their local enterprise agency. In addition to their use of enterprise agencies, 18 per cent (n = 14) of respondents had used their local TEC for business advice/training. The establishment of TECs in England during the early 1990s has been one of the major changes to have taken place in the provision of advisory support and training to small businesses (Bennett and McCoshan, 1993; Curran and Blackburn, 1994; Curran *et al.*, 1994). However, as the present survey and other research by Curran and Blackburn (1991), Woods *et al.* (1993) and Bennett (1995) reveals, in general TECs are failing to reach small firms, despite their local orientation. Indeed, according to research by Curran *et al.* (1994), the percentage of service sector businesses approaching local TECs for help or advice in 1994 was just 18.1 per cent.

As shown in Table 6.1, exactly the same number of male and female respondents were found to have used public/semi-public sector sources of advice and assistance. In addition, there were negligible differences between the male and female sample in terms of their use of enterprise agencies and TECs. There was no evidence to suggest that differences in the use of public/semi-public sources of advice and assistance might explain the differences between male and female business owners in terms of the financing of their businesses and the banking relationship.

6.3.3   Membership of industrial associations and business groups

Another important way in which business owners gain information, advice and assistance in the running of their businesses is through

Table 6.2 Membership of external associations or local business groups (% of total sample of respondents)

	Total	Female	Male	Sig X^2
Trade association/Professional body	21 (26)	11 (28)	10 (25)	No
Business group/club	17 (21)	11 (28)	6 (15)	No
Chamber of Commerce	15 (19)	8 (20)	7 (18)	No
Rotary/Round Table	4 (5)	0	4 (10)	—[b]
National small business association	4 (5)	3 (8)	1 (3)	—[b]
Total no. of respondents[a]	46 (58)	23 (58)	23 (58)	No

Notes: [a] Total number of respondents who were members of any organisation. May not equal total for column as respondents could mention more than one organisation; [b] it was not possible to test the statistical significance of these differences because, in order to perform a *chi*-square analysis, the *expected* number for each cell must not be less than 5 (Clegg, 1994)

their membership of external associations and local business groups. As indicated in Table 6.2, 58 per cent of the business owners interviewed belonged to one or more external groups or associations. Similarly, 57 per cent of small business owners in a survey by Curran and Blackburn (1994) were found to be members of external associations/groups. Overall, the respondents were most strongly affiliated with trade associations and professional bodies, 26 per cent of all respondents being a member of one or more. These tend to be national associations and membership is strongly associated with industrial sector (Curran and Blackburn, 1994). Some types of firm are legally obliged to belong to a professional body, for example financial services. Given the large number of professional service firms included in the survey, it is therefore not surprising to find over a quarter of respondents belonging to a trade association/professional body.

In addition, just over one-fifth of respondents were found to be members of one or more business groups/clubs. The most popular business group was found to be the Gosport and Fareham Small Business Club, of which 11 per cent of the total sample were members.[4] One of the respondents was found to be a co-founder of the Gosport and Fareham Small Business Club and he explained that the main aim of the group was to encourage inter-trading between its members, facilitated by the existence of a directory of its members. A further 4 per cent of respondents were members of other local small business clubs. In addition, 13 per cent of the female sample were found to be members of women's networks (The Breakfast Club, The Business and Professional Women's Association and Women 2000).

Just 20 per cent of respondents were members of a chamber of commerce. This is low compared to membership in Guildford, for example, where Curran and Blackburn (1994) found a 37.5 per cent membership rate among small business owners. However, it is recognised in the literature that there are often wide differences in the strength and resources of particular chambers (Bennett and McCoshan, 1993) and some are less energetically run and therefore attract fewer members than others. In the present survey, one respondent explained how the president of his particular chamber 'did not really put much time into attracting new members'.

The Rotary Club, another locally based institution, was also found to have a low membership – only 10 per cent of the male sample and none of the female sample were members. The latter is not surprising because, as pointed out in the introduction to the chapter, The Rotary Club is notorious for being male-dominated (Smeltzer and Fann, 1989). However, it is acknowledged that the low overall membership may also be influenced by geographical location, membership being stronger in certain towns/cities than others.

Finally, it was found that only 5 per cent of business owners were members of a national small business association, in this case the Federation of Independent Business. This compares quite closely with a membership rate of 9 per cent among small business owners in a study by Curran and Blackburn (1994).

As predicted, once structural differences between the male and female business owners had been held constant, there were no significant differences in the membership patterns of male and female business owners (Table 6.2). Since membership of most business groups and associations is sector-specific (Curran and Blackburn, 1994), it follows that differences in membership will be eliminated once sector is controlled for.

However, although based on very small numbers, there is evidence to suggest that female entrepreneurs in the survey were, or felt they were excluded from The Rotary Club, as none of the female respondents but 10 per cent of the male respondents were found to be members. This finding might also go some way towards explaining why significantly fewer of the female respondents in the survey had used friends/business colleagues in their networks. Membership of business groups such as The Rotary Club generally provide small business owners with the opportunity to socialise with a group of like-minded people, often other business people, with whom they can share information. Nevertheless, it does not explain why female business owners used more bank finance and had a more favourable experience of the banking relationship. In fact, according to Carter and Rosa (1995) one would expect female entrepreneurs with less access to traditional, male-dominated business clubs such as The Rotary Club to have a less satisfactory banking relationship and less access to bank finance. Indeed, they found that small business owners are more likely to be refused bank finance if they are not members of The Rotary Club or similar organisations. This is primarily due to the fact that bank managers are often part of these business networks themselves and use them to meet potential small business clients and to find out more about them as an aid to the financial decision-making process. The findings of this survey therefore challenge those of Carter and Rosa (1995) and suggest that membership of The Rotary Club may not be as important in raising finance or in the banking relationship as they have suggested.

6.4 CONCLUSION

This chapter has provided an insight into the networking behaviour of male and female small business owners. As speculated in section 6.1.5, there are many more similarities than differences between the male and female respondents in their use of external assistance and advice. Indeed, neither the female, nor the male business owners had an extensive network of contacts from whom they sought advice and assistance in the running of their businesses. The majority preferred to 'go it alone' and avoided turning to anyone else for help or advice. The profiles of male and female networks were also found to be quite similar, both being dominated by friends/business colleagues and accountants. In addition, they exhibited a similar membership of industrial associations and business groups.

Overall, there was no evidence to suggest that female business owners faced more problems in establishing networks than their male counterparts, as suggested in the literature (Hisrich and Brush, 1984; Turner, 1989; Reuber *et al.*, 1991; Carter and Cannon, 1992). Furthermore, there was no evidence that female entrepreneurs lack access to external business groups and organisations (Reskin and Hartmann, 1986). Although there were no female members of the male-dominated Rotary Club, many of the female business owners in this sample had joined and even formed their own women's networks. Only two female respondents had faced what they perceived to be gender-related problems in their networking activity. One of the female respondents complained about lack of consideration for women's child-care responsibilities in the scheduling of meetings by business organisations and another felt that the business adviser she had worked with was patronising towards women.

It is therefore likely that the differences in the networking behaviour of male and female business owners uncovered in previous networking research may have been a reflection of the methodology adopted rather than true gender-based differences. As with previous research into the financing of women-owned businesses, if a matched pairs method is not adopted, then it is likely that any differences between male- and female-owned businesses are the result of systematic structural differences between the general populations of male- and female-owned businesses, rather than gender-based differences.

Nevertheless, the survey did reveal some significant differences between the male and female business owners. First, the female respondents were found to have significantly larger networks than their male counterparts. Second, the female respondents had significantly fewer friends and business associates in their networks than the male respondents. Third, the female business owners were found to have used family members for advice significantly more than the male business owners. Fourth, in terms of formal advice sources, the female business owners were found to have used the bank more than their male counterparts (finding of chapter 5). It therefore appears that, while the male business owners were content to rely on one particular source of advice and assistance (friends/business colleagues), the female business owners had developed a much wider range of contacts, including their family and the banks. These findings therefore suggest that female entrepreneurs may be more likely than male entrepreneurs to perceive a large network of contacts to be valuable/important. Equally, they may suggest that female entrepreneurs are more aware of the wide range of sources advice available to small business owners. However, these suggestions need to be explored in more detail by future researchers.

The question is, what are the implications of these differences for the financing of women-owned businesses? In terms of the differences found between the male and female business owners in the financing of their businesses, it is likely that the finding that significantly more of the female business owners had used the bank for advice may have resulted in them experiencing a better overall banking relationship than their male counterparts (as discussed in chapter 5). The female respondents were also found to have a significantly wider range of contacts in their networks which may explain why they were also found to use a wider range of sources of finance, in particular more external sources of finance than their male counterparts. In addition, it also appears that, because significantly more of female business owners use family members in their networks, they may have greater access to family sources of finance than the male business owners. However, the fact that more of the female respondents had used family for advice and finance is more likely to be a reflection of their young age rather than any gender-related factor.

Nevertheless, it is noted that this study is based on a very small sample of business owners, concentrated in the service sector, over half of which were selected from the Enterprise Agency Directory. Therefore, the views of the business owners towards networking may not be representative of the population of small businesses as a whole. As indicated in chapters 4 and 5, it is also recognised that the respondents in the present study only included those that had successfully started and run a business. Future research is therefore needed to examine the relationship between networking behaviour and the financing of women-owned businesses from a wider range of sectors, and including both nascent female entrepreneurs and female entrepreneurs whose businesses have failed, using the matched pairs methodology.

7 Conclusions, implications and an agenda for future research

7.1 INTRODUCTION

The purpose of this concluding chapter is to summarise and discuss the findings of the book in the light of the main research questions which form the basis of the study. Suggestions are made regarding the ways in which the findings might be used to improve our theoretical understanding of the financing of women-owned businesses and how they might be used by female entrepreneurs, the banks and policy makers to improve the process of raising finance for female entrepreneurs. Finally, questions arising from this study are used to propose an agenda for future research.

7.1.1 Justification for research

Since the 1970s, there has been a rapid growth in the number of women starting their own businesses. Indeed, women-owned businesses currently account for approximately one-third of the total small business population. However, research suggests that many women face barriers in starting up and running their own businesses, the greatest of which is that of raising finance. The ability to raise finance is a critical factor in the formation and growth of small businesses; therefore the fact that women are found to face barriers in their access to finance has wide ranging implications and the identification and examination of these barriers is therefore a research priority.

In chapter 2 of the book, an in-depth review of the literature revealed that there is widespread anecdotal evidence that female business owners perceive themselves to be discriminated against in their access to business finance, particularly bank finance, because of their gender. This conclusion is supported by empirical evidence from research into the behaviour of financial organisations which suggests that banks may not treat female business owners in the same way as male business owners. However, chapter 2 also highlighted the fact that other research provides contradictory findings.

In an attempt to explain these contradictions, it was noted that one of the major problems with existing research is the lack of an appropriate theoretical framework. A re-interpretation of small firm finance theory from a gender perspective was therefore adopted as a valuable method by which to explore the problems faced by women in the financing of their businesses.

Another major reason for the contradictory nature of previous research findings has been the methodological weaknesses of existing studies. One of the most serious methodological shortcomings in existing research has been the frequent lack of a group of male business owners with whom to compare the experiences of female business owners. Even when male 'control' groups have been included, researchers have frequently failed to compare like with like (i.e. male- and female-owned businesses of the same sector, size, age etc.), even though it is widely acknowledged that the populations of male- and female-owned businesses differ on many structural characteristics and that structural characteristics are an important influence on the financing of small businesses. It has therefore been almost impossible to examine the extent to which sex of ownership is the explanatory variable in observed differences between men and women in the financing of their businesses and how far difficulties faced by women in the financing of their businesses are caused by gender discrimination or are merely a function of the characteristics of their businesses.

The technique used to overcome this problem was the 'matched pairs' approach. This allowed two samples of forty male- and female-owned businesses to be compared. Having identified the key matching criteria – factors which were most likely to distort the comparison (i.e. business age, employment size, sector and premises) – pairs of male- and female-owned businesses were selected across the two samples, matched on these key criteria. By holding the match criteria constant, it was possible to isolate the effect of gender and to attribute any statistically significant differences between the two samples to the owner-manager being a male or a female.

7.1.2 Summary of research findings

In chapter 2, five questions were posed which formed the basis of the research undertaken in this study. To summarise the findings of the study, each of these questions will be addressed in turn.

- How do women finance their businesses and does this differ from the way in which men finance their businesses?

Overall, the research indicates that female business owners start their businesses with very modest amounts of capital which they raise from a limited number of sources. Indeed, the amount most frequently used to start a business was between £1,000 and £4,999, and the sources of finance used were almost entirely 'internal', dominated by personal and family savings. Post-start-up, the most frequently used sources of finance were retained profits and bank overdrafts/loans. Apart from bank finance, the female respondents in this survey were found to use very few external sources finance, either at start-up or post-start-up.

There were more similarities than differences between the male and female business owners in the financing of their businesses. Indeed, there were no significant differences between the male and female respondents in the amount, number of sources, and type of finance used, both at start-up and post-start-up.

Nevertheless, there were two notable differences between the male and female respondents. First, in contrast to previous research that has found that female business owners borrow less frequently from the banks than their male counterparts (e.g. Hisrich, 1985), the present survey found that significantly more of the female business owners had used bank finance than the male business owners. It is suggested that the female business owners may be more reliant on bank finance because they have less access to personal savings (because they are younger than their male counterparts and therefore would have had less time to accumulate large savings, and because of the position of women in the labour market more generally which sees them concentrated in low-paid jobs). In addition, it was found that more of the male business owners had access to redundancy payments or early retirement settlements, which is likely to have reduced their need for additional finance from the banks.

The second difference was that the female respondents borrowed significantly smaller amounts of bank finance in the form of overdrafts than the male respondents, a finding which supports existing research (e.g. Brown and Segal, 1989). By way of an explanation, previous studies have found that female business owners are generally less inclined to take risks in their businesses than male business owners. They are therefore more likely to avoid debt finance from the banks (e.g. overdrafts) because it might mean them risking personal assets in the form of security/collateral. There was no evidence, however, to suggest that the female respondents had been restricted in their access to larger overdrafts.

• What problems do female entrepreneurs face in the financing of their businesses and how do these compare with the problems faced by male entrepreneurs?

Half the sample of female entrepreneurs were found to have faced problems relating to undercapitalisation. The majority had experienced cash-flow problems because of late payment and bad debts. However, only five of the female respondents had ever been refused finance, mainly because of insufficient turnover, collateral, and poor cash-flow. In total, just over 40 per cent of the female respondents were required to provide security/guarantees on bank overdrafts and almost 70 per cent on bank loans. Only six of the female respondents were required to provide spousal co-signatures on loans and overdrafts.

Contrary to what is suggested in the literature (e.g. Schwartz, 1976; Hisrich and O'Brien, 1982; Hisrich and Brush, 1983; 1984; 1985; 1987; Collerette and Aubry, 1990; Department of Industry, Technology and Commerce, 1991; Carter and Cannon, 1992), this study found no evidence to suggest that female business owners face more problems raising finance than their male counterparts. The female respondents were not found to suffer more from the problem of undercapitalisation. Exactly the same number of male and female respondents had been refused finance. In particular, there was no evidence to show that female entrepreneurs are more likely to be refused bank finance because they lack collateral (as suggested by Kaur and Hayden, 1993 and Carter and Rosa, 1995), and they were not required to provide the bank with security or guarantees more often than men (as suggested by Clutterbuck and Devine, 1987, Carter and Cannon, 1992, and Koper, 1993). In addition, the female business owners were not requested to provide spousal co-signatures on their bank borrowing more often than the male business owners (as suggested by Collerette and Aubry, 1990, Carter and Cannon, 1992, and Fabowale *et al.*, 1993). In only a very small number of instances were the problems faced by female entrepreneurs in the financing of their businesses blamed on 'perceived' discrimination by the banks.

• What kind of relationship do female business owners have with their banks? Is it different to the relationship male business owners have with their banks?

The female respondents in the study generally did not meet with their account manager at the bank on a frequent basis. Only 21 (52.5 per cent) of the female business owners saw their bank manager every 6 months or more frequently. Meanwhile, 22.5 per cent of the female business owners had never met with their bank manager or had not done so for over a year. However, in terms of the most important elements of the banking relationship, the female respondents rated the importance of the 'interpersonal' elements most highly ('bank manager is easy to talk to', 'bank manager makes me feel comfortable', 'bank manager treats me with respect'). In addition, the majority of female respondents were highly satisfied with the 'interpersonal' elements of the banking relationship. Nevertheless, the female respondents had faced a number of problems in the banking relationship. In total, 78 per cent of female respondents had faced problems in the banking relationship, primarily because of high charges, the unhelpful attitude of bank staff and the impersonal nature of the relationship.

However, here again, the results show that there were considerably more similarities than differences between the female and male business owners in their experiences of the banking relationship than would have been expected given the findings of previous research (e.g. Hisrich and Brush, 1984; Goffee and Scase, 1985; Carter and Cannon, 1992). Neither the female, nor the male business owners were in contact with their bank manager on a frequent basis. Both had faced similar types of problems when dealing with their banks and there was no evidence to suggest that the female business owners had to use 'straw men' in response to problems with the banking relationship (as found by Goffee and Scase, 1985 or Hertz, 1987).

Nevertheless, there were some noteworthy differences between the male and female small business owners. First, not only were the female business owners significantly more likely to take advice from their banks, but they also rated the importance of bank advice and the performance of their banks in the provision of advice significantly higher than the male business owners. By way of an explanation, many businesswomen are found in the literature to lack confidence and have a low self-assessment (chapter 2). The fact that more of the female respondents were prepared to take advice may reflect an underlying lack of confidence in their own abilities. However, it may also reflect the fact that male business owners perceive that they do not need to take advice. Indeed, it is generally accepted that businesswomen have less experience and fewer skills than businessmen, in particular, financial skills. Female business owners might therefore be more aware of their need to take external advice.

Second, the female respondents also rated the importance of the bank 'offering a wide range of services' and 'providing specialised small business bankers' significantly more highly than the male respondents. Given that the female respondents in the study were more willing to seek and take advice from the bank, it is therefore not surprising that they require specialised small business bankers in order to supply them with the necessary advice. The provision of a wide range of services may reflect the fact that the female respondents place more importance on convenience in the banking relationship than their male counterparts. Indeed, more of the female respondents were found to have chosen their bank because they already had their personal account there, suggesting a greater desire for convenience than the male respondents. Similarly, if their bank provides all the financial services that they might require, it saves the female business owners the inconvenience of looking elsewhere.

Third, the female respondents were significantly more satisfied with the overall banking relationship and the overall quality of service provided. On the ten separate performance indicators, the female respondents rated their bank's performance higher than the male respondents on every factor. Using the satisfaction index developed by Fabowale *et al.* (1993), the female respondents were found to be significantly more satisfied with their bank's provision of specialised small business bankers, helpful business advice and with the bank knowing their business. The suggestion made in chapter 4 is that, because female business owners are more 'participative' in the banking relationship (they use the bank for advice more than the male business owners), they have a better experience of it than their 'non-participative' male counterparts. However, it is also possible that the female respondents had lower expectations as to the quality of relationship they could expect. Therefore, when they did not experience any problems, they rated the relationship more highly than if they had gone in without any expectations.

Fourth, contrary to the body of existing research on the financing of women-owned businesses (e.g. Goffee and Scase, 1983; Hisrich and Brush, 1987; Carter and Cannon, 1992), the male respondents were found to have experienced significantly more problems in the banking relationship than the female respondents. This is an important finding as it contradicts the expectation that women usually face more problems in the banking relationship (see chapter 2). A likely explanation for this finding is the fact that the male respondents were found to have experienced a significantly higher level of staff turnover than the female respondents, a factor which is known for causing problems in the banking relationship (Wynant and Hatch, 1990). Another possible explanation is that, because the male respondents were less 'participa-

tive' in the banking relationship, they may have had a more problematic experience of the relationship (Binks, 1995).

- Is there any evidence to suggest women feel discriminated against in
  the banking relationship because of their gender?

Although the male business owners were found to have experienced
significantly more problems in the banking relationship, 20 per cent of
the female respondents but none of the male respondents felt that they
had been patronised or not taken seriously by their account managers
in the banking relationship because of their gender. As expected, the
results indicate that female respondents who had faced patronising or
sexist attitudes in the banking relationship rated the interpersonal
dimensions of the relationship significantly lower than those female
respondents who had not faced such attitudes. In particular, they were
less satisfied with the bank manager making them feel comfortable,
treating them with respect, and knowing them and their business.

- Do female entrepreneurs have a similar level of access to sources of
  advice and assistance in raising finance, compared with their male
  counterparts?

Networking is of utmost importance in the financing of small businesses for three main reasons. First, networks give entrepreneurs
access to vital resources, in particular finance. Second, they are also
an important way in which many small business owners compensate
for the fact that they lack the necessary financial skills to successfully
manage their business finances and to raise finance. Third, it has also
been argued that networking activity improves the small business–
banking relationship.

The findings of chapter 6 indicate that the female respondents have
significantly larger networks than their male counterparts. However,
as suggested in the networking literature (e.g. Aldrich, 1989), they have
significantly fewer informal sources of advice and assistance in their
networks, in particular friends and business associates, than the male
respondents. Nevertheless, the female business owners were found to
have used family members for advice significantly more than the male
business owners and, as outlined in chapter 5, they also used the bank
for advice significantly more than their male counterparts.

It therefore appears that, while the male business owners were
content to rely on one particular source of advice and assistance
(friends/business colleagues), the female business owners had developed a much wider range of contacts, including their family and the
banks. These findings therefore suggest that female entrepreneurs may

be more likely than male entrepreneurs to perceive a large network of contacts to be valuable/important. Equally, they may suggest that female entrepreneurs are more aware of the wide range of sources of advice available to small business owners. Although the male and female business owners in this study were found to be embedded in subtly different networks, there was no evidence to suggest that the female respondents faced more problems in establishing networks than the male respondents, as suggested in the literature (e.g. Hisrich and Brush, 1984; Turner, 1989; Reuber *et al.*, 1991; Carter and Cannon, 1992).

The fact that the female respondents were found to have a significantly wider range of contacts in their networks may explain why they were found to use a wider range of sources of finance, in particular more external sources of finance than their male counterparts. In addition, there also appears to be a relationship between the use of family members for advice and also for finance. Indeed, significantly more female business owners use family members in their networks and they also have greater access to family sources of finance than male business owners. Although female business owners had significantly fewer friends and business colleagues in their networks, it did not appear to have any significant implications for their access to business finance (chapter 4).

In summary therefore, the findings of the research indicate that, when matched on business age, size, sector and premises, there are more similarities than differences between male and female business owners in terms of the way in which they finance their businesses, in the banking relationship and in their networking behaviour. Moreover, there is little evidence to support the view that female business owners are discriminated against in the financing of their businesses and it appears that Buttner and Rosen (1989) are right in concluding that 'other things equal, bankers are not significantly influenced by sex stereotypes in funding decisions' (p. 259). Only a very small minority of female business owners felt that they had been treated in a patronising or sexist manner by individual bank managers.

7.2 RESEARCH IMPLICATIONS

7.2.1 Theoretical and methodological implications

As pointed out in chapter 2, the main problem with previous research on this issue has been the lack of a sound theoretical framework. In chapter 2 it was argued that, although traditional economic theory (agency theory) is a very valuable way in which to examine the financing of small firms generally, it fails to consider the role of gender. It is therefore impossible to use small firm finance theory to explain the gender-related differences found in existing literature on the financing of women-owned businesses. Indeed, it has been argued that even factors which appear to be non gender-specific (e.g. business sector, size or age) often have an important gender dimension (Jennings and Cohen, 1993). A theoretical approach was therefore required in which traditional economic thinking on small firm financing could be combined with current theories about female entrepreneurship (the integrated perspective), which recognise that female entrepreneurs have a different experience of business ownership than male entrepreneurs. By combining notions from both theoretical frameworks, a 'gendered' small firm finance theory was adopted.

The results of the research have highlighted the complexity of issues surrounding the financing of women-owned businesses and the fact that small firm financing cannot be examined in isolation of factors such as gender and social interaction. Therefore, the 'gendered' finance theory approach has proved to be a very useful lens through which to study the financing of women-owned businesses. The main implication of this finding is to suggest that future research into the financing of small businesses should also consider working with and refining a 'gendered' theoretical framework of study.

The research also has some important methodological implications. As highlighted in chapter 3, one of the main problems with existing research into the financing of women-owned businesses is the fact that it is far from clear as to whether differences between male and female business owners in the financing of their businesses are caused by gender-related factors or whether they are merely a function of systematic differences in the characteristics of male and female business owners and the types of businesses that they start. Therefore, in order to determine the extent to which women are discriminated against in the financing of their businesses, the present study faced the challenge of disentangling the effects of gender bias from other systematic structural differences between male-and female-owned businesses. In order to meet this challenge, the study adopted a matched pairs approach, allowing pairs of male-and female-owned businesses, matched on the key structural criteria, to be compared. By holding the match criteria constant in this way, significant differences between the two samples could be attributed more meaningfully to the role of gender.

The fact that this study found more similarities than differences between male and female business owners and that many of the significant differences found between them were contrary to what existing research had predicted (see section 7.1.2), once structural criteria had been held constant, therefore has important implications for the interpretation of previous research which failed to consider the role of structural factors, other than gender, in the financing of small businesses. This study has shown that Fabowale *et al.* (1993) are right to question studies which do not take into account the potentially confounding effects of other variables, which may or may not be related to gender. The findings also suggest that structural factors (e.g. business size, age, sector and type of premises) are more important in the financing of small businesses than gender. Indeed, once these are held constant, many gender-based differences disappear. The implication of this research for future studies is therefore to illustrate that meaningful comparisons between male-and female-owned businesses are not possible unless the role of factors, other than gender, are controlled for.

7.2.2 Implications for female business owners

The findings of this study have raised some important implications, not least for female business owners. One of the most significant is for the perceptions held by female entrepreneurs. The results of the survey suggest that the perception that banks are 'anti-women' and do not treat female business owners seriously is largely unfounded. There is therefore no need for female business owners to feel apprehensive about entering the banking relationship.

However, a very small minority of female business owners do face patronising treatment and this can result in a less satisfactory banking relationship. Therefore, female business owners should be aware of the fact that they might face sexist comments or that they might not be taken seriously in the banking relationship. However, where such 'sexist' treatment does occur, female business owners should also be aware that they can adopt strategies to address such scepticism, as demonstrated by the female business owners in the present study. The example set in this study by female entrepreneurs who had received sexist treatment by the banks is not to be put off but to persist with the relationship and to 'lay down the ground rules' as one female respondent put it. For example, one businesswoman felt that she was not being treated fairly and therefore confronted her bank manager in the following way,

> my general feeling was that he was not giving me the credibility that I deserved because I am a woman and so I confronted him and

asked if he actually believed in backing women at all...yes, I
suppose I became more forceful in my approach.

(survey respondent)

The advice for female entrepreneurs is therefore persistence and the
confidence to demand better treatment in the face of sexist behaviour.
Similarly, Clutterbuck and Devine (1987) argue that businesswomen
need to decide whether their gender is going to be a positive or a
negative aspect of their business (p. 140). It has been argued that 'only
when a person thinks something is a barrier that it becomes a barrier'
(Department of Alberta, 1990: p. 131). Many of the barriers faced by
female business owners in raising finance may therefore be solved by
more positive thinking. It is also argued that female entrepreneurs can
often dispel the sexist stereotypes held by many bank managers by
demonstrating a capacity to act independently and confidently (Buttner and Rosen, 1988a). Similarly, one of the female respondents in the
present survey pointed out,

> the key to getting what I wanted was I think in the determined way
> I went about getting it. So often women are in awe of bank
> managers and are too 'coy' about asking for what they want.
> Men stride in, put their plans on the table and look the bank
> manager in the eye.

(survey respondent)

When first choosing a bank, female business owners would be well
advised to 'shop around' if they are not completely satisfied with the
treatment received at one particular bank or branch (Godfrey, 1992).
In addition, new female business owners might consider seeking
advice from other businesswomen, friends or women's networks who
might be able to recommend the best bank or bank manager. In order
to avoid problems later on in the banking relationship, the general
advice given to all small business owners is equally applicable to
female business owners – they should be assertive, well prepared and
seek advice in those areas in which they have fewer skills or less
experience. Indeed, Berry *et al.* (1993) have argued that small business
owners who go into the banking relationship with a well-prepared
business plan, who are confident with their proposal, and who can
speak the bank's language are more likely to be offered the finance
they require and to have a more favourable experience of the banking
relationship.

Of course, if any business owner, regardless of sex, is not satisfied
with their banking relationship and are sure that they have done all

they can to fulfil their side of the relationship, they should exercise their right to change branches or banks. Although it may not be easy to change banks, the respondents in this survey have proved that it is possible.

7.2.3 Implications for the banks

The fact that 20 per cent of women in the sample felt that they had not been treated seriously in the banking relationship also raises some important implications for the banks. First, women-owned businesses are a significant and growing market segment (see chapter 1). They therefore represent an increasingly important source of new business for the banks. However, if the banks want to reap the benefits of a growing market, they cannot afford to be perceived to be 'women-unfriendly' by even a small number of women, especially as banks have already been the target of much unfavourable recent media attention with regard to their treatment of small businesses more generally (chapter 5). Many female business owners, as with small business owners more generally, are part of local business networks and tend to take the advice of business colleagues and friends very seriously. For instance, in this survey, the second most important factor influencing the choice of banks for female business owners was found to be personal recommendation (chapter 5). Even if the experiences of a female business owner are based on the attitude of just one manager at her particular branch, it can create a poor image of the bank as a whole and banks cannot afford to be singled out as being 'anti-female' on the local businesswomen's 'grapevine'.

Second, not only are women-owned businesses continuing to grow in numbers, but research indicates that they are proving to be better lending prospects than male-owned businesses. It has been reported that 'women plan and research their enterprises more thoroughly than their male counterparts and, as a result, tend to be more successful' (Thomas, 1991: p. 92; Carter and Cannon, 1992) and are also more likely to survive (*The Times*, 1992b). Indeed, White (1984) found women to be more successful than men at getting their businesses off the ground and to have clearer objectives from the start. Business-women are also found to be more realistic and pragmatic than busi-nessmen, more likely to achieve their first year financial forecasts and less inclined to overspend and over borrow (*The Times*, 1992a). In the eyes of one financial company, 'women are excellent risks, far safer than men' (*The Independent on Sunday*, 1993: p. 14) and have also been found to 'have a better track record of repayment overall than men' (*Sunday Times Magazine*, November 4, 1990: p. 6). In an environment of growing competition and because of the need to reduce lending risk (chapter 5), the ability of a bank to retain low-risk small business customers such as female entrepreneurs is therefore a competitive advantage.

Third, it is widely acknowledged that bank advice and other financial services are no longer peripheral to bank income generation. It is therefore highly significant that female entrepreneurs rate the importance of advice more highly than male entrepreneurs and use their banks for advice more than the men; not least because greater frequency of contact has the potential to 'unlock the door to selling many other [bank] services' (Bannock, 1994: p. 23). Indeed, the trust built up in a good banking relationship is known to help the bank sell more of its financial services to the small business (Howcroft and Bennett, 1993). In addition, women appear to be less averse than men to the idea of the bank providing a wider range of financial services. However, what this survey suggests is that the banks are not making full use of these opportunities to market their financial products and services to small women-owned businesses. Indeed, they are jeopardising important working relationships with many female entrepreneurs because of sexist attitudes and behaviour. The findings of this study show that those female business owners who had faced sexist treatment were significantly less satisfied with the interpersonal dimensions of the banking relationship and it is the interpersonal dimensions of the relationship, such as trust, which will be vital if the bank is to successfully sell the female business owner other financial products such as insurance or pensions (Howcroft and Bennett, 1993).

The question is, what should the banks be doing to address these problems? In 1989, the Equal Opportunities Commission produced a booklet call 'Women's Business Matters', which consisted of good practice guidelines for providers of training, advice and finance to women entrepreneurs. In particular, the booklet gave recommendations to banks about avoiding misunderstandings with their female clients (e.g. 'Don't appear to be patronising. Many women are expert in handling financial matters and are sensitive to your attitudes'). It may be that written guidelines are not explicit enough in explaining how 'not to appear patronising', for example. Many bank managers will be unaware as to how their words or body language might be interpreted by their female clients. It is argued, therefore, that there is a need for bank managers to undertake training in how to deal with and understand the needs of businesswomen as a specific customer group, in order to avoid those situations which leave some women feeling patronised or discriminated against. Many banks such as the National Westminster Bank have already recognised the need to respond to problems in the general small business–banking relationship and have taken part in courses such as those run by the Durham University Business School (DUBS), the purpose of which are to 'enable... managers to better understand what makes owner-managers tick, and therefore be in a better position to help them, rather than see them purely as a series of financial statistics' (*Networker*, 1994: p. 4).

However, according to the director of the training courses run by DUBS, Robert Sentance,[1] they do not cover issues of gender or what makes female owner-managers in particular 'tick'. This study therefore argues that there is a need for the female entrepreneur–banking relationship to be a prominent feature of such courses. Establishing contact with local women's business groups and networks would also be valuable in determining the needs of women in business, establishing how the banks could improve the banking relationship, and finding out how they are viewed by female entrepreneurs.

The banks are saddled, to some extent, by the stereotypical perception among many female business owners that all banks are 'anti-women'. While studies such as this go some way towards dispelling, or at least questioning the accuracy of some of these stereotypes, it may be that the banks need to take some positive steps themselves; for example, marketing themselves to the existing and potential female entrepreneur more effectively. A greater representation of women in promotional and informational material (e.g. through photographs or case studies of women in business) is one way forward, as long as it is not presented as a 'tokenism'. In Canada, for example, the banks started to realise that, because of the rapid increase in the number of female entrepreneurs, there was a growing pool of potential small business customers who were not being targeted. The Canadian Imperial Bank of Commerce therefore designed advertisements to appeal specifically to the female entrepreneur (Leitch, 1989). Similarly, in the UK, many of the high street banks have begun to feature female business owners in their promotional material; for example, in the Midland Bank television advertisement for their small business banking service. However, as found in research undertaken for Scottish Enterprise (1993b), 'where women are features, it tends to feature them doing stereotypical "girlie" things' (p. 3). Indeed, the Midland Bank advertisement features a female café owner. Promotional material could therefore be less stereotypical in its portrayal of business-women.

In addition, many women still see the banks as male-dominated organisations. As suggested by Koper (1989) and Hertz (1987), a greater representation of female small business bankers/advisors might convince many businesswomen that the banks are accessible to women and they are also likely to be able to empathise more easily with many of the particular challenges faced by female entrepreneurs.

7.2.4   For policy makers

Good small business–banking relations also have important implications for the economy. According to a study by the Forum of Private Business (1994), in order for small firms to fulfil their potential as the wealth and job creators of the UK economy, they need 'an efficient working relationship with their banks that is based on good communication and mutual trust' (p. 2). This applies equally to male-and female-owned small businesses.

It is therefore in the interests of the economy that policy makers should concentrate on removing the barriers to increased levels of female entrepreneurship, one of the greatest barriers being access to finance. However, one of the main reasons for undertaking the present study, as discussed in chapter 2, was that existing information on the financing of women-owned businesses is inadequate to assist public policy makers in dealing with the problem of finance, not least because it is unclear as to whether women face specific, gender-related problems in their access to sources of finance. In the light of research that claims it has found evidence for the existence of gender-related problems in the financing of women-owned businesses, it has been suggested that there should be specific schemes targeted at women seeking financial assistance to establish businesses (Carter and Cannon, 1992). For example, in the state of Victoria, Australia, the Victorian Women's Trust, initially set up using $1 million donated from the Victorian Government, not only offers grants to innovative business projects that enhance women's employment opportunities, but also provides loans to female entrepreneurs who are unable to raise finance elsewhere (LEDIS, 1990). Similarly, the Women's Economic Development Corporation (WEDCO) in Minnesota (USA), which grew out of a public education programme, administers loan funds which include The Seed Fund (offering loans of last resort to low-income businesswomen who lack a credit history) and The Growth Fund (investing in existing WEDCO clients' businesses that are expanding but which lack access to traditional venture capital) (LEDIS, 1989). Both of these programmes also offer support and encouragement, other than finance (e.g. networking opportunities, professional advice, seminars and business counsellors).

For the female respondents in this survey, however, it does not appear that there is a need for 'women-only' sources of finance. The survey results show that there are more similarities than differences between matched pairs of male and female business owners in terms of their access to traditional sources of business finance and that the female respondents were found to have used significantly more bank finance than their male counterparts. The policy-making role does not therefore appear to be one of 'facilitating' women's access to finance. Nevertheless, it is recognised that there is still a need for general financial assistance aimed at those businesses where the owners lack credit history or lack access to collateral, for example, and that women should have equal access to such assistance.

In addition, the present study offers no evidence to suggest that female business owners have a need or desire for 'women only' training, education or advice. Indeed, a small number of the female respondents were hostile towards the idea of single-sex provision of advice and networks (chapter 6). Nevertheless, some concern was shown that training and advice should be sensitive to the needs and constraints of women in business. For example, two of the female respondents felt that there was not enough consideration for women with young children in the scheduling of training courses at the enterprise agency, or chambers of commerce meetings. Indeed, both women had faced problems attending courses and meetings because they either clashed with the 'school run' or were late in the evening.

7.3 LIMITATIONS AND AN AGENDA FOR FUTURE RESEARCH

This study provides the first matched pairs analysis of the financing of women-owned businesses to be undertaken in the UK. Previous academic research and anecdotal studies in the field of female entrepreneurship have largely ignored the importance of comparing the experiences of male entrepreneurs in a way which controls for the systematic differences that occur between male- and female-owned businesses. In addition, the majority of previous studies have been undertaken without reference to an underlying theoretical framework (Brush 1992; Fischer *et al.*, 1993). While this book has gone some way to furthering our knowledge of the financing of women-owned businesses, addresses many of the theoretical and methodological weaknesses of previous studies, and reaches some important conclusions which are contrary to previous findings, the study has raised and identified a number of issues which would benefit from further study.

An important question raised in the research concerns the role of the bank manger's gender in the banking relationship. In this study, there were not enough examples of female bank managers to be able to make any such analyses. However, work by Palmer and Bejou (1994) on gender and the financial services industry has found that some aspects of relationship development between clients and financial advisors are significantly dependent on the gender of the 'buyer' and 'seller'. A valuable area of future research might therefore be to explore whether there are any fundamental differences between the experiences of male and female business owners in the banking relationship, depending on the sex of their bank managers; for example, does sexism in the banking relationship disappear when a female entrepreneur has a female bank manager? What is the effect of a female bank manager on the relationship with male and female small business owners?

It is widely acknowledged that business owners of both sexes frequently have domestic partners who contribute significantly to their business, even though they may not be legal co-owners or partners (Rosa and Hamilton, 1994). In the present study, it was found that domestic partners contribute to the financing of small businesses in terms of advice, financial and emotional support and in the banking relationship. However, the role of domestic partners in the banking relationship is an area in which future research could provide some more interesting insights. It has already been found, for example by Scase and Goffee (1980), that the wives of male business owners often jeopardise their own career prospects in order to help in their husband's business; meanwhile the husbands of female business owners offer limited, if any, help which is usually restricted to financial matters and only when the business succeeds (Goffee and Scase, 1985). Indeed, in the present survey, one of the female business owners explained how her husband 'had only decided to take a part in the business when it started to make a good profit. However, he then wanted to take over and pretend it was his business' (survey respondent).

Taking this research further, it would be valuable to explore the attitudes of domestic partners towards the financial commitments of being married to a small business owner and to compare the attitudes of male and female domestic partners.

It has been acknowledged throughout that this study only concentrated on those male and female business owners who had successfully launched a business enterprise. By only including the experiences of the 'successes', it fails to explore the financing attitudes and experiences of those women who take steps to initiate a business but fail to successfully start it ('nascent' female entrepreneurs – Reynolds and White, 1992) or of those women who start a business and later fail. It may be that more differences between the male and female samples would have been revealed had such groups been included. As pointed out by Bowman-Upton *et al.* (1987), 'if the sample had included unsuccessful entrepreneurs, they might have been more likely to attribute their failure to external factors, such as the lack of bank co-operation' (p. 7). Future research into the financing of women-owned businesses therefore needs to be complemented by research which examines 'nascent' and 'failed' female entrepreneurs, again in a matched pairs context.

A possible limitation of the study has been its focus on small firms which are almost entirely based in Hampshire, in particular South East Hampshire. As pointed out by Mason (1991), there is evidence to suggest that there are spatial variations in the need for, attitudes towards and availability of finance (Robson Rhodes, 1984; Harrison and Mason, 1986). For example, the economic conditions of a region influence the financial situation of the entrepreneur and often the lending policies of the banks in those regions (Bowman-Upton *et al.*, 1987; Buttner and Rosen, 1992). It has been argued that, even though UK banks are centralised, they nevertheless exhibit considerable variations in their lending practices because of the traditional independence[2] of the branch manager and the lag-time for policies to be implemented in the branches (Mason, 1991). In addition, clearing banks often rely on local enterprise agencies to help new firm founders to prepare their business plans; however, not all enterprise agencies are capable of the same level of support to new firm founders. Future research might therefore address these spatial issues in the financing of women-owned businesses and draw a sample of businesses from a much wider geographical scale than was possible in this study.

Similarly, attitudes to finance and financing behaviour change over time as well as space. However, this is a 'snapshot' study and is therefore not the best indicator of underlying small business characteristics, problems and attitudes because so many small business issues are dynamic. It is acknowledged that, because the businesses in the study were of varying ages, they will have raised finance at different times and therefore many of the findings may be historically specific. Indeed, there is little doubt that the bad press which banks were receiving at the time of interviewing (see chapter 5 for details) had an effect on the answers given. The interviews were also conducted during a period of recession, in the year following the peak in small firm failures (1993). It was therefore a time of great uncertainty for many of the respondents, especially financial uncertainty, and this will have undoubtedly been reflected in their use of external finance, particularly secured finance. In addition, as pointed out by Mason and Harrison (1994), the early 1990s witnessed a sharp drop in asset values which is likely to have impinged on the ability of the respondents to provide the bank with security on loans/overdrafts. The early 1990s were also characterised by an inherent conservatism on the part of the banks (see chapter 5) which is likely to have strained small business–banking relations further.

Another limitation of the study is the fact that the sample of businesses is drawn from a limited diversity of industries. The businesses in the study are primarily service-oriented. Even though it is the service sector in which most female-owned businesses are traditionally concentrated (Brush, 1992), by only looking at industries in which women are well represented, the study neglects the problems and attitudes of female entrepreneurs in 'non-traditional sectors' such as manufacturing. This has important implications for the findings as Hisrich and O'Brien (1982) have shown that female business owners in non-traditional sectors face more problems in the financing of their businesses and Buttner and Rosen (1988b) have found loan officers to be less supportive of 'non-traditional' female-owned businesses. It is therefore important for future research to include a wide range of women-owned businesses from all sectors of the economy.

It is also acknowledged that the matched pairs methodology has a number of flaws (as outlined in chapter 3), not least the fact that the pairs of female and male entrepreneurs were only matched on four structural criteria (business age, employment size, sector and premises). Other factors were not included because of the inherent limitations to the number and type of matching criteria that can be used. However, as discussed in chapter 3, the final choice of criteria was theoretically defensible. Nevertheless, future research might consider matching male and female business owners on alternative criteria such as the personal characteristics of the business owners.

In summary, the present study has dispelled many of the myths surrounding the financing of women-owned businesses, but has raised some important avenues for future research (e.g. the effect of bank manager gender on the banking relationship); and, as pointed out by Carter and Rosa (1995), the future for research into the financing of women-owned businesses lies in exploring the 'more specific and manageable sub-issues' such as those suggested in this chapter (p. 15).

Notes

1 THE GROWTH AND CHARACTERISTICS OF FEMALE ENTREPRENEURSHIP

1 Throughout the book, the terms entrepreneur, self-employed and small business owner are used interchangeably.
2 The Central Statistical Office (1995) *An Official Look at Ms Britain*, August.

2 THE FINANCING OF WOMEN-OWNED BUSINESSES

1 Included rates of loan turndown, rates of request for spousal co-signature, collateral required, amount of loan finance received relative to amount applied for, and interest rates charged.
2 The Theory Building Conference on Entrepreneurship (University of Illinois, October 1991).
3 It has consistently been argued that the financial needs of small businesses are not well served by existing financial institutions (Macmillan Committee, 1931; Bolton Report, 1971; Wilson Committee, 1979; Burns and Dewhurst, 1983; ACOST 1989) and that small firms face a 'finance gap' – defined as an 'unwillingness on the part of suppliers of finance to supply it (finance) on the terms and conditions required by small businesses' (Storey, 1984: p. 239).

3 RESEARCH INTO THE FINANCING OF WOMEN-OWNED BUSINESSES

1 In discussion at an ESRC Seminar Group: The Financing of Small Firms (New Developments in the Financing of New and Small Firms), University of Paisley, March, 1995.
2 A minimum of 35–40 matched pairs is suggested in order for the analysis to be meaningful (O'Farrell, 1993: personal communication).
3 Structured questions complemented by open-ended questions.
4 The South East Hampshire Enterprise Agencies Small Business Directory and The Market Location Directory (Hampshire).

5 A number of business owners were found to have business partners of the opposite sex when interviewed. However, these partners had joined the businesses since start-up and the principal owner-managers were still in charge of the finances and dealing with the bank.
6 Given the fact that the most important source of external finance for all small firms is the banks and that the banks are frequently accused of discriminating against women in business.
7 The potential problems of matching purely on structural characteristics and not on personal characteristics are acknowledged and discussed in chapter 7.
8 Business age (years) [up to 1 / 2–4 / 5–9 / 10–20 / 20 and over]; Business size (employees) [0 / 1 / 2–3 / 4–10 / 11–20 / 21 and over].
9 It also gave them too much time to think of reasons why they could not be interviewed!

4   RAISING FINANCE

1 Amounts shown are real adjusted figures based on the 1992 Retail Price Index.
2 N = 32; excludes any pairs whose difference was found to be 0.
3 As the categories in Table 4.2 are not independent (many respondents expressed multiple problems), Oppenheim's (1968) suggestion is followed (as suggested by Cromie, 1991), whereby each category of problem is tested against all the others put together in a series of 2×2 *chi*-squared tests.
4 In order to perform a *chi*-square analysis, the expected number for each cell must not be less than 5 (Clegg, 1994).
5 Excludes extreme outlier (£277,200).

5   THE CHARACTERISTICS OF THE BANKING RELATIONSHIP

1 Using a four-point scale (4 – 'very satisfied'; 3 – 'quite'; 2 – 'not very'; 1 – 'not at all satisfied').
2 Refers to the person at the bank with whom owner-managers would discuss their business affairs.
3 N = 19 excludes any pairs whose difference was found to be 0.
4 There were no statistical differences between the men and the women in terms of the actual problems faced (Table 5.11).
5 $X^2 = 0.392(\text{df} = 1)$ not a significant difference.
6 Significant at the 0.01 level (two-tailed test) using the Wilcoxon Test (T = 34; N = 16).
7 It is also acknowledged that the experience of discrimination depends largely on the type of woman involved. Some women are more aware than others of gender-related problems. Carter and Cannon (1992) found that, while women share similar experiences, some attribute them to gender discrimination while others do not.

6 THE ROLE OF NETWORKING IN THE FINANCING OF MALE AND FEMALE-OWNED BUSINESSES

1 External assistance was defined in this survey as 'help relating to either specific business problems or the general running of the business which was received from individuals or organisations outside the firm'.
2 Almost all businesses included in the directory are those which have had contact with their local enterprise agency.
3 This figure is almost certainly higher than that of the UK small business population as a whole reflecting the fact that approximately half of the businesses in the sample were drawn from the South East Hampshire Enterprise Agencies Small Business Directory.
4 Likely to reflect the fact that approximately half of the businesses in the sample were drawn from the South East Hampshire Enterprise Agencies Small Business Directory and that the Gosport and Fareham Small Business Club is run by the enterprise agency.

7 CONCLUSIONS, IMPLICATIONS AND AN AGENDA FOR FUTURE RESEARCH

1 Personal communication (September, 1995).
2 Less so in recent years.

Bibliography

Accountancy (1991) 'Fonds pour femmes', November, p. 60.

ACOST (Advisory Council on Science and Technology) (1990) *The Enterprise Challenge: Overcoming Barriers to Growth in Small Firms*, HMSO: London.

Aglietta, M. (1979) *A Theory of Capitalist Regulation*, New Left Books: London.

——(1982) 'World capitalism in the eighties', *New Left Review*, 136, pp. 25–36.

Aldrich, H. (1989) 'Networking among women entrepreneurs', in O. Hagan, C. Rivchun and D. Sexton (eds) *Women-Owned Businesses*, London: Praeger, pp. 103–132.

Aldrich, H. and Zimmer, C. (1986) 'Entrepreneurship through social networks', in D.L. Sexton and R.W. Smilor (eds) *The Art and Science of Entrepreneurship*, Ballinger: Cambridge, MA, pp. 3–23.

Aldrich, H., Reese, P. R., Dubini, P., Rosen, B. and Woodward, B. (1989) 'Women on the verge of a breakthrough?: networking among entrepreneurs in the US and Italy', *Entrepreneurship and Regional Development*, 1(4), pp. 339–356.

Allen, S. and Truman, C. (1988) 'Women's work and success in women's business', paper presented to the 11th National Small Firms Policy and Research Conference (Cardiff, 1988).

Allen, S. and Truman, C. (1991) 'Prospects for women's business and self-employment in the year 2000', in J. Curran and R.A. Blackburn (eds) *Paths of Enterprise: The Future of the Small Business*, Routledge: London, pp. 114–127.

Allen, S. and Truman, C. (1993a) 'Women and men entrepreneurs: life strategies, business strategies', in S. Allen and C. Truman (eds) *Women in Business: Perspectives on Women Entrepreneurs*, Routledge: London, pp. 1–13.

Allen, S. and Truman, C. (1993b) *Women in Business: Perspectives on Women Entrepreneurs*, Routledge: London.

Allen, S., Truman, C. and Wolkowitz, C. (1992) 'Home-based work: self-employment and small business', in P. Leighton and A. Felstead (eds) *The New Entrepreneurs: Self-employment and Small Business in Europe*, Kogan Page: London, pp. 123–141.

Ang, J. S. (1991) 'Small business uniqueness and the theory of financial management', *The Journal of Small Business Finance*, 1(1), pp. 1–13.

——(1992) 'On the theory of finance for privately held firms', *Journal of Small Business Finance*, 1(3), pp. 185–203.

Atkinson, J. (1984) *Flexibility, Uncertainty and Manpower Management*, Institute of Manpower Studies Report No. 89, University of Sussex, Brighton.

——(1985) 'Planning for an uncertain future', *Manpower, Policy and Practice*, 1, pp. 26–29.

Atlantic Canada Opportunities Agency (1992) *The State of Small Business and Entrepreneurship in Atlantic Canada – 1992*, Atlantic Canada Opportunities Agency: Moncton, New Brunswick.

Bacon, D. C. (1989) 'Look who's working at home', *Nation's Business*, October, pp. 20–31.

Bank of England (1994) *Finance for Small Firms*, note by the Bank of England, January.

——(1995) *Finance for Small Firms: A Second Report*.

Bannock, G. (1993) *Small Businesses and Their Banks: Executive Summary*, January.

——(1994) *The Future of Small Business Banking*, a report by Graham Bannock and Partners Ltd.

Barclays Bank (1992) *Starting Up – A Barclays Report on Britain's Small Business Men and Women*, Paragon Communications: London.

Barnea, A., Haugen, R. and Senbet, L. (1981) 'Market imperfections, agency problems and capital structure: a review', *Financial Management*, Summer, pp. 7–22.

Barrett, M. (1995) 'Feminist perspectives on learning for entrepreneurship: the view from small business', paper presented at the 1995 Babson College Kauffman Foundation Entrepreneurship Research Conference, London.

Barton, S. L. and Matthews, C. H. (1989) 'Small firm financing: implications from a strategic management perspective', *Journal of Small Business Management*, 27(1), pp. 1–7.

Batchelor, C. (1987) 'Women take charge', *Financial Times*.

——(1993) 'From lender to investor', *Financial Times*, 23 March, p. 15.

Belcourt, M. (1991) 'From the frying pan into the fire: exploring entrepreneurship as a solution to the glass ceiling', *Journal of Small Business and Entrepreneurship*, 8(3), pp. 49–55.

Belcourt, M., Burke, R. J. and Lee-Gosselin, H. (1991) *The Glass Box: Women Business Owners in Canada*, background paper, Canadian Advisory Council on the Status of Women, Ontario, Ottawa, February.

Bellu, R. R. (1993) 'Task role motivation and attributional style as predictors of entrepreneurial performance: female sample findings', *Entrepreneurship and Regional Development*, 5(4), pp. 331–344.

Bennett, J. (1995) 'The re-focusing of small business services in enterprise agencies: the influence of TECs and LECs', *International Small Business Journal*, 13(4), pp. 35–55.

Bennett, R. J. and McCoshan, A. (1993) *Enterprise and Human Resource Development: Local Capacity Building*, Paul Chapman: London.

Berry, A., Faulkner, S., Hughes, M. and Jarvis, R. (1993) *Bank Lending: Beyond the Theory*, Chapman and Hall: London.

Berry, A., Jarvis, R., Lipman, H. and Macallan, H. (1990) *Leasing and the Smaller Firm*, Research Paper No. 3, the Chartered Association of Certified Accountants.

Bhide, A. (1992) 'Bootstrap finance: the art of start-ups', *Harvard Business Review*, 70(6), pp. 109–117.

Binks, M. (1991) 'Banks and the provision of finance to small businesses', in J. Stanworth and C. Gray (eds) *Bolton 20 Years On: The Small Firm in the 1990s*, Paul Chapman: London, pp. 50–75.

——(1993) *The Financing of Small and Medium Sized Enterprises in the UK: 1993*, a summary report on the findings of a CBI discussion group, February.

——(1995) 'Changing banks for UK SMEs', paper presented at the ESRC Seminar Group – Banks and Small Firms: Developing Best Practice, Stirling, June.

Binks, M. R. and Vale, P. A. (1990) *Entrepreneurship and Economic Change*, McGraw-Hill: London.

Binks, M. R., Ennew, C. T. and Reed, G. V. (1988) 'The survey by the Forum of Private Businesses on banks and small firms', in G. Bannock and E. V. Morgan (eds) *Banks and Small Businesses: A Two Nation Perspective*, Forum of Private Businesses/National Federation of Small Business.

Binks, M. R., Ennew, C. T. and Reed, G. V. (1992) *Small Businesses and Their Banks: An International Perspective*, National Westminster Bank.

Birley, S. (1985) 'The role of networks in the entrepreneurial process', *Journal of Business Venturing*, 1, pp. 107–117.

——(1989) 'Female entrepreneurs: are they really any different?', *Journal of Small Business Management*, 27(1), pp. 32–37.

Birley, S., Moss, C. and Saunders, P. (1986) 'The differences between small firms started by male and female entrepreneurs who attended small business courses', in R. Ronstadt, J. A. Hornaday, R. Peterson and K.H. Vesper (eds) *Frontiers of Entrepreneurship Research*, Babson College: Wellesley, MA, pp. 211–222.

Blackburn, R. A., Curran, J. and Jarvis, R. (1992) 'Small firms and local networks: some theoretical and conceptual explorations', in M. Robertson, E. Chell and C. Mason (eds) *Towards The 21st Century: The Challenge For Small Businesses*, Nadamal Books: Macclesfield, Cheshire, pp. 105–122.

Bolton Report (1971) *Report of the Committee of Inquiry on Small Firms*, Cmnd 4811, HMSO: London.

Bowlin, O.D. (1984) 'Lease financing: an attractive method of financing for small firms', in P. M. Horvitz and R.R Pettit (eds) *Small Business Finance*, JAI Press: Greenwich, Connecticut, pp. 155–62.

Bowman-Upton, N., Carsrud, A. L. and Olm, K. W. (1987) 'New venture funding for the female entrepreneur: a preliminary analysis', in N. C. Churchill, J. A. Hornaday, B. A. Kirchhoff, O. J. Krasner and K.H. Vesper (eds) *Frontiers of Entrepreneurship Research*, Babson College: Wellesley, MA, pp. 200–201

Bradford, J. (1993) 'Banks and small firms: an insight', *National Westminster Bank Quarterly Review*, May, pp. 13–16.

Brophy, D. J. (1989) 'Financing women-owned entrepreneurial firms', in O. Hagan, C. Rivchun and D. Sexton (eds) *Women-Owned Businesses*, Praeger: London, pp. 55–75.

Brown, S. A. and Segal, P. (1989) 'Female entrepreneurs in profile', *Canadian Banker*, 96(4), pp. 32–34.

Brush, C. (1990) 'Women and enterprise creation, in OECD (Organisation for Economic Co-operation and Development)', *Local Initiatives for Job Creation: Enterprising Women*, HMSO: London, pp. 37–55.

——(1992) 'Research on women business owners: past trends, a new perspective and future directions', *Entrepreneurship, Theory and Practice*, 16(4), pp. 5–30.

Brush, C. G. and Hisrich, R. D. (1988) 'Women entrepreneurs: strategic origins impact on growth', in B. A. Kirchhoff, W. A. Long, W. E. McMullan, K. H. Vesper and W.E. Wetzel Jr (eds) *Frontiers of Entrepreneurship Research*, Babson College: Wellesley, MA, pp. 612–625.

Brush, C. G., Rajin, D. P. and Francisco, I. (1995) 'Participation patterns of women in franchising: the moderating effects of size', paper presented at the 1995 Babson College Kauffman Foundation Entrepreneurship Research Conference, London.

Burns, P. and Dewhurst, J. (1983) *Small Business: Finance and Control*, Macmillan: London.

Buttner, E. H. and Rosen, B. (1988a) 'Bank loan officer's perceptions of the characteristics of men, women, and successful entrepreneurs', *Journal of Business Venturing*, 3, pp. 249–258.

——(1988b) 'The influence of entrepreneur's gender and type of business on decisions to provide venture capital', *Proceedings*, Southern Management Association, Atlanta.

——(1989) 'Funding new business ventures: are decision makers biased against women entrepreneurs', *Journal of Business Venturing*, 4, pp. 249–261.

Buttner, E. H. and Rosen, B. (1992) 'Rejection in the loan application process: male and female entrepreneurs' perceptions and subsequent intentions', *Journal of Small Business Management*, 30(1), pp. 58–65.

BVCA (British Venture Capital Association) (1993) *Report on Investment Activity 1993*, BVCA: London.

Cachon, J. (1989) Laurentian University, personal correspondence, September.

Campbell, K. (1991) 'Women and their business partners: some research issues', *Journal of Small Business and Entrepreneurship*, 8(2), pp. 39–50.

Caplan, P. (1978) (ed.) *Women United, Women Divided: Cross-Cultural Perspectives on Female Solidarity*, Fontana: London.

Carland, J. C. and Carland, J. W. (1991) 'An empirical investigation into the distinctions between male and female entrepreneurs and managers', *International Small Business Journal*, 9(3), pp. 62–72.

Carswell, M. (1990) 'Small firm networking and business performance', paper presented to the 13th UK Small Firms Policy and Research Conference, Harrogate, November.

Carter, S. (1993) 'Female business ownership: current research and possibilities for the future', in S. Allen and C. Truman (eds) *Women in Business: Perspectives on Women Entrepreneurs*, Routledge: London, pp. 148–160.

Carter, S. and Cannon, T. (1988) *Female Entrepreneurs: A Study of Female Business Owners; Their Motivations, Experiences and Strategies for Success.* Department of Employment, Research Paper No. 65, HMSO: London.

——(1992) *Women as Entrepreneurs: A Study of Female Business Owners, Their Motivations, Experiences and Strategies for Success*, Academic Press: London.

Carter, S. and Rosa, P. (1995) 'The financing of male and female owned businesses', paper presented to the ESRC seminar on New Developments in the Finance of New and Small Firms, University of Paisley, Craigie Campus, Ayr (March).

Carty, P. (1994) 'The economics of expansion', *Accountancy*, March, pp. 42–44.

CBI (Confederation of British Industry) (1994) *Finance provision for small firms*, in association with Cleveland County Council and the University of Teesside.

Central Statistical Office (1995) *An Official Look at Ms Britain*, August.

Chaganti, R. (1986) 'Management in women-owned enterprises', *Journal of Small Business Management*, October, pp. 18–29.

Chapman, J. (1987) *Women Working it Out*, Manpower Services Commission: Sheffield.

Chapman, J. R. (1976) (ed.) *Economic Independence for Women*, Beverly Hills: Sage.

—— (1976) 'Sex discrimination in credit: the backlash of economic dependency', in J. R. Chapman (ed.) *Economic Independence for Women*, Beverly Hills: Sage, pp. 263–281.

Charbonneau, F. J. (1981) 'The woman entrepreneur', *American Demographics*, 3(6), pp. 21–23.

Chaston, I. (1993) 'Delivering customer satisfaction within the SME client–banker relationship', *The Service Industries Journal*, 13(1), pp. 98–111.

—— (1994) 'Rebuilding small business confidence by identifying and closing service gaps in the bank/SME relationship', *International Small Business Journal*, 13(1), pp. 54–62.

Chrystal, K. A. (1992) 'Don't shoot the messenger: do banks deserve the recent adverse publicity?', *National Westminster Review*, May, pp. 44–54.

Churchill, N. C. and Lewis, V. L. (1983) 'The five stages of small business growth', *Harvard Business Review*, 61(3), May–June, pp. 30–50.

Clark, T. A. and James, F. J. (1992) 'Women-owned businesses: dimensions and policy issues', *Economic Development Quarterly*, 6(1), pp. 25–40.

Clegg, F. (1994) *Simple Statistics: A Course Book for the Social Sciences*, Cambridge University Press: Cambridge.

Cleveland, D. (1993) 'New factor drives business growth', *Sunday Times*, 29 August, p. 3.8.

Clutterbuck, D. and Devine, M. (1987) (eds) *Businesswoman: Present and Future*, Macmillan: London.

Clutterbuck, D. and Devine, M. (1987) 'Is entrepreneurship the way ahead for women?', in D. Clutterbuck and M. Devine (eds), *Businesswoman: Present and Future*, Macmillan: London, pp. 130–141.

Collerette, P. and Aubry, P. (1990) 'Socio-economic evolution of women business owners in Quebec (1987)', *Journal of Business Ethics*, 9, pp. 417–422.

Collinson, D. (1987) 'Banking on women: selection practices in the finance sector', *Personnel Review*, 16(5), pp. 12–20.

Cooke, P. (1992) 'Computing and communications in the U.K. and France: innovation, regulation and spatial dynamics – an introduction', in P. Cooke, F. Moulaert, E. Swyngedouw, O. Weinstein and P. Wells (eds) *Towards Global Localization*, UCL Press: London, pp. 1–18.

Cooper, A., Dunkelberg, W. C. and Furuta, S. (1985) 'Incubator organization background and founding characteristics', in J. A. Hornaday, E. B. Schils,

J. A. Timmons and K. H. Vesper (eds) *Frontiers of Entrepreneurship Research*, Babson College: Wellesley, MA, pp. 61–79.

Cosh, A. and Hughes, A. (1994) 'Size, financial structure and profitability: UK companies in the 1980s', in A. Hughes and D. J. Storey (eds) *Finance and the Small Firm*, Routledge: London, pp. 18–63.

Cosmopolitan Magazine (1995), July.

Cressy, R. (1992) 'Overdraft lending and business starts: an empirical investigation on UK data', in F. Chittenden, M. Robertson and D. Watkins (eds) *Small Firms, Recession and Recovery*, Paul Chapman Publishing: London, pp. 188–201.

Cromie, S. (1987a) 'Motivations of aspiring male and female entrepreneurs', *Journal of Occupational Behaviour*, 8, pp. 251–261.

——(1987b) 'Similarities and differences between women and men who choose business proprietorship', *International Small Business Journal*, 5(3), pp. 43–60.

——(1991) 'The problems experienced by young firms', *International Small Business Journal*, 9(3), pp. 43–61.

Cromie, S. and Birley, S. (1992) 'Networking by female business owners in Northern Ireland', *Journal of Business Venturing*, 7(3), pp. 237–251.

Cromie, S. and Hayes, J. (1988) 'Towards a typology of female entrepreneurs', *The Sociological Review*, 36(1), pp. 87–113.

Cromie, S., Birley, S. and Callaghan, I. (1993) 'Community brokers: their role in the formation and development of business ventures', *Entrepreneurship and Regional Development*, 5, pp. 247–264.

Crompton, R. (1989) 'Women in banking: continuity', *Employment and Society*, 3(2), pp. 141–156.

Cuba, R., DeCenzo, D. and Anish, A. (1983) 'Management practices of successful female business owners', *American Journal of Small Business*, 8(2), pp. 40–46.

Curran, J. (1986) *Bolton Fifteen Years On: A Review and Analysis of Small Business Research in Britain, 1971–1986*, Small Business Research Trust.

Curran, J. and Blackburn R. A. (1991) (eds) *Paths of Enterprise: The Future of the Small Business*, Routledge: London.

Curran, J. and Blackburn R. (1994) *Small Firms and Local Economic Networks: The Death of the Local Economy?*, Paul Chapman: London.

Curran, J. and Burrows, R. (1988) *Enterprise Britain: A National Profile of Small Business Owners and the Self-Employed*, Small Business Research Trust: London.

Curran, J. and Roberts, L. (1989) 'Why single-minded operators reap rewarding benefits', The *Guardian*, 28 March.

Curran, J., Blackburn, R. A. and Klett, M. (1994) *Small Firms in Services – the 1994 Survey*, Small Business Research Centre, Kingston University, May.

Curran, J., Blackburn, R. A. and Woods, A. (1991) 'Profiles of the small enterprise in the service sector', ESRC Centre for Research on Small Service Sector Enterprises, Kingston Polytechnic, Surrey.

Curran, J., Burrows, R. and Evandrou, M. (1987) *Small Business Owners and the Self-employed in Britain: An Analysis of General Household Survey Data*, Small Business Research Trust: London.

Dalgleish, M. (1993) 'An evaluation of the Prince's Youth Business Trust', *Employment Gazette*, January, pp. 661–666.

208   Bibliography

Daly, M. (1990) 'The 1980s – a decade of growth in enterprise: data on VAT registrations and deregistrations', *Employment Gazette*, November, pp. 553–565.

——(1991) 'Registrations and deregistrations in 1990', *Employment Gazette*, November, pp. 579–588.

Davidson, M. J. and Cooper, C. L. (1992) *Shattering the Glass Ceiling*, Paul Chapman Publishing: London.

Davies, L. G. and Gibbs, A. A. (1991) (eds), *Recent Research in Entrepreneurship*, Avebury: Aldershot.

Deakins, D. and Hussain, G. (1991) 'Risk assessment by bank managers: a report on the importance of different criteria used in making a lending decision by bank managers and equivalent staff who have responsibility for lending to small businesses', Birmingham Polytechnic Business School, mimeo.

Deakins, D. and Hussain, G. (1992) 'Overcoming the adverse selection problem', paper presented at the 15th UK Small Firms Conference, Southampton.

Department of Alberta Economic Development and Trade (1990) *A Study of Barriers Faced by Albertan Women in Business,* Department of Alberta Economic Development and Trade.

Department of Employment (1991) *Small Firms in Britain 1991*, HMSO: London.

Department of Industry, Technology and Commerce (1991) *First Annual Report: Small Business in Australia*, The Australian Government Publishing Service.

Devine, M. and Clutterbuck, D. (1985) 'The rise of the entrepreneuse', *Management Today*, January, pp. 63–107.

Dickson, T. (1983) 'Why companies go bust', *Financial Times*, 8 March.

Dolinsky, A. L., Caputo, R. K., Pasumarty, K. and Quazi, H. (1993) 'The effects of education on business ownership: a longitudinal study of women', *Entrepreneurship: Theory and Practice*, Fall, pp. 43–53.

Donckels, R. and Lambrecht, J. (1995) 'Networks and small business growth: an explanatory model', *Small Business Economics*, 7, pp. 273–289.

Drucker, P. F. (1985) *Innovation and Entrepreneurship*, Heinemann: London.

DTI (The Department for Enterprise) (1991) *Constraints on the Growth of Small Firms*, a report of a survey of financial institutions and other organisations by Cousins Stephens Associates, HMSO: London.

——(1995) *Small Firms in Britain Report 1995*, HMSO: London.

Dubini, P. and Aldrich, H. (1991) 'Personal and extended networks are central to the entrepreneurial process', *Journal of Business Venturing*, 6, pp. 305–313.

Eagly, A. M. and Carli, L. L. (1981) 'Sex of researchers and sex-typed communications as determinants of sex differences in influenceability: a meta-analysis of social influence studies', *Psychological Bulletin*, 90, pp. 1–20.

Easterday, L., Papademas, D., Schorr, L. and Valentine, C. (1977) 'The making of a female researcher: role problems in field work', *Urban Life*, 6(3), pp. 333–348.

Eichler, M. (1988) *Non-Sexist Research Methods: A Practical Guide*, Allen and Unwin: London.

Employment Gazette (1992) 'Women and the labour market: results from the 1991 labour force survey', September, pp. 433–459.

——(1993) 'Labour Force Survey Help-Line: women in employment', October, p. LFS2.

——(1995) 'Labour Force Survey Help-Line', p. LFS33.

Ennew, C. and Binks, M. B. (1993) 'Financing entrepreneurship in recession: does the banking relationship constrain performance?', paper presented at the 13th Babson Entrepreneurship Research Conference, University of Houston, Texas.

Entrepreneurial Woman (1993) 'Helping hands', 1, p. 11

Equal Opportunities Commission (1988) *Women and Men in Britain: A Research Profile*, HMSO: London.

——(1989) *Women and Men in Britain, 1989*, HMSO: London.

Evans, D. S. (1987) 'The relationship between firm growth, size and age', *Journal of Industrial Economics*, 35, pp. 567–581.

Fabowale, L., Orser, B., Riding, A. and Swift, C. (1993) 'Gender, structural factors, and credit terms between Canadian small businesses and financial institutions', Carleton University.

Fandt, P. M. and Stevens, G. E. (1991) 'Evaluation bias in the business classroom: evidence relating to the effects of previous experiences', *The Journal of Psychology*, 125(4), pp. 469–477.

Fausnaugh, C. J. and Hofer, C. W. (1993) 'Cognitive mapping as a research technique for entrepreneurship research: an exploratory study', paper presented at the International Council for Small Business 38th World Conference, Las Vegas, Nevada, June.

Fay, M. and Williams, L. (1991) 'Sex of applicant and the availability of business "start-up" finance', *Australian Journal of Management*, 16(1), pp. 65–72.

Fay, M. and Williams, L. (1993) 'Gender bias and the availability of business loans', *Journal of Business Venturing*, 8, pp. 363–376.

Fertuck, L. (1982) 'Survey of small business lending practices', *Journal of Small Business Management*, October, pp. 32–41.

Financial Times (1994) 'Banking gloom for small businesses', 10 May, p. 12.

Fischer, C. S. and Oliker, S. J. (1983) 'A research note on friendship, gender, and the life cycle', *Social Forces*, 62, pp. 124–133.

Fischer, E. M., Reuber, A. R. and Dyke, L. S. (1993) 'A theoretical overview and extension of research on sex, gender and entrepreneurship', *Journal of Business Venturing*, 8, pp. 151–168.

Fletcher, M. (1995) 'Decision making by Scottish bank managers', *International Journal of Entrepreneurial Behaviour and Research*, 1(2), pp. 37–53.

Fogarty, M. P. (1972) 'Women at work: the small child gap and other problems', *Personnel Management*, February, pp. 18–22.

Forth, E. (1992) 'Bridging the capital gap for small businesses', *Venture Capital Report*, March.

Forum of Private Business (1994), *Small Businesses and Their Banks 1994 – Report Two*, Executive Summary, November.

Fothergill, S. and Gudgin, G. (1982) *Unequal Growth: Urban and Regional Employment Change in the UK*, Heinemann: London.

Gapper, J. (1993) 'Lessons of the 80s spark policy reviews', *Financial Times*, 27 February, p. 5.

George, E. A. J. (1994) 'The financing of small firms', speech given by the Governor of the Bank of England, 17 June, Glasgow.

Gertler, M. S. (1992) 'Flexibility revisited: districts, nation-states, and the forces of production', *Transactions of the Institute of British Geographers*, 17, pp. 259–278.

Gibb, A. A. (1992) 'Can academe achieve quality in small firms policy research?', *Entrepreneurship and Regional Development*, 4, pp. 127–144.

—— (1993) 'Key factors in the design of policy support for the small and medium enterprise (SME) development process: an overview', *Entrepreneurship and Regional Development*, 5(1), pp. 1–24.

Gilligan, C. (1982) *In a Different Voice,* Cambridge, MA: Harvard University Press.

Godfrey, J. (1992) *Our Wildest Dreams: Women Entrepreneurs Making Money, Having Fun, Doing Good*, Harper Collins: New York.

Goffee, R. and Scase, R. (1983) 'Business ownership and women's subordination: a preliminary study of female proprietors', *Sociological Review*, 31, pp. 625–648.

—— (1985) *Women in Charge: The Experiences of Female Entrepreneurs*, George Allen and Unwin: London.

Goldberg, P. (1968) 'Are women prejudiced against women?', *Transaction*, 6, pp. 258–264.

Goss, D. (1991) *Small Business and Society*. Routledge: London.

Gould, S. and Parzen, J. (1990) 'Conclusions, recommendations and a framework for action', in OECD (Organisation for Economic Co-operation and Development) *Local Initiatives for Job Creation: Enterprising Women*, HMSO: London, pp. 85–99.

Gregg, G. (1985) 'Woman entrepreneurs: the second generation', *Across the Board*, 22(1), pp. 10–18.

Guardian, the (1991a) 'Signpost', 11 November, p. 16.

—— (1991b) 'UK firms lag on paying bills', 16 December, p. 14.

—— (1991c) 'Codes of conduct little comfort while small firms are at the mercy of banks', 16 September, p. 12.

—— (1991d) 'Tin bath and spade days are numbered', 30 September, p. 12.

—— (1991e) 'Signpost', 11 November, p. 16.

—— (1991f) 'Big four's coded messages "need unscrambling"', 16 December, p. 14.

—— (1992a) 'More women crack the "glass ceiling"', 13 July, p. 14.

—— (1992b) 'Bank rates rancour obscures deeper problems in firms', 23 November, p. 16.

—— (1993a) 'Signpost', 10 May, p. 10.

—— (1993b) 'TECs "fail to meet the needs of their local small firms"', 19 July, p. 12.

—— (1994) 'A bigger factor is funding', 21 February, p. 12.

Gumpert, D. E. (1985) 'Wanted: women entrepreneurs for high-tech opportunities', *Working Women*, December, pp. 37–39.

Gurney, J. N. (1990) 'Female researchers in male-dominated settings: implications for short-term versus long-term research', in Shaffir, W. B. and Stebbins, R. A. (eds) *Experiencing Fieldwork: An Inside View of Qualitative Research*, Sage: London.

Hagan, O., Rivchun, C. and Sexton, D. (eds) (1989) *Women-Owned Businesses*, Praeger: New York.

Hall, J. and Hofer, C. W. (1993) 'Venture capitalists' decision criteria in new venture evaluation', *Journal of Business Venturing*, 8, pp. 25–42.

Halpern, M. and Szurek, J. (1989) *Business Creation by Women: Motivations, Situations and Perspectives*, Final Report of a Study for the Commission of the European Communities Equal Opportunities Office.

Hamilton, D. (1993) ' "Ecological" basis for the analysis of gender differences in the predisposition to self-employment', in H. Klandt (ed.) *Entrepreneurship and Business Development*, Avebury: Aldershot, pp. 199–210.

Hamilton, D., Rosa, P. and Carter, S. (unpublished) 'The impact of gender on the management of small businesses: some fundamental problems', Scottish Enterprise Foundation, Stirling.

Hand, J. H., Lloyd, W. P. and Rogow, R. B. (1982) 'Agency relationships in the close corporation', *Financial Management*, 11(1), pp. 25–30.

Harris, D. (1994) 'Family firms can be a woman's world', *The Times*, 13 September, p. 32.

Harrison, R. T. and Mason, C. M. (1986) 'The regional impact of the small firms Loan Guarantee Scheme in the UK', *Regional Studies*, 20, pp. 535–550.

Harrison, R. T. and Mason, C. M. (1991) 'Informal investment networks: a case study from the United Kingdom', *Entrepreneurship and Regional Development*, 3 (3), pp. 269–279.

Harvey, D. (1989) *The Condition of Postmodernity*, Basil Blackwell: Oxford.

Hay, A. and Peck, F. (1984) 'An alternative to the sign test in a matched pairs design', *The Statistician*, 33, pp. 201–204.

Healey, M. J. and Rawlinson, M.B. (1993) 'Interviewing business owners and managers: a review of methods and techniques', *Geoforum*, 24(3), pp. 339–355.

Herod, A. (1993) 'Gender issues in the use of interviewing as a research method', *Professional Geographer*, 45(3), pp. 305–317.

Hertz, L. (1987) *The Business Amazons*. Methuen: London.

Hisrich, R. D. (1985) 'The woman entrepreneur: characteristics, skills, problems , and prescriptions for success', in D.L. Sexton and R.W. Smilor (eds), *The Art and Science of Entrepreneurship*, Ballinger: London, pp. 61–81.

—— (1986) 'The woman entrepreneur: a comparative analysis', *Leadership and Organisational Development Journal*, 7(2), pp. 1–16.

Hisrich, R. D. and Brush, C. (1983) 'The woman entrepreneur: implications of family educational, and occupational experience', in J. A. Hornaday, J. A. Timmons and K. H. Vesper (eds) *Frontiers of Entrepreneurship Research*, Babson College: Wellesley, MA, pp. 255–270.

Hisrich, R. D. and Brush, C. (1984) 'The woman entrepreneur: management skills and business problems', *Journal of Small Business Management*, 22(1), pp. 30–37.

Hisrich, R. D. and Brush, C. G. (1985) 'Women and minority entrepreneurs: a comparative analysis', in J. A. Hornaday, E. B. Schils, J. A. Timmons and K.H. Vesper (eds) *Frontiers of Entrepreneurship Research*, Babson College: Wellesley, MA, pp. 566–587.

Hisrich, R. D. and Brush, C.G. (1986) *The Woman Entrepreneur: Starting, Financing and Managing a Successful New Business*, Lexington Books: Massachusetts.

—— (1987) 'Women entrepreneurs: a longitudinal study', in N. C. Churchill, J. A. Hornaday, B. A. Kirchhoff, O. J. Krasner and K. H. Vesper (eds)

Frontiers of Entrepreneurship Research, Babson College: Wellesley, MA, pp. 187–199.

Hisrich, R. D. and Fan, Z. (1991) 'Women entrepreneurs in the People's Republic of China: an exploratory study', *Journal of Managerial Psychology*, 6(3), pp. 3–12.

Hisrich, R. D. and Fuldop, G. (1993) 'Women entrepreneurs in controlled economies: a Hungarian perspective', in N.C. Churchill, S. Birley, W.D. Bygrave, J. Doutriaux, E.J. Gatewood, F.S. Hoy and W.E. Wetzel Jr. (eds) *Frontiers of Entrepreneurship Research*, Babson College: Wellesley, MA, pp. 590–591.

Hisrich, R. D. and O'Brien, M. (1981) 'The woman entrepreneur from a business and sociological perspective', in K.H. Vesper (ed.) *Frontiers of Entrepreneurship Research*, Babson College: Wellesley, MA, pp. 21–39.

Hisrich, R. D. and O'Brien, M. (1982) 'The woman entrepreneur as a reflection of the type of business', in K.H. Vesper (ed.) *Frontiers of Entrepreneurship Research*, Babson College: Wellesley, MA, pp. 54–67.

Holmes, S. and Kent, P. (1991) 'An empirical analysis of the financial structure of small and large Australian manufacturing enterprises', *The Journal of Small Business Finance*, 1(2), pp. 141–154.

Honig-Haftel, S. and Martin, L. R. (1986) 'Is the female entrepreneur at a disadvantage?', *Thrust* (Journal for Employment and Training), 1(2), pp. 49–64.

House of Representatives Report, No. 100–736 (1988) *New Economic Realities: The Rise of Women Entrepreneurs*, US Government Printing Office: Washington, DC.

Howcroft, B. and Beckett, A. (1993) 'Change in UK bank branch networks: a customer perspective', *The Service Industries Journal*, 13(4), pp. 267–288.

Hughes, A. and Storey, D. J. (1994) 'Introduction: financing small firms', in A.Hughes and D.J. Storey (eds) *Finance and the Small Firm*, Routledge: London., pp. 1–17.

Hutchinson, P. and Ray, G. (1986) 'Surviving the financial stress of small enterprise growth', in J. Curran, J. Stanworth and D. Watkins (eds) *The Survival of the Small Firm, Volume I – The Economics of Survival and Entrepreneurship*, Gower: Aldershot, pp. 53–71.

Hymounts, C. (1986) 'The corporate women – the glass ceiling', *Wall Street Journal*, 7 December, p. 7.

Imrie, R. (1994) ' "A strategy of the last resort?" Reflections on the role of the subcontract in the United Kingdom', *OMEGA*, 22(6), pp. 569–578.

Inc. (1993) 'For women only', September, p. 35.

Independent, The (1991) 'They're doing it their way', 24 October, p. 22.

Independent on Sunday, The (1993) 'Divorced women offered help to buy partners out', 5 December, p. 14.

Jankowicz, A. D. and Hisrich, R. D. (1987) 'Intuition in small business lending decisions', *Journal of Small Business Management*, July, pp. 45–52.

Jarillo, I. C. (1989) 'Entrepreneurship and growth: the strategic use of external resources', *Journal of Business Venturing*, 4, pp. 133–147.

Jennings, P. L. and Cohen, L. (1993) 'Invisible entrepreneurs', paper presented to the 16th National Small Firms Policy and Research Conference, Sheffield.

Jensen, M. C. and Meckling, W. H. (1976) 'Theory of the firm: managerial behaviour, agency costs and ownership structure', *Journal of Financial Economics*, 3(4), pp. 305–60.

Johannisson, B. (1990) 'Economies of overview – guiding the external growth of small firms', *International Small Business Journal*, 9(1), pp. 32–44.

Johnson, S. and Storey, D. (1993) 'Male and female entrepreneurs and their businesses: a comparative study', in S. Allen and C. Truman (eds) *Women in Business: Perspectives on Women Entrepreneurs*, Routledge: London, pp. 70–85.

Jones, T., McEvoy, D. and Barrett, G. (1992) *Raising Capital for the Ethnic Minority Small Business*, prepared for the 11th researcher's meeting: ESRC Small Business Initiative, University of Warwick.

Journal of Business Venturing (1993), Vol. 8(3).

Kalleberg, A. L. and Leicht, K. T. (1991) 'Gender and organizational performance: determinants of small business survival and success', *Academy of Management Journal*, 34(1), pp. 136–161.

Kane, E. W. and Macaulay, L. J. (1993) 'Interviewer gender and gender attitudes', *Public Opinion Quarterly*, 57, pp. 1–28.

Kane, F. and Whitebloom, S. (1993) 'Bankers sick as parrots over £6bn bad debt', The *Guardian*, 6 March, p. 40.

Kanter, R. (1977) *Men and Women of the Corporation*, Basic Books: New York.

—— (1981) 'Women and the structure of organisations: explorations in theory and behaviour', in O. Grunsky and G. A. Miller (eds) *The Sociology of Organisations*, 2nd edition, Free Press: New York.

Kaplan, E. (1988) 'Women entrepreneurs: constructing a framework to examine venture success and failure', in B. A. Kirchhoff, W. A. Long, W. E. McMullan, K. H. Vesper and W.E. Wetzel Jr. (eds) *Frontiers of Entrepreneurship Research*, Babson College: Wellesley, MA, pp. 643–653.

Kaplan, R. S. and Atkinson, A. A. (1989) *Advanced Management Accounting*, Prentice-Hall: Englewood Cliffs, NJ.

Katz, J. A. (1994) 'Markers for entrepreneurship knowledge: identifying opportunities and forums for new exchanges of findings from research and practices', working paper, Jefferson Smurfitt Center for Entrepreneurial Studies.

Kaur, D. and Hayden, C. (1993) 'Not just for pin money: a case study of the West Midlands clothing business start-up project', in S. Allen and C. Truman (eds) *Women in Business: Perspectives on Women Entrepreneurs*, Routledge: London, pp. 101–120.

Keasey, K. and Watson, R. (1993a) (eds) *Small Firm Management: Ownership, Finance and Performance*, Blackwell: Oxford.

Keasey, K. and Watson, R. (1993b) 'Banks and small firms: is conflict inevitable?', *National Westminster Bank Quarterly Review*, May, pp. 30–40.

Keeble, D. (1990) 'Small firms, new firms and uneven regional development in the United Kingdom', *Area*, 22(3), pp. 234–245.

Keeble, D. and Wever, E. (1986) (eds) *New Firms and Regional Development in Europe*, Croom Helm: Beckenham, Kent.

Keeble, D., Bryson, J. and Wood, P. (1991) 'Small firms, business services growth and regional development in the UK: some empirical findings', *Regional Studies*, 25, pp. 439–457.

Keeble, D., Tyler, P., Broom, G. and Lewis, J. (1992) *Business Success in the Countryside: The Performance of Rural Enterprise*, HMSO: London.

Kets de Vries, M. F. R. (1977) 'The entrepreneurial personality: a person at the cross roads', *Journal of Management Studies*, February, pp. 34–57.

Knoke, D. and Kuklinski, J. H. (1983) *Network Analysis*, Sage Publications: Beverley Hills.

Koper, G. (1989) 'Women entrepreneurs and business credit granting: constraints and possibilities', paper presented at the International Conference on Female Entrepreneurship, University of Bradford, March.

——(1993) 'Women entrepreneurs and the granting of business credit', in S. Allen and C. Truman (eds) *Women in Business: Perspectives on Women Entrepreneurs*, Routledge: London.

Kraus-Harper, U. (1992) 'Towards a typology of enterprising women in poor communities', in N. C. Churchill, S. Birley, W. D. Bygrave, D. F. Muzyka, C. Wahlbin and W. E. Wetzel Jr. (eds) *Frontiers of Entrepreneurship Research*, Babson College: Babson Park, MA, p. 160.

Kryzanowski, L. and Bertin-Boussu, E. (1984) 'Equal access to credit: lenders' attitudes toward an applicant's sex and marital status', *International Journal of Women's Studies*, 4(3), pp. 213–233.

Landström, H. (1992) 'The relationship between private investors and small firms: an agency theory approach', *Entrepreneurship and Regional Development*, 4, pp. 199–223.

Landström, H. and Winborg, J. (1995) 'Small business managers' attitudes towards and use of external financial sources', paper presented at the 1995 Babson College–Kauffman Foundation Entrepreneurship Reesearch Conference, London.

Lash, S. and Urry, J. (1987) *The End of Organised Capitalism*, Polity Press: Cambridge.

——(1994) *Economies of Signs and Space*, Sage: London.

Lawton Smith, H., Dickson, K. and Smith, S. C. (1991) ' "There are two sides to every story": innovation and collaboration within networks of large and small firms', *Research Policy*, 20, pp. 457–468.

Lavarack, D. (1994) 'Support for business', *Business Counselling Review*, 4(1), pp. 5–7.

Lavoie, D. (1984) 'A new era for female entrepreneurship in the 80's', *Journal of Small Business Canada*, 2(3), pp. 34–43.

LEDIS (Local Economic Development Information Service) (1989) 'Women's Economic Development Corporation, Minnesota, USA', Overseas, May, E52.

——(1990) 'Victorian Women's Trust – Australia', Overseas, April, E72.

Lee-Gosselin, H. and Grisé, J. (1990) 'Are women owner-managers challenging our definitions of entrepreneurship? An in-depth survey', *Journal of Business Ethics*, 9, pp. 423–433.

Leitch, C. (1989) 'Chastened bankers seeing women afresh', *The Globe and Mail*, August 14, p. C2.

Lerner, M., Brush, C. G. and Hisrich, R. D. (1995) 'Factors affecting performance of Israeli women entrepreneurs: an examination of alternative perspectives', paper presented at the 1995 Babson College Kauffman Foundation Entrepreneurship Research Conference, London.

Levin, R. and Trevis, V. (1987) 'Small company finance', *Harvard Business Review*, 65(6), pp. 30–32.

Lipietz, A. (1986) 'New tendencies in the international division of labour: regimes of accumulation and modes of social regulation', in A. J. Scott and M. Storper (eds) *Production, Work and Territory*, Allen and Unwin: London, pp. 16–40.

——(1987) *Mirages and Miracles: The Crises of Global Fordism*, Verso: London.

Lloyds Bank/Small Business Research Trust (1994) 'Management succession', *Quarterly Small Business Management Report*, 2(3).

Lonsdale, S. (1985) *Work and Inequality*, Longman: London.

Loscocco, K. A. and Robinson, J. (1991) 'Barriers to women's small-business success in the United States', *Gender and Society*, 5(4), pp. 511–532.

Loscocco, K. A., Robinson, J., Hall, R. H. and Allen, J. K. (1991) 'Gender and small business success: an inquiry into women's relative disadvantage', *Social Forces*, 70(1), pp. 65–85.

Low, M. and MacMillan, I. (1988) 'Entrepreneurship: past research and future challenges', *Journal of Management*, 14(2), pp. 139–161.

McDowell, L. (1991) 'Life without father and Ford: the new gender order of post-Fordism', *Transactions of the Institute of British Geographers*, NS.16, pp. 400–419.

——(1992) 'Valid games? A response to Erica Schoenberger', *Professional Geographer*, 44(2), pp. 212–215.

McMahon, R. G. P., Holmes, S., Hutchinson, P. J. and Forsaith, D. M. (1993) *Small Enterprise Financial Management: Theory and Practice*, Harcourt Brace: London.

Macmillan Committee (1931) *Report of the Committee on Finance and Industry*, Cmd 3897, HMSO: London.

MacMillan, I. C., Siegel, R. and Narasimha, P. N. S. (1985) 'Criteria used by venture capitalists to evaluate new venture proposals', *Journal of Business Venturing*, 1, pp. 119–128.

Maidment, C. (1994) 'Aid on tap for green shoots', The *Observer*, March 20, p. 8.

Malecki, E. J. (1995) 'Flexibility and industrial districts', *Environment and Planning A*, 27, pp. 11–14.

Malveaux, J. (1990) 'Women in the labour market: the choices women have', in OECD (Organisation for Economic Co-operation and Development) *Local Initiatives for Job Creation: Enterprising Women*, HMSO: London, pp. 21–35.

Mason, C. M. (1983) 'Some definitional difficulties in new firms research', *Area*, 15(1), pp. 53–59.

——(1991) 'Spatial variations in enterprise: the geography of new firm formation', in R. Burrows (ed.) *Deciphering the Enterprise Culture: Entrepreneurship, Petty Capitalism and the Restructuring of Britain*, Routledge: London, pp. 74–106.

Mason, C. and Harrison, R. (1990) 'Informal risk capital: a review and research agenda', Venture Finance Research Project, Working Paper 1, University of Southampton (Urban Policy Research Unit, Department of Geography) and University of Ulster (Centre for Executive Development, Ulster Business School).

Mason, C. and Harrison, R. (1991) 'A strategy for closing the small firm's finance gap', Venture Finance Research Project, Working Paper 3,

University of Southampton (Urban Policy Research Unit, Department of Geography) and University of Ulster (Centre for Executive Development, Ulster Business School).

Mason, C. M. and Harrison, R. T. (1993) 'Strategies for expanding the informal venture capital market', *International Small Business Journal*, 11(4), pp. 23–38.

Mason, C. and Harrison, R. (1994) 'Informal venture capital in the UK', in A. Hughes and D.J. Storey (eds) *Finance and the Small Firm*, Routledge: London, pp. 64–111.

Mason, C., Harrison, R. and Chaloner, J. (1991) 'Informal risk capital in the UK: a study of investor characteristics, investment preferences and investment decision-making', Venture Finance Research Project, Working Paper 2, University of Southampton (Urban Policy Research Unit, Department of Geography) and University of Ulster (Centre for Executive Development, Ulster Business School).

Massey, D. (1984) *Spatial Divisions of Labour*, Macmillan: London.

Meager, N. (1989) 'Who are the self-employed?', Anglo-German Self-Employment Project, Working Paper No. 1, Institute of Manpower Studies, University of Sussex.

Miles, R. E. and Snow, C. C. (1992) 'Causes of failure in network organizations', *California Management Review*, Summer, pp. 53–72.

Miskin, V. and Rose, J. (1990) 'Women entrepreneurs: factors related to success', in N. C. Churchill, W. D. Bygrave, J. A. Hornaday, D. F. Muzyka, K. H. Vesper and W. E. Wetzel Jr. (eds) *Frontiers of Entrepreneurship Research*, Babson College: Babson Park, MA, pp. 27–38.

Mitchell, J. C. (1973) 'Networks, norms and institutions', in J. Boissevain and J.C. Mitchell (eds) *Network Analysis: Studies In Human Interaction*, Monton: The Hague.

Moore, D. P., Buttner, E. H. and Rosen, B. (1992) 'Stepping off the corporate track: the entrepreneurial alternative', in K. Sekaran and F. T. L. Leong (eds) *Womanpower: Managing in Times of Demographic Turbulence*, Sage: London, pp. 85–109.

Moore, S. (1993) 'Once upon a time in the nuclear family', The *Guardian*, 5 March, p. 11.

Murray, G. (1990) *Change and Maturity in the UK Venture Capital Industry 1990–95*, Warwick Business School: Coventry.

——(1993) 'Venture Capital', paper presented at a CBI workshop on finance for SMEs.

Myers, S. C. (1984) 'The capital structure puzzle', *Journal of Finance*, 39(3), pp. 575–592.

National Foundation for Women Business Owners (USA) (1992) *Women-Owned Businesses: The New Economic Force*.

Nelson, G. W. (1987) 'Information needs of female entrepreneurs', *Journal of Small Business Management*, July, pp. 38–44.

——(1989) 'Factors of friendship: relevance of significant others to female business owners', *Entrepreneurship: Theory and Practice*, Summer, pp. 7–18.

Nelson, L. (1978) 'Women must help each other: female beer producers in Kenya', in P. Caplan (ed.) *Women United, Women Divided: Cross-Cultural Perspectives on Female Solidarity*, Fontana: London.

Nelton, S. (1990) 'The challenge to women', *Nations Business*, July, pp. 16–21.

Network (1994) 'The bank manager cometh', 2, pp. 4–5.
Networker (1994) The Newsletter of the Small Business Centre, Durham University Business School, No. 2, p. 1.
New Earnings Survey – Northern Ireland (1985) Department of Economic Development, Belfast.
Nguyen, T. (1986) 'Credit and finance: are women getting anywhere?', *Australian Quarterly*, 58(3), pp. 220–229.
Nicholson, N. and West, J. (1988) *Managerial Job Change*, Cambridge University Press: Cambridge.
Nieva, V. F. and Gutek, B. A. (1980) 'Sex effects on evaluation', *Academy of Management Review*, 5(2), pp. 267–276.
Noe, R. A. (1988) 'Women and monitoring: a review and research agenda', *Academy of Management Review*, 9, pp. 35–45.
Norton, E. (1991a) 'Capital structure and small public firms', *Journal of Business Venturing,* 6(4), pp. 287–303.
——(1991b) 'Capital structure and small growth firms', *Journal of Business Venturing*, 1(2), pp. 161–177.
Oakley, A. (1981) 'Interviewing women: a contradiction in terms', in H. Roberts (ed.) *Doing Feminist Research*, Routledge and Kegan Paul: London, pp. 30–61.
——(1982) *Subject Women*, Fontana: London.
Observer, The (1994a) 'Hats off to the recession beaters', 20 March, p. 7.
——(1994b) 'Banks take some of the credit', 20 March, p. 3.
——(1994c) 'Lenders mend their ways', 20 March, p. 6.
——(1994d) 'The view from the trenches: small firms report back on prospects and problems', 20 March, p. 8.
O'Farrell, P. N. and Crouchley, R. (1983) 'Industrial closures in Ireland 1973–1981: analysis and implications', *Regional Studies*, 17(6), pp. 411–427.
O'Farrell, P. N. and Hitchens, D. M. W. N. (1988a) 'Inter-firm comparisons in industrial research: the utility of a matched pairs design', *Tijdschrift voor Economische en Sociale Geografie*, 79(1), pp. 63–69.
O'Farrell, P. N. and Hitchens, D. M. W. N. (1988b) 'The relative competitiveness and performance of small manufacturing firms in Scotland and the mid-west of Ireland: an analysis of matched pairs', *Regional Studies*, 22(5), pp. 399–415.
O'Farrell, P. N., Hitchens, D. M., and Moffat, L. A. R. (1993) 'The competitive advantage of business service firms: a matched pairs analysis of the relationship between generic strategy and performance', *The Services Industries Journal,* 13(1), pp. 40–64.
O'Hare, W. and Larson, J. (1991) 'Women in business: where, what, and why', *American Demographics*, July, pp. 34–38.
OECD (Organisation for Economic Co-operation and Development) (1986) 'Local initiatives for employment creation', ILE Notebook, No. 6, Paris.
——(1990) *Local Initiatives for Job Creation: Enterprising Women*, HMSO: London.
Olm, K. W., Carsrud, A. L. and Alvey, L. (1988) 'The role of networks in new venture funding for the female entrepreneur: a continuing analysis', in B. A. Kirchhoff, W.A. Long, W.E. McMullan, K.H. Vesper and W.E. Wetzel (Jr.) (eds) *Frontiers of Entrepreneurship Research*, Babson College: Wellesley, MA, pp. 658–659.

Oppenheim, A. N. (1968) *Questionnaire Design and Attitude Measurement*, Heinemann: London.

Orser, B. J. and Foster, M. K. (1992) 'Lending practices and women in micro-based businesses', paper presented to the Global Research Conference on Women and Management, Fall.

Orser, B. J., Riding, A. L. and Swift, C. S. (1993) 'Banking experiences of Canadian micro-businesses', *Journal of Enterprising Culture*, 1(3).

Ostgaard, T. A. and Birley, S. (1994) 'Personal networks and firm competitive strategy – a strategic or coincidental match', *Journal of Business Venturing*, 9, pp. 281–305.

Owens, P. L. (1986) 'Social survey methods in geographical teaching', *Journal of Geography*, 85, pp. 57–61.

Palmer, A. and Bejou, D. (1994) 'The effects of gender on the development of relationships between clients and financial advisers', paper submitted to the International Journal of Bank Marketing, in revision.

Patel, K. (1994) 'Women escape bias by business', *The Times Higher Education Supplement*, 30 September.

Peck, F. W. (1985) 'The use of matched-pairs research design in industrial surveys', *Environment and Planning A*, 17, pp. 981–989.

Pellegrino, E. T. and Reece, B. L. (1982) 'Perceived formative and operational problems encountered by female entrepreneurs in retail and service firms', *Journal of Small Business Management*, pp. 15–24.

Pettit, R. R. and Singer, R. F. (1985) 'Small business finance: a research agenda', *Financial Management*, 14(3), pp. 47–60.

Pinder, D. A. (1990) (ed.) *Challenge and Change in Western Europe*. Bellhaven: London.

Piore, M. and Sabel, C. (1984) *The Second Industrial Divide: Possibilities For Prosperity*, Basic Books: New York.

Price, C. and Monroe, S. (1992) 'Educational training for women and minority entrepreneurs positively impacts venture growth and development', in N. C. Churchill, S. Birley, W. D. Bygrave, D. F. Muzyka, C. Wahlbin, and W. E. Wetzel Jr. (eds) *Frontiers of Entrepreneurship Research*, Babson College: Babson Park, MA, pp. 216–230.

Price, C. and Monroe, S. (1993) 'Educational training for women and minority entrepreneurs positively impacts venture growth and development', paper presented at the 1993 Babson College Entrepreneurship Conference, Houston, Texas.

Read, L. H. (1994) 'The financing of women-owned businesses: a review and research agenda', Venture Finance Working Paper No. 8, University of Southampton (Urban Policy Research Unit, Department of Geography).

Redclift, N. and Sinclair, M. T. (1991) (eds) *Working Women: International Perspectives on Labour and Gender Ideology*, Routledge: London.

Rees, T. (1992) *Women and the Labour Market*, Routledge: London.

Reese, P. R. (1992) 'Resource acquisition: does gender make a difference?', mimeo, University of North Carolina, NC.

Reilly, M. (1989) 'The problems of being a businesswoman', *Accountancy*, July, pp. 24–25.

Reskin, B. and Hartmann, H. (1986) *Women's Work, Men's Work: Sex Segregation on the Job*, National Academy Press: Washington, DC.

Reuber, A. R., Dyke, L. S. and Fischer, E. M. (1991) 'Gender role stereotypes regarding women business owners: impacts on external resource provision by consultants', *Canadian Journal of Administrative Sciences*, 8, pp. 244–250.

Reynolds, P. D. and White, S. B. (1992) 'Finding the nascent entrepreneur: network sampling and entrepreneurship gestation', paper presented to the 12th annual Babson Entrepreneurship Research Conference, INSEAD, Fontainebleau, France.

Riding, A. L. and Swift, C. S. (1990) 'Women business owners and terms of credit: some empirical findings of the Canadian experience', *Journal of Business Venturing*, 5, pp. 327–340.

Roberts, E. B. (1991) *Entrepreneurs in High Technology: Lessons from MIT and Beyond*, Oxford University Press: New York.

Robertson, M., Chell, E. and Mason, C. (1992) (eds), *Towards the 21st Century: The Challenge for Small Business*, Nadamal Books: Macclesfield, Cheshire.

Roberts-Reid, L. and Curran, J. (1992) 'Women and the one person enterprise: a flexible form of self-employment for the 1990s?', in M. Robertson, E. Chell and C. Mason (eds), *Towards the 21st Century: The Challenge for Small Business*, Nadamal Books: Macclesfield, Cheshire, pp. 249–267.

Robson Rhodes (1984) *A Study of Businesses Financed Under the Small Business Loan Guarantee Scheme*, DTI: London.

Rosa, P. and Hamilton, D. (1994) 'Gender and ownership in UK small firms', *Entrepreneurship Theory and Practice*, 18(3), pp. 11–27.

Rosa, P., Hamilton, D. and Burns, H. (1994) 'Gender and ownership in UK small firms', in J. M. Veciana (ed.) *SMEs: Internationalization, Networks and Strategy*, Avebury: Aldershot, pp. 615–636.

——(unpublished) 'Gender and ownership in UK small firms', draft paper from the Scottish Enterprise Foundation, University of Stirling.

Ross, S., Westerfield, R., Jordan, B. and Roberts, G. (1993) *Fundamentals of Corporate Finance: First Canadian Edition,* Irwin: Homewood, Ill.

Rothwell, R. (1992) 'Successful industrial innovation: critical factors for the 1990s', *R&D Management*, 22(3), pp. 221–239.

Sapienza, H. J. (1989) 'Variations in venture capitalist–entrepreneur relations: antecedents and consequences', unpublished doctoral thesis, University of Maryland at College Park.

Sargent, M. and Young, J. E. (1991) 'The entrepreneurial search for capital: a behavioural science perspective', *Entrepreneurship and Regional Development*, 3, pp. 237–252.

SBA (US Small Business Administration) (1988) *Small Business in the American Economy*, US Government Printing Office: Washington, DC.

SBRC (1992) *The State of British Enterprise: Growth Innovation and Competitive Advantage in Small and Medium Sized Firms*, Small Business Research Centre, University of Cambridge.

Scase, R. and Goffee, R. (1980) *The Real World of the Small Business Owner*, Croom Helm: London.

Scase, R. and Goffee, R. (1982) *The Entrepreneurial Middle Class*, Croom Helm: London.

Scherbaum, C. J. and Shephard, D. H. (1987) 'Dressing for success: effects of color and layering on perceptions of women in business', *Sex Roles*, 16(7/8), pp. 391–399.

Scherr, F. C., Sugrue, T. F. and Ward, J. B. (1993) 'Financing the small firm start-up: determinants of debt use', *Journal of Small Business Finance*, 1(2), pp. 179–183.

Schoenberger, E. (1991) 'The corporate interview as a research method in economic geography', *Professional Geographer*, 43(2), pp. 180–189.

——(1992) 'Self-criticism and self-awareness in research: a reply to Linda McDowell', *Professional Geographer*, 44(2), pp. 215–218.

Schreier, J. and Komives, J. (1973) *The Entrepreneur and New Enterprise Formation: A Resource Guide*, Center for Venture Management: Milwaukee, WI.

Schwartz, E. B. (1976) 'Entrepreneurship: a new female frontier', *Journal of Contemporary Business*, 5(1), pp. 47–76.

Scott, C. E. (1986) 'Why more women are becoming entrepreneurs', *Journal of Small Business Management*, 24(4), pp. 37–44.

Scottish Enterprise (1993a) *Scotland's Business Birth Rate* (A National Enquiry by Scottish Enterprise), Scottish Enterprise in partnership with Scottish Business Insider, Glasgow.

——(1993b) *Women Starting Businesses: Making It Happen*, Glasgow.

Sekaran, K. and Leong, F. T. L. (1992) (eds) *Womanpower: Managing in Times of Demographic Turbulence*, Sage: London.

Sexton, D. L. and Bowman, N. B. (1986) 'Validation of a personality index: comparative psychological characteristics analysis of female entrepreneurs, managers, entrepreneurship students and business students', in R. Ronstadt, J. A. Hornaday, P. Peterson and K. H. Vesper, *Frontiers of Entrepreneurship Research*, Babson College: Wellesley, MA, pp. 40–51.

Sexton, D. L. and Bowman-Upton, N. (1988) 'Sexual stereotyping of female entrepreneurs: a comparative psychological trait analysis of female and male entrepreneurs', in B. A. Kirchoff, W. A. Long, W.E. McMullan, K. H. Vesper and W.E. Wetzel Jr. (eds) *Frontiers of Entrepreneurship Research*, Babson College: Wellesley, MA, pp. 654–655.

Sexton, D. L. and Bowman-Upton, N. (1990) 'Female and male entrepreneurs: psychological characteristics and their role in gender-related discrimination', *Journal of Business Venturing*, 5, pp. 29–36.

Sexton, D. L. and Bowman-Upton, N. B. (1991a), *Entrepreneurship: Creativity and Growth*, Macmillan: London.

Sexton, D. L. and Bowman-Upton, N. B. (1991b) 'The female entrepreneur', in D. L. Sexton and N.B. Bowman-Upton, *Entrepreneurship: Creativity and Growth*, Macmillan: London, pp. 285–299.

Sexton, D. L. and Kent, C. A. (1981) 'Female executives and entrepreneurs: a preliminary comparison', *Frontiers of Entrepreneurship Research* (Proceedings of the 1981 Babson College Entrepreneurship Research Conference), pp. 40–55.

Sexton, D. L. and Smilor, R. W. (1985) (eds), *The Art and Science of Entrepreneurship*, Ballinger: London.

Shutt, J. and Whittington, R. (1987) 'Fragmentation strategies and the rise of small units: cases from the North West', *Regional Studies*, 21(1), pp. 13–23.

Siegel, B. (1993) 'Business creation and local economic development: why entrepreneurship should be encouraged', in S. Allen and C. Truman (eds) *Women in Business: Perspectives on Women Entrepreneurs*, Routledge: London, pp. 11–20.

Simpson, S. M. (1991) 'Women entrepreneurs', in J. Firth-Cozens and M. A. West (eds) *Women at Work: Psychological and Organizational Perspectives*, Open University Press: Milton Keynes, pp. 113–130.

Smallbone, D. (1990) 'Success and failure in new business start-ups', *International Small Business Journal*, 8(2), pp. 34–47.

Small Business Secretariat (1982) 'Canadian Women Owner/Managers', Small Business Secretariat Working Paper (Policy Research and Formulation Unit).

Smeltzer, L. and Fann, G. L. (1989) 'Gender differences in external networks of small business owner/managers', *Journal of Small Business Management*, 27(2), pp. 25–32.

Smith, A. M. (1989) 'Service quality: relationships between banks and their small business clients', *International Journal of Bank Marketing*, 7(5), pp. 28–35.

Smith, N. R., McCain, G. and Warren, A. (1982) 'Women entrepreneurs really are different: a comparison of constructed ideal types of male and female entrepreneurs', in K.H. Vesper (ed.) *Frontiers of Entrepreneurship Research*, Babson College: Wellesley, MA, pp. 68–77.

Smith, P. L., Smits, S. J. and Hoy, F. (1992) 'Female business owners in industries traditionally dominated by males', *Sex Roles*, 26(11/12), pp. 485–496.

Sowman, M. (1994) 'Finding the right advice', *Business Money*, July, pp. 4–5.

Srinivasan, R., Woo, C. Y. and Cooper, A. C. (1994) 'Performance determinants for male and female entrepreneurs', paper presented at the 1995 Babson College Kauffman Foundation Entrepreneurship Research Conference, London.

Stanworth, R. and Curran, J. (1976) 'Growth and the small firm: an alternative view', *Journal of Management Studies*, 13, pp. 95–110.

Starr, J. A. and MacMillan, I. C. (1990) 'Resource cooptation via social contracting of resource acquisition strategies for new ventures', *Strategic Management Journal*, 11, pp. 79–92.

Steier, L. and Greenwood, R. (1995) 'Venture capitalist relationships in the deal structuring and post-investment stages of new firm creation', *Journal of Management Studies*, 32(3), pp. 337–357.

Stevenson, L. (1983) 'An investigation of the entrepreneurial experience of women: implications for small business policy in Canada', research document from the Fred C. Manning School of Business, Acadia University, Wolfville, Nova Scotia.

——(1986) 'Against all odds: the entrepreneurship of women', *Journal of Small Business Management*, 24(1), pp. 30–36.

Still, L. V. and Guerin, C. D. (1991) 'Barriers facing self-employed women: the Australian experience', *Women in Management Review and Abstracts*, 6(6), pp. 3–8.

Stoner, C. R., Hartman, R. T. and Arora, R. (1989) 'Work–home role conflict in female-owned small businesses: an exploratory study', *Journal of Small Business Management,* 28(1), pp. 30–38.

Storey, D. J. (1994) *Understanding the Small Business Sector*, Routledge: London.

Storey, D. and Johnson, S. (1987) *Job Generation and Labour Market Change*, Macmillan: London.

Storey, D. J. and Strange, A. (1992) *Entrepreneurship in Cleveland, 1979–1989: A Study of the Effects of the Enterprise Culture*, Research Series No. 3, Centre for Small and Medium Sized Enterprises, Warwick Business School, University of Warwick.

Storey, D., Watson, R. and Wynarczyk, P. (1992) *Fast Growth Small Businesses: Case Studies of 40 Small Firms in North East England*, Department of Employment, Research Paper No. 67, HMSO: London.

Summers, D. (1992) 'Bank managers' eyes glaze over', *Financial Times*, 28 July, p. 9.

Sunday Times, The (1994) 'Bulletin', 13 March, p. 13.

Sunday Times Magazine, The (1990) 'New York: making a women's bank balance', 4 November, p. 6.

Sundin, E. and Holmquist, C. (1991) 'The growth of women entrepreneurship – push or pull factors?', in L. G. Davies and A. A. Gibbs (eds), *Recent Research in Entrepreneurship*, Avebury: Aldershot, pp. 106–114.

Szarka, J. (1990) 'Networking and small firms', *International Small Business Journal*, 8(2), pp. 10–22.

Taub, R. P. and Gaglio, C. M. (1995) 'Entrepreneurship and public policy: beyond solving the credit crunch', paper presented at the 1995 Babson College–Kauffman Foundation Entrepreneurship Research Conference, London.

Therrien, L., Carson, T., Hamilton, J. and Hurlock, J. (1986) 'What do women want? A company they can call their own', *Business Week*, 22 December, pp. 54–56.

Thomas, H. (1991) 'The pleasure of their own company', *Accountancy*, February, pp. 91–92.

Thompson, S. (1988) 'Agency theory', in S. Thompson and M. Wright (eds) *Internal Organisation, Efficiency and Profit*, Philip Allan: Oxford.

Thornhill, S. (1989) 'Small business is big business', *Banking World*, 7(6).

Times, The (1992a) 'Women are better in business than men', October 12, p. 8.

—— (1992b) 'Wise words given to businesswomen', August 7, p. 22.

—— (1994a) 'Don't whine, walk', 18 October, p. 27.

—— (1994b) 'Small firms favour accountants for advice', 6 September, p. 33.

—— (1995) 'Couple's defeat of Lloyds could rebound on borrowers', 5 September, p. 2.

Truman, C. (1993) 'Good practice in business advice and counselling', in S. Allen and C. Truman (eds) *Women in Business: Perspectives on Women Entrepreneurs*, Routledge: London, pp. 121–132.

Turner, C. (1989) 'Support for women entrepreneurs across the member-states of the EEC', paper presented to the Women in Enterprise/University of Bradford Women Entrepreneurs Conference, University of Bradford, April.

Turner, C. (1993) 'Women's businesses in Europe: EEC initiatives', in S. Allen and C. Truman (eds) *Women in Business: Perspectives on Women Entrepreneurs*, Routledge: London, pp. 133–147.

Turner, C. F. and Martin, E. (1984) (eds) *Surveying Subjective Phenomenon*, Russell Sage Foundation: New York.

Turok, I. and Richardson, P. (1989) *Supporting the Start-Up and Growth of Small Firms: A Study in West Lothian*, Strathclyde Papers on Planning, No. 14, University of Strathclyde, Centre for Planning, Glasgow.

——(1991) 'New firms and local economic development: evidence from West Lothian', *Regional Studies*, 25(1), pp. 71–86.

USSBA (US Small Business Administration) (1985) *The State of Small Business: A Report of the President*, US Government Printing Office: Washington, DC.

——(1986) *The State of Small Business: A Report of the President*, US Government Printing Office: Washington, DC.

——(1988) *The State of Small Business: A Report of the President*, US Government Printing Office: Washington, DC.

——(1990) *The State of Small Business: A Report of the President*, US Government Printing Office: Washington, DC.

——(1991) *Small Business in the American Economy*, US Government Printing Office: Washington, DC.

Van der Meer, L. (1986) 'A survey of women entrepreneurs and support organisations in the Netherlands', European Centre for the Development of Vocational Training, Rotterdam, September.

Walker, D. A. (1989) 'Financing the small firm', *Small Business Economics*, 1, pp. 285–296.

Watkins, J. and Watkins, D. (1984) 'The female entrepreneur: background and determinants of business choice – some British data', *International Small Business Journal*, 2(4), pp. 21–31.

Weiss, C. (1990) 'The role of intermediaries in strengthening women's self-employment activities', in OECD (Organisation for Economic Co-operation and Development) *Local Initiatives for Job Creation: Enterprising Women*, HMSO: London, pp. 58–74.

Welsch, H. and Young, E. (1984) 'Male and female entrepreneurial characteristics and behaviours: a profile of similarities and differences', *International Small Business Journal*, 2(4), pp. 11–20.

West, J. (1982) (ed.) *Work, Women and the Labour Market*, Routledge and Kegan Paul: London.

Westhead, P. (1995a) 'Exporting and non-exporting small firms in Great Britain', *International Journal of Entrepreneurial Behaviour and Research*, 1(2), pp. 6–36.

——(1995b) 'New owner-managed businesses in rural and urban areas in Great Britain: a matched pairs comparison', *Regional Studies*, 29(4), pp. 367–380.

White, J. (1984) 'The rise of female capitalism – women as entrepreneurs', *Business Quarterly*, Spring, pp. 133–135.

Wilkins, E. (1995) 'Equal pay "50 years away for women"', *The Times*, 26 June, p. 5.

Wilson Committee (1979) *The Financing of Small Firms: Interim Report of the Committee to Review the Functioning of the Financial Institutions*, Cmnd 7503, HMSO: London.

Woodcock, C. (1992) 'Creditors run out of patience', The *Guardian*, 27 July, p. 14.

Woods, A., Blackburn, R. and Curran, J. (1993) 'A longitudinal study of small enterprises in the service sector', 1993 Survey Report, Small Business Research Programme, Kingston University (Small Business Research Centre) and Brunel University (Department of Management Studies).

Wynant, L. and Hatch, J. (1990) *Banks and Small Business Borrowers*, The Western Business School, University of Western Ontario.

Young, M. (1995) 'Banks and smaller firms: the British experience from the banks' viewpoint', paper presented to the seminar on Financing Small and Medium Sized Enterprises, Brussels, September.

Zhao, L. and Aram, J. D. (1995) 'Networking and growth of young technology-intensive ventures in China', *Journal of Business Venturing*, 10, pp. 349–370.

Index

access: to businesses 80–1; to reliable data 81–3
accountants 161, 172–3
accumulation 3
achievement oriented women 10–11, 20
adverse selection 36, 41–2, 45, 116
advice: bank 130–3, 155–7; formal 166–8, 186–7; informal 166–8, 186; *see also* networking
age: of business owner 106–7
age of business *see* business age
agency costs 37, 127
agency theory 33–7, 41, 116, 123, 188
androcentrism 64
asymmetric information 34–7, 41, 120, 123, 162
Australia: increasing women-owned businesses 1–2; Victorian Women's Trust 15, 194
autocratic style 21
autonomy 39
awareness 56–9

bad debts 22, 41, 121, 182
bank: advice 172–4; changing 152–5; as financial source 101–5, 182; relationship 61, 120–57, 182–6; research implications 191–4; services 126; staff turnover 147; treatment 26–31
bank charges 112–13, 146, 151
bank finance: non-use 111

bank finance analysis 113–17; amount 114–15; terms and conditions 115–17
bank use 128–36; choice of bank 128–30; external parties and bank finance 135–6; frequency of contact 133–5; source of advice 130–3
Banking Acts 1979, 1987 125
Banking Ombudsman 151
banking relationship 25, 120–57, 162, 165; characteristics 136–55, 158–9; dealing with problems 151–5; important elements 136–40; problems 145–51; research findings 181–7; satisfaction 140–5; small business overview 122–8; use of banks 128–36
banks: Canada 28, 43, 193; USA 28
Barclays Bank; bad debt provision 125–6; staff turnover 147; use 128
biotechnology 54
body language 59, 74
Body Shop 9
bonding arrangements 36–7
bootstrapping 95–6
borrowing: and women 44–5, 182 *see also* bank
BP 15
Breakfast Club 175
British Association of Women Entrepreneurs 9
broker 161; definition 161
building societies: use 128–9